Mobile OS Vulnerabilities

This book offers in-depth analysis of security vulnerabilities in different mobile operating systems. It provides methodology and solutions for handling Android malware and vulnerabilities and transfers the latest knowledge in machine learning and deep learning models towards this end. Further, it presents a comprehensive analysis of software vulnerabilities based on different technical parameters such as causes, severity, techniques, and software systems' type. Moreover, the book also presents the current state of the art in the domain of software threats and vulnerabilities. This would help analyze various threats that a system could face, and subsequently, it could guide the security engineer to take proactive and cost-effective countermeasures.

Security threats are escalating exponentially, thus posing a serious challenge to mobile platforms. Android and iOS are prominent due to their enhanced capabilities and popularity among users. Therefore, it is important to compare these two mobile platforms based on security aspects. Android proved to be more vulnerable than iOS. The malicious apps can cause severe repercussions such as privacy leaks, app crashes, financial losses (caused by malware-triggered premium rate SMSs), arbitrary code installation, etc. Hence, Android security is a major concern among researchers, as seen in the last few years. This book provides an exhaustive review of all the existing approaches in a structured format.

The book also focuses on the detection of malicious applications that compromise users' security and privacy, the detection performance of the different program analysis approach, and the influence of different input generators during static and dynamic analysis on detection performance. This book presents a novel method using an ensemble classifier scheme for detecting malicious applications, which is less susceptible to the evolution of the Android ecosystem and malware than previous methods. The book also introduces an ensemble multi-class scheme to classify malware into known families. Furthermore, we propose a novel framework of mapping malware to vulnerabilities exploited using Android malware's behavior reports leveraging pretrained language models and deep learning techniques. The mapped vulnerabilities can then be assessed on confidentiality, integrity, and availability on different Android components and subsystems and different layers.

Mobile OS Vulnerabilities

Quantitative and Qualitative Analysis

Shivi Garg and Niyati Baliyan

CRC Press is an imprint of the
Taylor & Francis Group, an **informa** business

First edition published 2024
by CRC Press
2385 Executive Center Drive, Suite 320, Boca Raton, FL 33431

and by CRC Press
4 Park Square, Milton Park, Abingdon, Oxon, OX14 4RN

CRC Press is an imprint of Taylor & Francis Group, LLC

Library of Congress Cataloging-in-Publication Data
Names: Garg, Shivi, author. | Baliyan, Niyati, author.
Title: Mobile OS vulnerabilities : quantitative and qualitative analysis / Shivi Garg and Niyati Baliyan.
Description: First edition. | Boca Raton : CRC Press, 2024. | Includes bibliographical references.
Identifiers: LCCN 2023007110 (print) | LCCN 2023007111 (ebook) | ISBN 9781032407463 (hardback) | ISBN 9781032407487 (paperback) | ISBN 9781003354574 (ebook)
Subjects: LCSH: Mobile computing—Security measures. | Operating systems (Computers)—Security measures.
Classification: LCC QA76.59 .G37 2024 (print) | LCC QA76.59 (ebook) | DDC 005.355—dc23/eng/20230331
LC record available at https://lccn.loc.gov/2023007110
LC ebook record available at https://lccn.loc.gov/2023007111

ISBN: 978-1-032-40746-3 (hbk)
ISBN: 978-1-032-40748-7 (pbk)
ISBN: 978-1-003-35457-4 (ebk)

DOI: 10.1201/9781003354574

Typeset in Caslon
by Apex CoVantage, LLC

Contents

ABOUT THE AUTHORS ix

CHAPTER 1 INTRODUCTION 1
1.1 Introduction 1
1.2 Evolution of Mobile Phones 1
1.3 Mobile Ecosystem and Threats 4
1.4 Motivation 7
1.5 Book Objectives 8
1.6 Book Organization 9

CHAPTER 2 BACKGROUND 11
2.1 Mobile Platforms 11
2.2 Mobile Security 11
2.3 Vulnerability 12
2.3.1 Based on the Techniques 15
2.3.2 Based on the Severity Levels 16
2.3.3 Based on the Causes of Vulnerabilities 17
2.3.4 Based on the Software Systems 18
2.4 Malware 26
2.4.1 Malware Attack Vectors 26
2.4.2 Anatomy of a Mobile Attack 29
2.4.3 Mobile Malware Risk Matrix 30
2.4.4 Malware Behavior 32

CHAPTER 3 RELEVANT WORKS AND STUDIES RELATED TO ANDROID AND iOS 35
3.1 Introduction 35
3.2 Android versus iOS Battle 36
3.2.1 System Architecture 36
3.2.2 Security 37
3.2.3 Isolation Mechanism 39
3.2.4 Encryption Mechanism 41
3.2.5 App Permissions 42
3.2.6 Auto-Erase Mechanism 43
3.2.7 Application Provenance 43
3.3 Security Assessment of Android 52
3.3.1 Taxonomy Construction 55
3.3.2 Discussions and Future Research Directions 73

CHAPTER 4 A PARALLEL CLASSIFIER SCHEME FOR VULNERABILITY DETECTION IN ANDROID 77
4.1 Introduction 77
4.2 Relevant Works 80
4.3 Dataset Description 86
4.4 Proposed Methodology 87
4.5 System Configuration and Experimental Setup 93
4.6 Results 93
4.6.1 Individual Classifiers 93
4.6.2 Parallel Classifiers 94
4.7 Conclusion and Future Directions 97

CHAPTER 5 CLASSIFICATION OF ANDROID MALWARE USING ENSEMBLE CLASSIFIERS 101
5.1 Introduction 101
5.2 Relevant Works 101
5.3 Proposed Methodology 102
5.4 Setting Up the Data 104
5.5 Results 106
5.6 Conclusion and Future Directions 113

CHAPTER 6 TEXT PROCESSING–BASED MALWARE-TO-VULNERABILITY MAPPING FOR ANDROID 115
6.1 Introduction 115
6.2 Relevant Works 116
6.3 Malware-to-Vulnerability Mapping 118
6.4 Proposed Methodology 119
6.5 Evaluation and Results 129
6.6 Conclusion and Future Directions 139

Chapter 7 Android Vulnerabilities Impact Analysis on the Confidentiality, Integrity, and Availability Triad at the Architectural Level 141
7.1 Introduction 141
7.2 Relevant Works 142
7.3 Design Approach 143
7.3.1 Vulnerability Extraction 143
7.3.2 Impact Analysis 144
7.4 Results 145
7.5 Conclusion and Future Directions 149

Chapter 8 Conclusion and Future Directions 151
8.1 Introduction 151
8.2 Future Directions 153

Appendix A Android Malware Behavior 157

References 167

About the Authors

Niyati Baliyan is assistant professor, Department of Computer Engineering, National Institute of Technology Kurukshetra, Haryana. She attained a Doctor of Philosophy degree from the Computer Science Department, Indian Institute of Technology (IIT), Roorkee, India. Her thesis title was "Quality Assessment of Semantic Web based Applications." She also has a post-graduate certificate in information technology from Sheffield Hallam University, Sheffield, UK. Niyati obtained the Chancellor's Gold Medal for being university topper during post-graduate studies at Gautam Buddha University. She is co-author of *Semantic Web-Based Systems: Quality Assessment Models, SpringerBriefs in Computer Science*, 2018. Her research interests include knowledge engineering, machine learning, healthcare analytics, recommender systems, information security, and natural language processing. Her publication and other details can be found at: https://sites.google.com/site/niyatibaliyan.

Shivi Garg received a Doctor of Philosophy degree in December 2021 from the Information Technology Department, Indira Gandhi Delhi Technical University for Women (IGDTUW), Delhi, India. Her thesis was titled "Design and Analysis of Mobile Application Vulnerabilities." She is also a post graduate in Information Security at Delhi Technological University (DTU) Delhi, India. She has teaching and research experience since August 2016. Currently, she is assistant professor at J.C. Bose University of Science & Technology, YMCA, Faridabad. Her research interests include information security, mobile security, cyber security, and machine learning. Her publication and other details can be found at https://sites.google.com/view/shivigarg/home.

1
Introduction

1.1 Introduction

In the present world of information technology, the invention of mobile phones has proven to be revolutionary. Mobile phones act as a major correspondence hub for humans' primary data. They have not only transformed communication but also enabled us to expand businesses and impart education to remote areas. In fact, mobile phones are equipped to do almost everything that can be done with a desktop computer. The mobile phone is not just a telephone but a much more powerful, handy, and easy-to-use device [1, 2].

1.2 Evolution of Mobile Phones

Breakthrough "generational" changes are seen in wireless mobile communication networks to support large numbers of users and to meet high demands for lower latency, higher data rates, and better quality of services (QoS). Mobile technology has evolved significantly over the last four decades: 1G was launched in the 1980s, was based on analog signals, and provided only voice call services. In the 1990s, 2G was launched and was based on digital communication to enable voice services via digital signals. It supported short message service (SMS). The second-to-third-generation bridge (2.5G) supported data (email and web search) along with voice. From 2000 onward, 3G operated in high-frequency bands and supported multimedia services such as smart TV, video calls, etc. In the 2010s, 4G was based on long-term evolution (LTE) technology and provided high data rate applications such as video gaming, cloud computing, HD TV, etc. In the 2020s, 5G was deployed, enabling the Internet of Things (IoT), augmented and virtual Reality (AR and VR), vehicular ad hoc networks (VANETs), etc. [3]. Figure 1.1 depicts the evolution of mobile phones and cellular technologies. Table 1.1 summarizes the comparison among these cellular technologies.

DOI: 10.1201/9781003354574-1

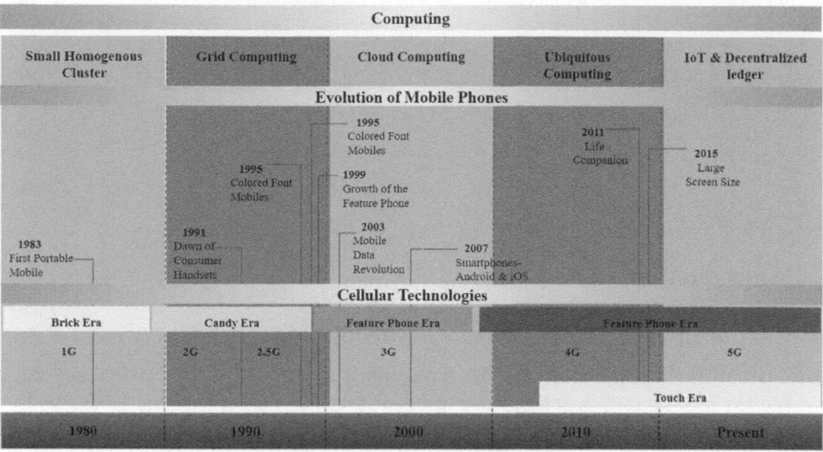

Figure 1.1 Evolution of mobile phones and cellular technologies.

With the changing cellular technology from 1G to 5G, mobile devices also changed and proved to be the right solution at the time. Mobile devices can provide all the services that users are availing with utmost ease and comfort from simply making a phone call from anywhere to today's personal pocket computers.

1. The Brick Era (1973–1988): Dr. Martin Cooper, a Motorola employee, made the first mobile phone call using a prototype DynaTAC phone. In 1973, mobile devices used an embedded system as an operating system (OS). This embedded system controlled operations. The phones in the brick era required enormous batteries. These phones were useful only to small segments of customers who needed constant communication, such as field workers, stockbrokers, realtors, etc. because they were big and expensive.
2. The Candy Bar Era (1988–1998): This era proved to be a significant leap in mobile technology. The phones were long, thin, and rectangular in shape and supported 2G. This era ushered in portability. The phones were used not only for making voice calls but also for sending SMSs.
3. The Feature Phone Era (1998–2008): The phones in this era opened the way for numerous services and diverse applications through the Internet, such as photography, music, videos, etc.

Table 1.1 Comparison among Cellular Technologies

FEATURES	1G	2G	3G	4G	5G
Launched/Deployed	1970/1984	1980/1999	1990/2002	2000/2010	2010/2015
Bandwidth	2 kbps	14-64 kbps	2 Mbps	200 Mbps	>1Gbps
Technology	Analog	Digital	Broad bandwidth, IP, CDMA	Undefined IP & combination of LAN/WAN/PAN/WLAN	4G + WWWW
Standards	AMPS, NMT, TACS	GSM, TDMA, CDMA	WCDMA, CDMA-2000	LTA, WiMAX	Not defined
Multiplexing	FDMA	TDMA, CDMA	CDMA	CDMA	CDMA
Switching	Circuit	Circuit and Packet	Packet	Packet	Packet
Service	Voice/telephony	Digital Voice/SMS	Integrated high-quality audio, video and data	Dynamic information access, wearable devices	Dynamic information access, wearable devices with AI capabilities
Core Network	PSTN	PSTN	Packet Network	Internet	Internet
Hands off	Horizontal	Horizontal	Horizontal	Horizontal & Vertical	Horizontal & Vertical
Physical Resources	Frequency	Time slots	Time slots/PN codes	Time/Frequency	Time/Frequency
Duplex Methods	FDD	FDD	FDD/ TDD	FDD/ TDD	FDD/ TDD

4. The Smartphone Era (2002–Present): Smartphones are on par with feature phones in terms of sending an SMS, making a phone call, capturing a photo, and accessing the mobile Internet. Smartphones mostly differ in terms of baseline OS, screen size, a stylus for input, QWERTY keyboard, and high-speed wireless connectivity/Wi-Fi. Nokia, Handspring, and Research in Motion (RIM) were the first companies to provide smartphones.
5. The Touch Era (2007–Present): In the fifth and final era, Steve Jobs introduced the iPhone and changed the mobile world immensely. Apple set new standards of people's expectations with the launch of iPhone, which offered new and advanced features for interaction and communication. Advanced features include location tracking, movement tracing, collecting real-time health data, etc.

1.3 Mobile Ecosystem and Threats

The mobile ecosystem is unique and comprises multiple devices (such as tablets, mobile phones, etc.), software (OS, development and testing tools), several device manufacturing companies (Apple, Samsung, Nokia, etc.), carrier companies (Airtel, Vodafone, etc.), and app stores (Google Play, the App Store). These components work together seamlessly for better end-to-end connectivity. Figure 1.2 depicts the mobile ecosystem.

Mobile phones started as simple devices for connecting people across different geographical locations by making phone calls. Now they are being used for handling multiple tasks such as computing, recording, exchanging, streaming, gaming, etc. These proved to be more powerful, more valuable, and therefore more vulnerable [4].

The mobile ecosystem consists of a series of interconnected systems and networks that support modern mobile devices. Software applications and cloud services greatly enhance the utility of mobile devices. App stores in mobile OS offer numerous and customized applications for end users' convenience. However, these applications (downloaded mainly from third-party app stores) are among the major vectors to easily distribute malicious software to mobile devices. Mobile applications generally pass through several communication networks and

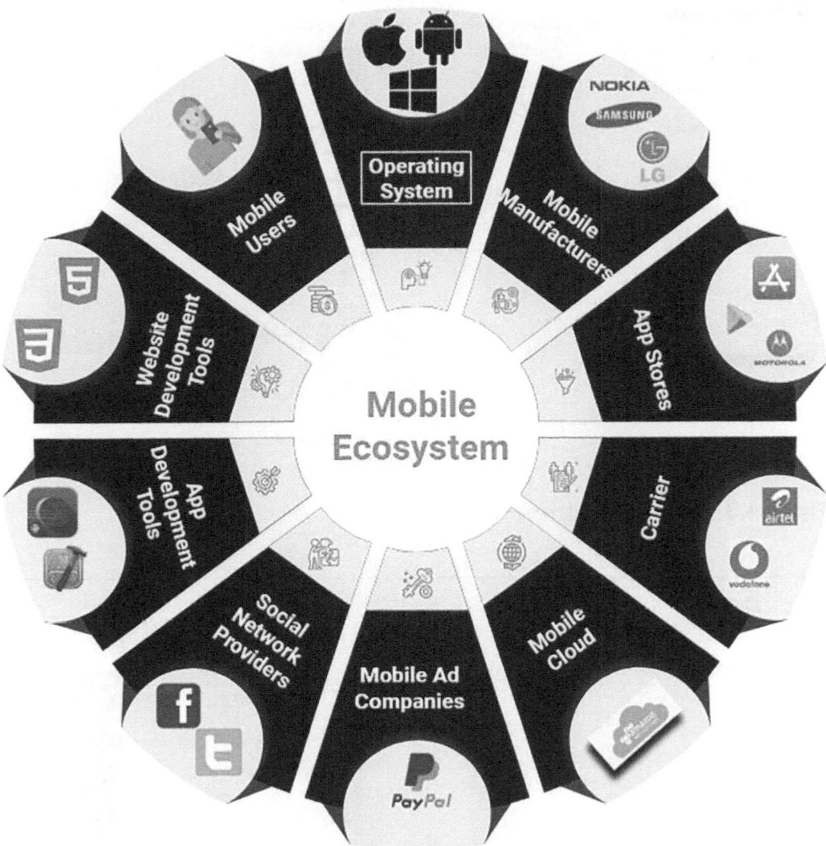

Figure 1.2 Mobile ecosystem.

interact with different systems maintained and controlled by other parties to achieve their intended goals [5]. This mobile ecosystem is depicted in Figure 1.3.

With the growing connectivity, mobile devices are exposed to multiple susceptibilities. Mobile OEM developers often use obsolete components and out-of-date system architectures that are prone to malicious attacks [6]. The COVID-19 pandemic geared up the digital transformation and led to the expansion of the attack surface histrionically, driven by the impetuous towards the cloud, operational technology (OT), and IT assets [7].

As per a Skybox Security report of 2022, zero-day attacks nearly doubled in 2021 [8]. The average time needed by the companies to detect and respond to cyber-attacks stretched to 280 days [9]. More than

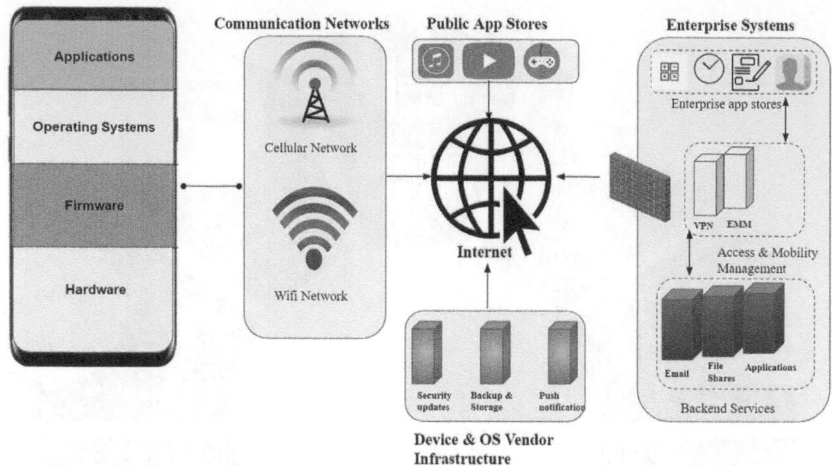

Figure 1.3 Threats to mobile ecosystem.

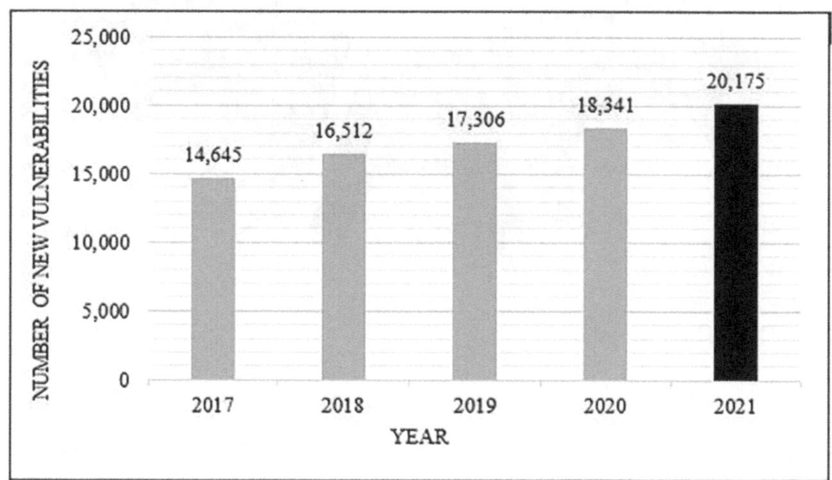

Figure 1.4 New vulnerabilities over last five years.

20,000 new vulnerabilities (an all-time high) were discovered in 2021; 20,175 common vulnerabilities and exposures (CVE) were published in 2021, 10% higher than in 2020 [7], as shown in Figure 1.4.

Nowadays, smartphones have technological capabilities that are on par with those of personal computers. With their improved computational capacity, smartphones have become fairly ingrained in our daily lives. According to a poll by Ericson, there are currently more than six billion smartphone subscriptions worldwide, and that number is expected

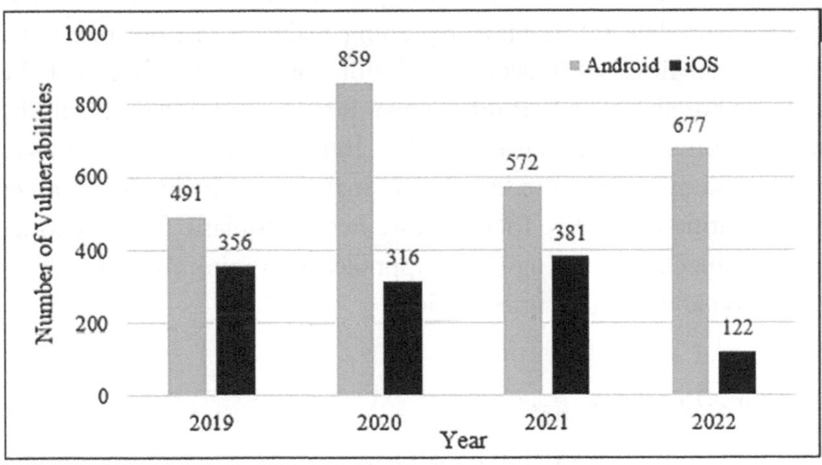

Figure 1.5 The number of vulnerabilities in Android and iOS (2019–2022).

to increase by several hundred million over the next several years. The three countries with the most smartphone users are China, India, and the United States [10]. Even where there were other mobile systems available, Google's Android and Apple's iOS together held 99% of the market as of 2020 [11]. As a result, the two most popular platforms for attacks are Android and iOS. The number of vulnerabilities in Android and iOS from 2019 to 2022 are shown in Figure 1.5 [12].

1.4 Motivation

Android OS forms the base of numerous computing platforms, such as mobile and Internet of Things devices (e.g., phones and tablets) [13]. Cyber-attackers generally target end users by publishing malicious applications (apps), which are easily deployable in mobile app stores and, therefore, compromise many mobile devices. Numerous security solutions are proposed against Android malware; however, they are not fool proof.

More powerful security solutions are needed to defend against malicious apps on mobile platforms and to overcome the shortcomings of prevailing malware-detection techniques and methods. First, the malware-detection mechanisms should be highly accurate. Second, these detection mechanisms must operate on different scales, such as IoT devices, smartphones, tablets, etc. Third, detection mechanisms should not only detect whether an app is malicious or benign but also provide complete information regarding malware to prioritize mitigation strategies. Lastly, security solution should not only detect the malware but also classify it into known families and determine all the possible threats a system is exposed to. In the past, manual analysis of malware samples were used to classify malware to the known families with identified patterns. Therefore, we need automatic feature extraction and machine learning (ML) approaches to minimize human intervention and be more time efficient.

1.5 Book Objectives

The prime objective of this book is to propose a novel end-to-end approach for assessing the impact of vulnerabilities on Android architecture, in order to improve secure coding mechanisms for Android applications and the underlying platform. Important background and key terms related to mobile OS security are discussed in Chapter 2. Android and iOS mobile platforms are compared in Chapter 3 from the standpoint of security, and important research gaps are identified.

The overall objectives of the book are:

1. To perform a comprehensive literature review of vulnerabilities in different mobile OS such as Android and iOS
2. To design and validate an approach for malware detection for Android using ensemble binary classifier
3. To design and assess an approach for Android malware classification using ensemble multi-class classifier
4. To develop and evaluate an approach for Android malware family mapping to vulnerabilities and assess the impact of Android vulnerabilities on the confidentiality, integrity, and availability (CIA) triad at the architectural level

The works presented in this book have been evaluated using benchmark datasets, standard validation methods, and performance analysis. We have identified the research gaps and challenges from the literature survey. The techniques and algorithms included in the thesis have been implemented using Python and related tools.

1.6 Book Organization

The remainder of the book is organized as follows: Chapter 2 gives an overview of basic terms related to mobile security. A statistical analysis is performed to compare Android and iOS from a security standpoint. A systematic literature review (SLR) presents various existing approaches in the domain of Android security and analyzes the gaps in current research, followed by the motivation for the study in Chapter 3. Chapter 4 proposes an ensemble binary classifier for malware detection in Android. Chapter 5 presents an ensemble multi-class classifier for malware classification into known families. Chapter 6 proposes a framework that maps malware to vulnerabilities using a 2D matrix. This framework models malware description reports using a bag-of-words (BoW) model and leverages natural language processing (NLP) and ML techniques to build ensemble ML-based models. Chapter 7 assesses the impact of mapped vulnerabilities on the CIA triad at the architectural level. Finally, Chapter 8 sums up the contributions made in the proposed work. Furthermore, open research challenges and possible directions for future research work are also presented in this concluding chapter.

2
Background

2.1 Mobile Platforms

There are many mobile platforms for smartphones, including Blackberry, Symbian, Sony Ericsson, Samsung, Windows, iOS, and Android; however, by 2022, Apple's iOS and Google's Android held a combined market share of 99% [14]. The market share of various mobile OS is shown in Figure 2.1 for the period of 2011 to 2022. In the mobile market, iOS (26.27%) and Android (72.95%) are in the lead, thanks to their improved features and customer popularity.

2.2 Mobile Security

Mobile security generally refers to protecting portable computing devices such as smartphones, laptops, IoT devices, and tablets from threats and vulnerabilities associated with wireless computing [15].

It is crucial to manage mobile devices across several business operations. Issues related to data privacy and security can be addressed through numerous mobile security products, such as mobile device management (MDM), enterprise mobility management (EMM), and unified endpoint management (UEM) [16], as depicted in Figure 2.2.

1. MDM refers to the remote management of devices and includes multiple features such as device security, enrollment, location tracking, and device provisioning. MDM can help wipe data in case of lost/stolen devices. A basic MDM tool enforces security policies, tracks inventory, and performs real-time monitoring and reporting.

The exponential usage of the smartphones and app markets led to the establishment of mobile application management (MAM), a solution that manages and controls major business applications for data security. MAM, unlike MDM specific to a device, is applicable to

DOI: 10.1201/9781003354574-2

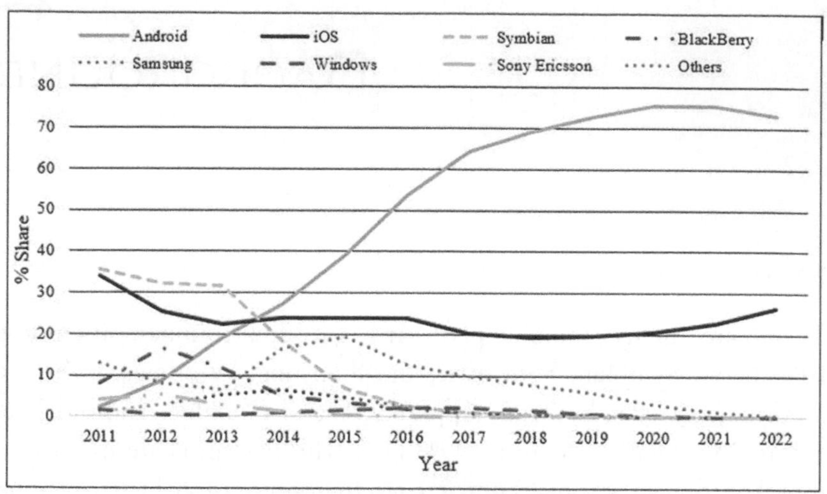

Figure 2.1 Market share of different mobile OS (2011–2022).

specific applications on a device. MAM helps in setting up an enterprise app store and pushes/updates vital apps on business devices remotely. MAM could not support the majority of native app stores; therefore, mobile information management (MIM) and mobile content management (MCM) came into existence. They primarily focus on the security of a specific file repository where employers and employees can access and share files without affecting the entire device or other applications.

2. EMM is a combination of MDM, MAM, and MCM along with app wrapping and containerization for securing data. It offers complete data security on bring-your-own devices (BYOD) and corporate-owned single-use (COSU) or dedicated devices for enterprises.
3. UEM helps manage all endpoints such as mobile phones, laptops, personal computers (PCs), tablets, printers, and wearables using a single comprehensive EMM solution.

2.3 Vulnerability

System vulnerabilities are defined as defects in the hardware/software that deteriorate the security of the device/system [17]. A vulnerability model can be depicted as an intersection of (i) an attacker's modus

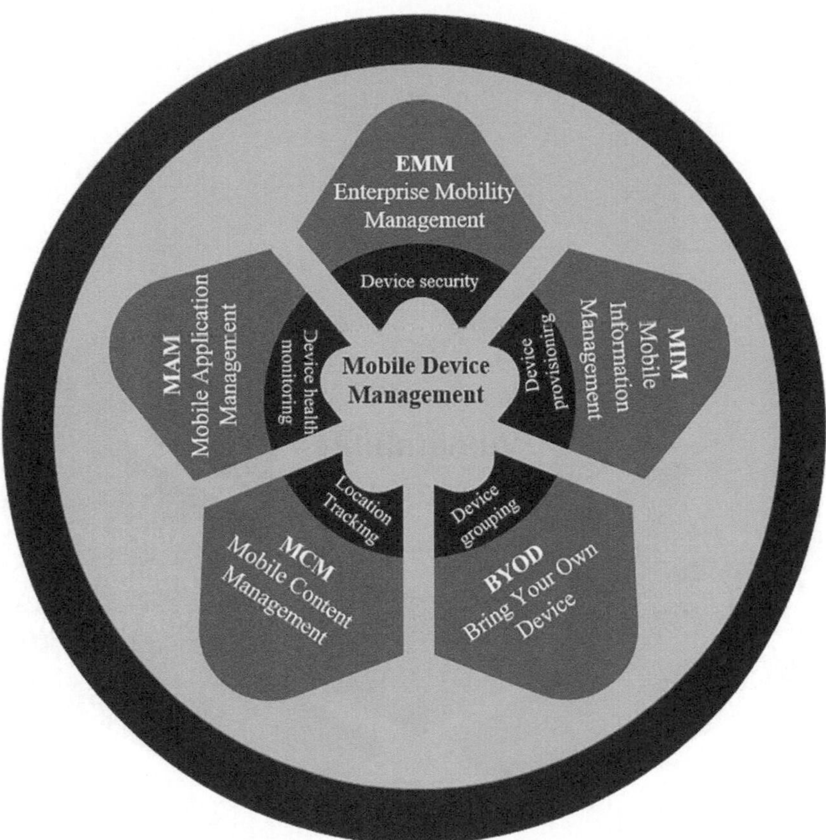

Figure 2.2 UEM, EMM, and MDM.

operandi for attack, (ii) a system's weakness, (iii) and an attacker's potential to exploit that weakness [18].

Vulnerabilities in a software system should be classified to understand the exact cause and subsequently take the appropriate cost- and time-effective measures. A comprehensive and holistic vulnerability classification model can help identify, analyze, and discover unknown vulnerabilities. Vulnerability modelling can be further used to build patching processes by estimating the number of vulnerability types and their severity levels. Several standard technical factors (based on past studies) are proposed for vulnerability classification in software systems. These factors are based on techniques used, severity levels, causes of vulnerabilities, and different types of software systems [19], as shown in Figure 2.4.

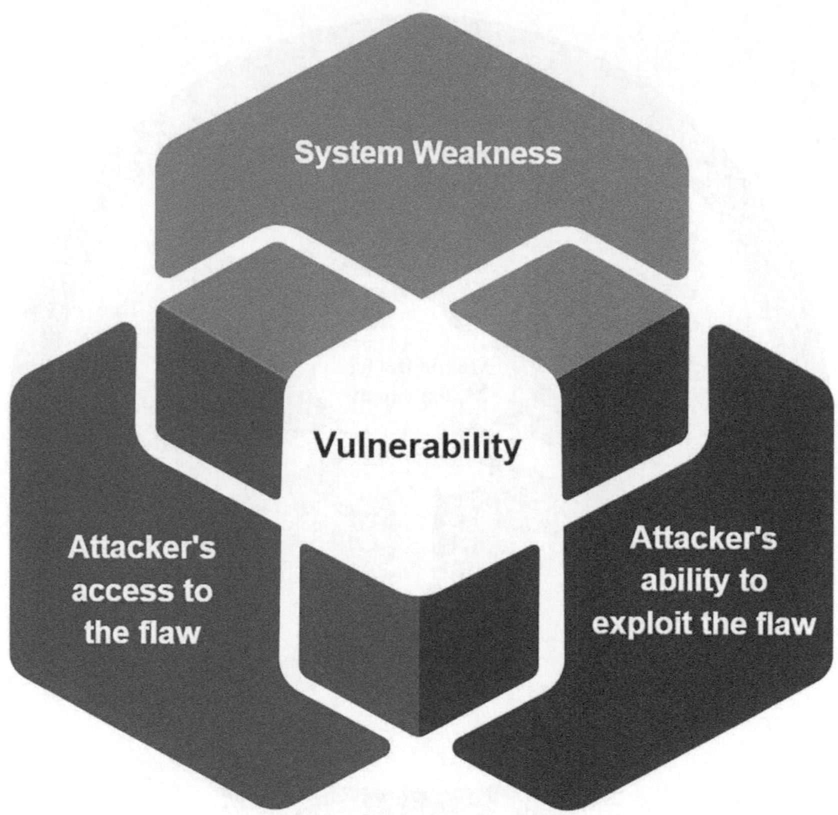

Figure 2.3 Vulnerability model.

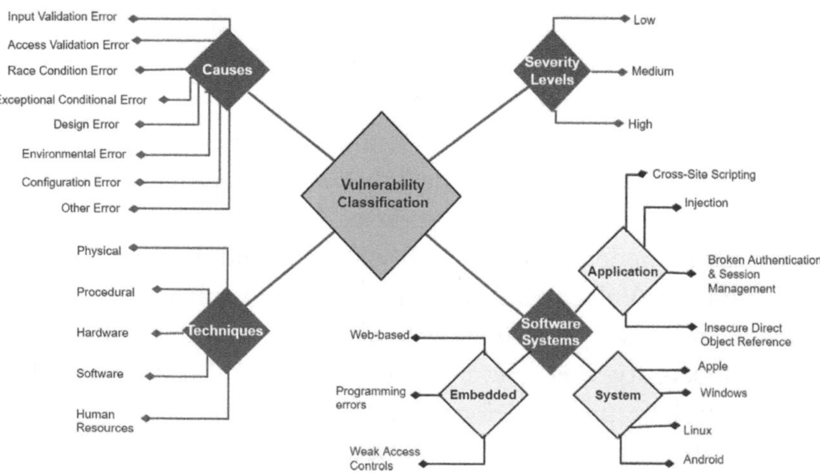

Figure 2.4 Software vulnerability classification.

2.3.1 Based on the Techniques

Numerous techniques can exploit system susceptibilities, including hardware, software, physical, procedural, and human resources [20].

1. Hardware techniques: The prime means to exploit system vulnerability using hardware are damaging equipment physically, implanting a bug within the hardware, and launching a hardware attack. For example, Thunderclap is a type of hardware vulnerability that resides in the Thunderbolt hardware interface produced by Intel. Attackers physically access the Thunderbolt port to hack a target system. They execute arbitrary code and gain access to sensitive information such as passwords, encryption keys, and other data.
2. Software techniques: Malicious software or malware can penetrate through application programs and utility routines. Software susceptibilities usually occur due to out-of-date OS and productivity software, obsolete legacy applications, unpatched web browsers, or out-of-date plug-ins.
3. Physical techniques: Physically entering a restricted place, such as a building, a computer room, or any other defined location, is referred to as a physical invasion. Physical vulnerabilities include undesirable site-specific actions, such as theft, vandalism, and trip hazards, whether on purpose or accidental. A vulnerability that can be exploited physically requires the attacker to interact with or control the affected component physically.
4. Procedural techniques: Numerous agendas, procedural guidelines, policies, and secure software development frameworks such as Microsoft Security Development Life Cycle (MSDLC), System Security Engineering Capability Maturity Model (SSECMM), Common Criteria (CC), Open Software Assurance Maturity Model (OpenSAMM), etc. are used to build software development processes. However, these models are not standardized, so security is compromised, leading to the inherent vulnerabilities in software development.
5. Human resource techniques: Software developers, I/O schedulers, and system analysts are authorized to access the system. These human resources can infringe on the system and

launch an attack. Human susceptibilities can cause technical vulnerabilities. A dearth of proper knowledge of software requirements and a lack of technical skills can lead to faulty system design.

Software developers should consider leakage points when designing software and its components. They should use protection mechanisms in the software, regardless of its configuration. These defense mechanisms can be leveraged for multiple leakage points.

2.3.2 Based on the Severity Levels

Severity levels can be used to classify vulnerabilities in software systems. A heuristic-based classification method called the Common Vulnerabilities Scoring System (CVSS) aims to focus on multiple vulnerability attributes. The National Institute of Standards and Technology (NIST) and the National Vulnerability Database (NVD) have defined CVSS as a standard scoring system. CVSS gives a score on a scale of 1–10 for each vulnerability. According to CVSS v3.0 ratings, a base score range of 0.0 indicates no risk, a score range 0.1–3.0 indicates low risk, 4.0–6.9 indicates medium risk, 7.0–8.9 indicates high risk, and 9.0–10.0 indicates critical risk. [21]. NIST defines the severity levels in NVD [22] as follows:

1. Critical severity: Vulnerabilities with critical severity are difficult to exploit and compromise root-level servers and infrastructure devices. For example, CVE-2022–27572 vulnerability has a CVSS score of 10.0. It is a heap-based buffer overflow generally found in Android library functions and allows attackers to execute arbitrary code [23].
2. High severity: These vulnerabilities are generally difficult to exploit and often result in exploitation of elevated privileges. These vulnerabilities lead to serious loss of data and downtime. For example, CVE-2019–8591 has a CVSS score of 8.8 and was seen in Apple iOS. This vulnerability led to system termination unexpectedly [24].
3. Medium severity: These vulnerabilities allowed the attackers to manipulate victims through social engineering tactics. The exploitation of such vulnerabilities provides limited access

[25]: e.g., CVE-2022–30721 in Android has a CVSS score of 5.0 and triggers crashes [26].

4. Low severity: The impact of these vulnerabilities on the organization is minimal. Physical or local access to the system is frequently required to exploit these vulnerabilities. For instance, the Android CVE-2022–33702 vulnerability results in inappropriate authorization, allowing a local attacker to disable Keyguard and circumvent the Knox Guard lock by performing a factory reset.

The severity of the vulnerability can be used to gauge the seriousness of an exploitation's effects. The influence on CIA can be calculated based on the CVSS severity-level ratings. Impact values can be marked as none, partial, or complete for various security categories (low, medium, high, and critical) and these values combined make up one value.

2.3.3 Based on the Causes of Vulnerabilities

Depending on the causes, vulnerabilities can be categorized. The eight classifications, as defined by NVD [27], are as follows:

1. Input validation error (comprises boundary condition error, buffer overflow): This vulnerability is caused when the input affecting the control or data flow is not validated or is incorrectly validated. Errors in coding are prime reasons for buffer overflows. Attackers exploit the buffer overflow vulnerability to inject malicious code that can overwrite a buffer. As a result, a system can be compromised by unauthorized access.
2. Access validation error: This is usually known as broken access control and allows the attackers to gain unauthorized access to private/sensitive information and resources: for instance, privilege escalation vulnerabilities.
3. Exceptional condition error: These vulnerabilities often occur when the system is able to handle undefined and unanticipated exceptions. Exceptions can be caused by the unavailability of the database, the failure of the system call, network timeouts, null pointer exceptions, etc. Exceptions may allow an attacker to induce unexpected as well as unnoticed behavior.

4. Design error: This vulnerability results from faulty program architecture, such as the Telnet protocol, which enables remote connections to machines without encryption.
5. Environmental error: These vulnerabilities are brought on by the particular constraints of the computational environment. For instance, multiple Telnet hazards brought on by environmental issues frequently result in packet snooping and session hijacking.
6. Configuration error: Incompatible system settings are to blame for certain vulnerabilities. Unpatched security issues, inappropriate file and directory permissions, improper authentication with external systems, and unpatched security problems are a few instances of configuration vulnerabilities.
7. Race condition error: Improper process serialization triggers race condition vulnerabilities These errors occur across shared resources such as local and global variables in multi-threaded programs, memory, files, etc.
8. Others: This group includes all the non-standard vulnerabilities that are not listed previously.

These eight classes are not completely mutually exclusive since some vulnerabilities can fit into multiple categories. Multiple vulnerabilities can therefore result in malware attacks and are referred to as "overlap vulnerabilities." Most of these flaws arise from design problems, followed by input validation errors [28].

2.3.4 Based on the Software Systems

Application, embedded, and system software all fall under one of three categories. The next sections examine each category's vulnerabilities.

1. Embedded system vulnerabilities: Embedded systems often suffer from numerous vulnerabilities:

   - Web-based vulnerability: These are also referred to as network intrusion attacks. Networked embedded systems are vulnerable to server and workstation attacks comparable to remote exploits. For instance, a buffer overflow attack occurs when malicious scripts are executed.

- Programming errors: These weaknesses can be taken advantage of via fabricated inputs and controlled hijacking. Unauthorized reprogramming of embedded devices is possible: for instance, if game consoles are made to run Linux.
- Weak access control or authentication: Manipulated inputs through sensors in the system can exploit these vulnerabilities: e.g., directory traversal vulnerabilities.
- Exhaustion attack: This is also known as energy drainage vulnerability. Increased system load, reduced sleep cycles, and intense use of sensors can cause such vulnerabilities.
- Physical tampering: These are typically brought on by system bus spying or power analysis attacks.
- Damage to peripherals and sensors: Inaccurate sensor calibration might result in damage to the functioning of peripherals or sensors, which can damage peripherals.

Embedded system vulnerabilities are primarily due to physical exposure, inadequate power availability and processing power, and network connectivity issues.

2. Application software vulnerabilities include the following:

- Injection vulnerabilities: These vulnerabilities may be caused by injection attacks, including light-weight directory access protocol (LDAP) injection, SQL injection, OS injection, and email injection. A query or instruction that contains malicious code or data is forwarded to another system, enabling an attacker to seize control of the target machine and execute a fraudulent database query.
- Cross-site scripting (XSS): This attack involves injecting malicious scripts into a trustworthy link. The embedded script runs when the user hits this link, giving access to the private data.
- Broken authentication and session management: When authentication actions are not properly implemented, hackers take over one or more accounts and compromise passwords, keys, and session IDs. Sometimes users forget to log out of a session where re-authentication is needed.

An attacker can identify these sessions and hack them. Two-factor verification is considered for transactions with high value.

- Format string: This vulnerability results from the application interpreting unfiltered user input as a command. For instance, the format string parameter used in C's scanf() and printf() methods is %d.
- Insecure direct object reference: These vulnerabilities occur when an application directly accesses objects based on user-supplied inputs. As a result, authentication mechanisms are bypassed, and resources are directly accessed, such as files, databases, etc. [28].

Web apps can range from simple to complicated. Application vulnerabilities are responsible for 90% and 99% of online and mobile application vulnerabilities, respectively, according to [29]. Some daily use apps, such as Facebook and Tinder, may be the kind that are simple to create but extremely sophisticated and prone to flaws.

3. OS vulnerabilities: An OS suffers from numerous vulnerabilities. We mainly concentrate on the flaws in Linux, Windows, Apple, and Android, which are described as follows:

   - Linux vulnerabilities
     i. Privilege escalation: Attackers target the victim computer and access the resources illegitimately. It allows someone with access to a computer to do much more than a regular user or software would be able to. For example, an application with these privileges could delete all the files on the computer without any other person being aware of the action.
     ii. DoS: Often, hacking and cybercrime involve making a resource inaccessible or unavailable. This can be done by manipulating network traffic or exploiting vulnerabilities in the code of a site or login.
     iii. IP spoofing: The IP address in an Internet packet can be forged to hide someone's identity. It also somctimes masquerades as a different machine, which can stop IP address–based authentication.

Linux is open source, so you can use it for free. This means that the code is available and can be used, modified, or changed for others to use. It also means that it's possible to install and run powerful programs on Linux in just a few minutes. Hence, we want to study and fix vulnerabilities in Linux because they can be exploited by malicious users.

- Apple vulnerabilities
  i. Password stealing: Malicious apps can steal a user's credentials. For example, they may steal passwords, authentication tokens, and web passwords that users have saved in their keychain while using the app.
  ii. Container cracking: This flaw enables a rogue app to access a different app's safe and data-hiding container and steal its data. Currently, this vulnerability is unknown and unpatched.
  iii. IPC interception: This means a malicious app can disguise itself as an authentic app, then intercept data and steals anything you thought was secure. For example, some apps/servers use a WebSocket connection that exposes important information about an app. If one is developed by a malicious developer, they could potentially intercept data and make it appear to be authentic. Apple devices have no means at all to authenticate this. The identity of a local app cannot be identified using an API call.
  iv. Scheme hijacking: URL scheme hijacking is another name for scheme hijacking. Apps on iOS and OS X can register for any URL schemes they want to handle, including those that can be used to start apps or transfer data payloads across apps. On iOS and OS X, there are numerous categories that an app could register for. For instance, many apps can register for any URI scheme. Multiple apps may share tokens (passwords, codes) via URL schemes if they share the same login through a third-party provider.

Apps installed from the iOS and Mac app stores are generally limited to a sandbox. They are only able to access resources outside their container if the user approves it. The four vulnerabilities mentioned earlier allow an unauthorized user to gain access to the device. These are also known as cross-app resource access (XARA) attacks.

v. Privilege escalation: Kernel memory corruption vulnerability on an OS X system often causes the escalation and privileges of the attacker. Mac OS X users are advised to apply any OS updates right away, once they become available.
vi. Extensible firmware interface (EFI): The EFI provides improved protection against malicious activities, but if that fails, then you have to make sure your system's memory is refreshed in order to prevent any corruption.
vii. Thunderstrike: A new vulnerability called Thunderstrike allows for the use of a bootkit on Macs. Basically, it can overwrite the SPI flash ROM and make your computer vulnerable to attacks from within. This can be done by only allowing Thunderbolt devices with a known serial number to connect.
viii. Root pipe: One of many privileges escalation vulnerabilities allowing the attacker full access to the system. The problem can be mitigated through improved input validation in the script and handling of redirects.
ix. AirDrop: AirDrop is an Apple product for transferring files. A directory traversal attack is used to compromise the device's core and install malware. The signed software being used in this attack has been given the trust seal. The malware is given a wide range of privileges, including the ability to read contacts, use the camera, and record location data. The latest versions of iOS and Mac OS X can be upgraded to help mitigate this threat.

- Windows vulnerabilities

i. Integer underflow: This is a software security issue that arises due to an improperly aligned table, which can lead to the remainder at a subtraction operation being underflowed. If a remote attacker entices the victim to open an affected TrueType font (TTF) file containing specially crafted data, they can take advantage of the vulnerability and exploit it.

ii. DNS use-after-free: An adversary could use Microsoft Windows to execute arbitrary damaging code due to domain name system (DNS) servers. The software's handling of DNS requests is the problem. By sending bogus DNS requests to a target machine, this vulnerability is taken advantage of. This could trigger a use-after-free state, allowing the attacker to run arbitrary code and take full control of the system.
iii. Graphics memory corruption: This occurs due to incorrect memory functions that contain manipulated fonts.
iv. Journal heap overflows: By opening a specially crafted journal file, the user can remotely execute code by taking advantage of this vulnerability. Users with administrative powers on the system are more negatively impacted than users with lower user rights.
v. Journal RCE: In this, arbitrary codes are executed via a specially manufactured journal notes file (.jnt).
vi. Use-after-free toolbar: This happens especially in Windows Server 2008, in which hackers run malicious code using a specially built toolbar object.
vii. Graphics component buffer overflow: This vulnerability is the most serious and allows malicious code to be executed at random when a specifically crafted OpenType font is read by an authorized user.
viii. Windows media center RCE: This vulnerability is exploited when a media center link (.mcl) file is opened and allows the execution of an arbitrary code.
ix. OpenType font parsing: When the atmfd.dll file in the Adobe Type Manager Library of Microsoft Windows Server 2008 is opened, this vulnerability is exploited, enabling an attacker to use a specifically crafted OpenType font to perform a DoS attack.
x. Server message block corruption: This problem appears in Windows Server 2008. Through the use of a carefully

designed string in a server message block (SMB) server error-logging action, it permits authenticated users to run any piece of code. The compromised software's improper logging practices are the cause of the vulnerability. By sending a specifically crafted string to the target device, an unauthorized attacker might take advantage of the vulnerability and completely compromise the machine.

xi. Password theft: Web browsers such as Google Chrome operating on Windows 10 are used to exploit this vulnerability in order to steal credentials. Google Chrome downloads files with non-printable characters and uses the MIME-sniffing technique for files that contain text or content that is similar to text. On the victim's website, the attackers can plant a Shell Command File (SCF) with non-printable characters.

Monolithic kernel designs are supported by Windows OS. In Windows, the graphical user interface (GUI) is given more consideration. Windows endpoints are vulnerable to malware attacks. Windows lacks the ability to handle complex changes and software updates.

- Android vulnerabilities

i. Bypass something: Attackers circumvent the authentication mechanisms to access unsecured files and applications.

ii. Code execution: Attackers execute arbitrary code and insert malicious code into the user's input. The software's flow control can be changed by arbitrary code execution, and sensitive data can also be modified.

iii. Denial of service (DoS): This vulnerability, when exploited, makes the resources unavailable to legitimate users. DoS can result from improper handling of resources such as files, records, memory, I/O devices, etc.

iv. Directory traversal: Path traversal vulnerability, also referred to as directory traversal, happens when an attacker creates a pathname to access a file or directory outside the restricted directory using predetermined input sequences. This means that the attacker can access any file on the target machine.

v. Gain information: This vulnerability, when exploited, takes control of sensitive information. Attackers can gain access to sensitive data by executing malicious scripts in the applications.
vi. Gain privileges: This vulnerability can result in gaining root or administrative privileges and happens when routine security checks are disabled by the OS.
vii. Memory corruption: When a program reads from or writes to a memory location outside the bound buffer, it crashes. As a result, an attacker can access confidential and sensitive data and change the control flow.
viii. Overflow: The cause of this vulnerability is the overwritten buffer. The data in the buffer is usually overwritten by malicious scripts. It can cause a system crash that can harm files and other sensitive information.
ix. SQL injection: An attacker can use SQL injection to insert malicious data into a database query, which can then be used to access sensitive information, bypass security checks, or alter the database. SQL injection is a common vulnerability in database-driven websites.

Android is vulnerable to attack due to a number of factors, such as its open-source nature, insecure Linux kernel, lightweight construction, slow rate of OS updates, and improper app selection. These vulnerabilities are not exclusive to Android; any operating system can be susceptible to the same type of attack. For instance, password theft can occur in both Windows and Apple, though for different reasons. SQL injection is considered a serious security threat and has been responsible for a number of high-profile breaches, including the 2012 Yahoo! data breach.

Vulnerabilities are exploitable risks and unsecured entry points that can be leveraged by various threat factors such as malware (malicious programs), hidden backdoor programs, etc. Further details about malware follow.

2.4 Malware

Malware is a type of software that is designed to harm or disrupt a computer system. It can perform actions like stealing sensitive information, bypassing access controls, and displaying unwanted advertisements. Malware is a serious threat to both individual users and businesses, and it is important to be aware of the dangers it poses [30]. Different types of malware have different purposes, as shown in Figure 2.5:

Various aspects related to malware are discussed next.

2.4.1 Malware Attack Vectors

Mobile devices can get malware from multiple sources called attack vectors, which pose serious risks. The attack vectors represent the means by which an attacker acquires access to the mobile device or injects malicious code into the device. Attack vectors can be viewed on physical and logical levels based on different pre-conditions [31]. Figure 2.6 represents the attack vectors for mobile devices.

1. Physical attack vectors: Physical attack vectors come into account when an attacker acquires or there are widespread local communication interfaces.
   a. Wireless interfaces: Malicious data packets are injected through wireless interfaces such as Wi-Fi, Bluetooth, etc.

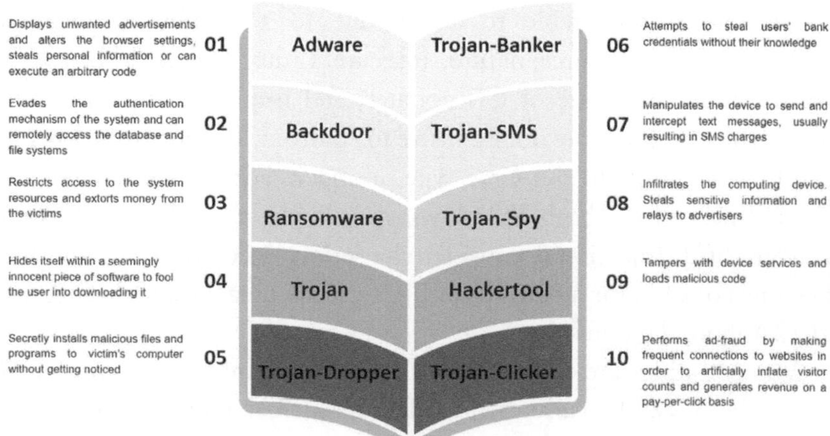

Displays unwanted advertisements and alters the browser settings, steals personal information or can execute an arbitrary code
01
Adware
Trojan-Banker
06
Attempts to steal users' bank credentials without their knowledge
Evades the authentication mechanism of the system and can remotely access the database and file systems
02
Backdoor
Trojan-SMS
07
Manipulates the device to send and intercept text messages, usually resulting in SMS charges
Restricts access to the system resources and extorts money from the victims
03
Ransomware
Trojan-Spy
08
Infiltrates the computing device. Steals sensitive information and relays to advertisers
Hides itself within a seemingly innocent piece of software to fool the user into downloading it
04
Trojan
Hackertool
09
Tampers with device services and loads malicious code
Secretly installs malicious files and programs to victim's computer without getting noticed
05
Trojan-Dropper
Trojan-Clicker
10
Performs ad-fraud by making frequent connections to websites in order to artificially inflate visitor counts and generates revenue on a pay-per-click basis

Figure 2.5 Types of malware.

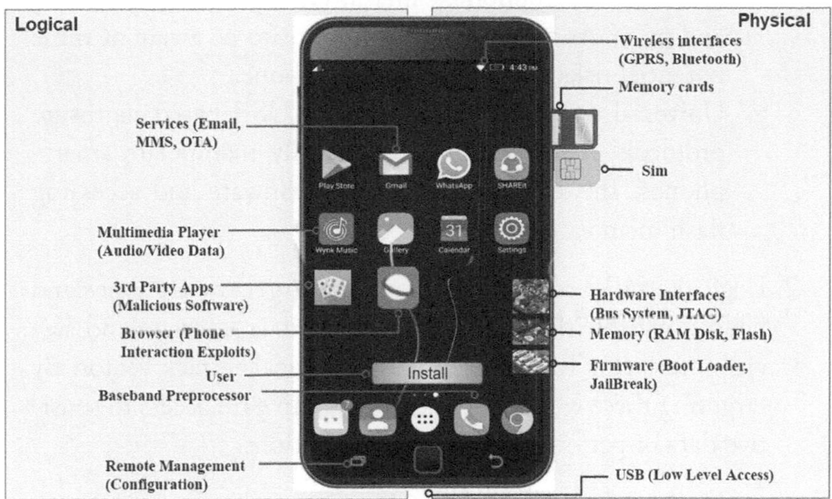

Figure 2.6 Mobile attack vectors

Attacker can decrypt (in the case of weak encryption, such as WEP) and read the transmitted data over the wireless transmission.

b. Storage cards: Data on external storage media is vulnerable to brute-force attack. Malicious users can read data from the storage media, and manipulated data can be implanted by exploiting the vulnerabilities in the victim's smartphone.
c. SIM card: Attackers can gain physical access to mobile devices and manipulate the communication between the mobile device and the SIM (subscriber identification module) card by exploiting SIM toolkit vulnerabilities in the specifications.
d. Hardware interfaces: Attackers are able to attain access to hardware elements of the smartphone, such as memory buses and hardware interfaces, (e.g., JTAG) and can bypass individual user interface protection mechanisms.
e. Storage: The attacker can access the data stored in the memory and bypass the protection mechanisms by manipulating OS functions in the flash memory.
f. Firmware: Because firmware can be manipulated by attackers (evil maid attack), this gives them complete remote control over a smartphone and its data. The attackers can

access the microphone, camera, GPS positioning system, and more. As a result, it is important to be aware of these potential risks when using a smartphone.

g. Universal serial bus (USB): Using USB-based hardware protocols, it is possible to physically manipulate smartphones. This enables exchanging firmware and accessing flash memory directly.

2. Logical attack vectors: Attackers can target smartphones and tablets by exploiting weaknesses in various software and service interfaces. This is known as a "logical" attack vector. By targeting these weaknesses, attackers can gain access to sensitive data or perform other malicious actions.

   a. Communication services: Communication services can be used to transfer malicious data to end devices over the Internet. This includes email, SMS, MMS, instant messaging, and VoIP services.
   b. Browser: Web browser applications in smartphones are the major source of malware propagation and can exploit vulnerabilities in the browser to access private and confidential data.
   c. Baseband processor: The baseband processor has been identified as a point of attack from two different sides. First, an attack from outside the mobile radio interface for end devices, which violates availability and confidentiality. Second, an attack from the smartphone itself against mobile radio network base stations or its users, which violates availability of the mobile radio service.
   d. Apps: Apps downloaded from untrusted sources such as third-party libraries are often pirated or contain malware. On installing these applications, private and sensitive information can be accessed such as GPS locations, call records, microphones, etc.
   e. Multimedia player: Multimedia data downloaded from dubious sources poses a serious risk to smartphone devices and exploits vulnerabilities from compressed multimedia data streams such as MP3, MP4, GIF, TIFF, PDF, etc.

f. Remote maintenance: Key aspects such as an unsafe device configuration, lack of software updates, or the use of enterprise services via non-registered devices can be addressed using remote control interfaces. However, such interfaces with OS functions pose serious risks. Attackers can often penetrate and manipulate security mechanisms by exploiting vulnerabilities in the interfaces to the remote device management.
g. Users: Users can also unwittingly act as agents for an attacker. Attackers may exploit a user's lack of knowledge about proper responses to the system and warning messages. Additionally, they may use OS vulnerabilities to trick the user into confirmations that result in malicious software distribution (e.g., ZeuS-in-the-Mobile [ZitMo], Cabir).

2.4.2 Anatomy of a Mobile Attack

As mobile devices become increasingly prevalent, cybercriminals more actively exploit vulnerabilities in these devices. In order to protect user data, it is crucial to understand the mobile technology chain and the points where malicious attacks can occur. Figure 2.7 shows

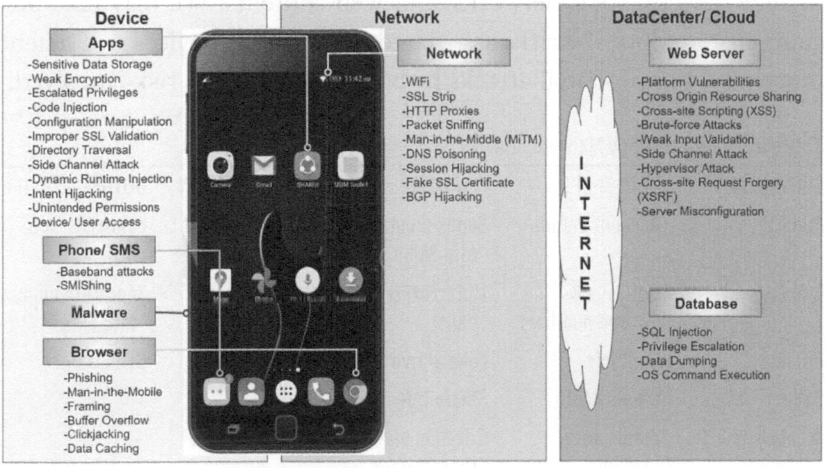

Figure 2.7 Anatomy of a mobile attack.

the three key points in the mobile technology chain—device, network, and data center/cloud—where vulnerabilities can be exploited by attackers.

Malware can perform several notorious activities once it infects a mobile device and thus, the mobile device becomes a surveillance system. Malware can access the audio, camera, GPS location, and text messages and can take over the privacy of the user. It can lead to data theft and financial losses by stealing login credentials, international mobile equipment identity (IMEI) information, and transaction authentication numbers (TAN), extortion via ransomware, sending premium-rate SMSs, etc. Malware can carry out illegal activities such as distributed denial of service (DDoS) attacks [32], clicking on fraudulent emails, thus posing a serious risk to the device. Moreover, impersonating attacks can gain the trust of the users to send and redirect emails and posts on social media. Table 2.1 summarizes the activities by malware attacks.

2.4.3 Mobile Malware Risk Matrix

Malware and other security issues are rapidly affecting mobile devices. The mobile risk matrix (MRM) clarifies the range of risks associated with mobile devices and illustrates their prevalence [33]. Figure 2.8 illustrates how MRM encompasses a variety of attack routes, including malware, vulnerabilities, and behavioral setups. These attack vectors include devices, apps, networks, and web contents. We may take precautions to reduce the risks associated with mobile devices and defend ourselves from potential attacks by being aware of the risks involved.

Table 2.1 Activities by Malware Attacks

SURVEILLANCE	DATA THEFT	FINANCIAL	IMPERSONATION	BOTNET ACTIVITY
Audio	Account details	Sends premium rate SMSs	SMS redirection	Launches DDoS attacks
Call Logs	Call logs & phone numbers	Makes expensive calls	Posts to social media	Sends premium rate SMSs
Camera	Contacts	Fake antivirus	Sends emails	Click fraud
SMS	Steals IMEI	Steals TAN	–	–
Location	Steals data via app vulnerabilities	Extortion via ransomware	–	–

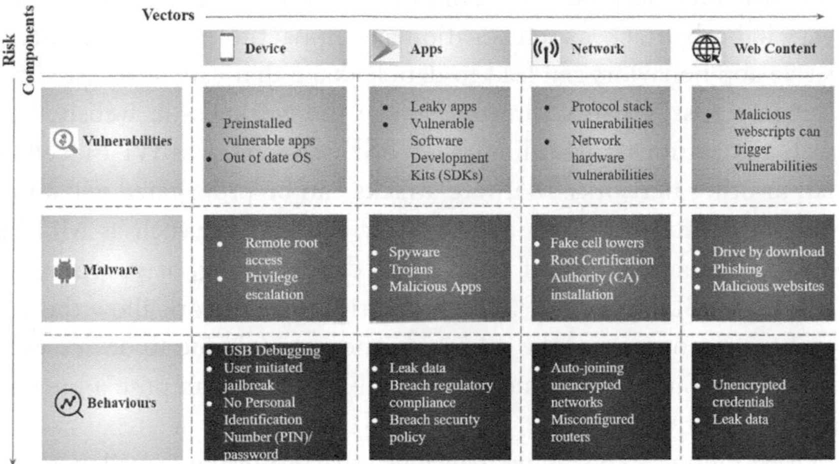

Figure 2.8 Mobile risk matrix showing the spectra of mobile risks.

Malware affecting mobile device firmware and OS potentially causes serious data loss and surveillance issues since malicious users can obtain higher permissions levels than usually granted to apps. As an example, the Pegasus [34] spyware targets Android devices and is prevalent due to its high impact. Pegasus activates by a single click on a phishing SMS and spies on the conversations taking place around the device by accessing the phone's cameras and microphones. It can steal end-to-end encrypted messages between clients and can also trace victims' movements. Mobile devices are also affected by multiple known vulnerabilities. Security bulletins released by Google at regular intervals detail the fixes for the latest device vulnerabilities. Risk can be measured by tracking the vulnerability half-life from device vulnerabilities. The half-life of a vulnerability is defined as the time required to reduce its occurrence by 50% [35]. Most of the device configurations and behaviors are device specific and consist of installing apps from non-official app stores and USB debugging for Android.

Malicious mobile apps can steal sensitive information and physically damage devices. Malware can get into legitimate mobile apps when the apps are injected with malicious code or on a device when user permissions are exploited. As an example, a flashlight app in Android with masked intent can access users' personal information for malicious purposes [36]. Android application vulnerabilities can vary in both attacker sophistication and impact to the end user. Sensitive app behaviors can lead to data leakage that can be accessed by certain apps. Network threats leverage the weakness in websites or web applications establishing TLS/SSL sessions over Wi-Fi, cellular, or other networks. Malware attacks can be propagated via automated methods or direct execution by the attacker such as MiTM attacks, impersonation of certificates, downgrading, or stripping of the TLS/SSL cipher suite. Vulnerabilities in a network allow the attacker to compromise the device via the network due to device vulnerability. End users connecting to public Wi-Fi can pose a greater risk to enterprise data.

Text messages containing malicious links or phishing emails can direct users to websites that appear to be legitimate but have malicious content. Malicious content in the form of images, videos, or web pages can exploit Android applications or OS components to gain unauthorized access to a device by triggering vulnerabilities. Generally, low-reputation websites do not encrypt user credentials, leak enterprise data, and increase the likelihood of malicious activity. Different variants of malware exist, and they follow specific behavioral patterns. Behavior-based detection has proven to be highly effective in detecting malware attacks.

2.4.4 Malware Behavior

The inherent properties of malware can be determined by analyzing the malware behavior. Similar malware categories may have different malware behavior [37]. To understand Android malware behavior, it is imperative to identify whether the whole app is standalone malware, or some components belong to the malware payload. Various aspects of malware behavior, such as installation, composition, activation, anti-analysis techniques, etc., are listed for 150 malware in Appendix A and further illustrated in Figure 2.9. These are further discussed next.

1. Installation: There are multiple methods by which malware gets into mobile devices.

    - Drop (DR): Malware can trick the user into downloading and installing malicious applications containing the malware's payload.

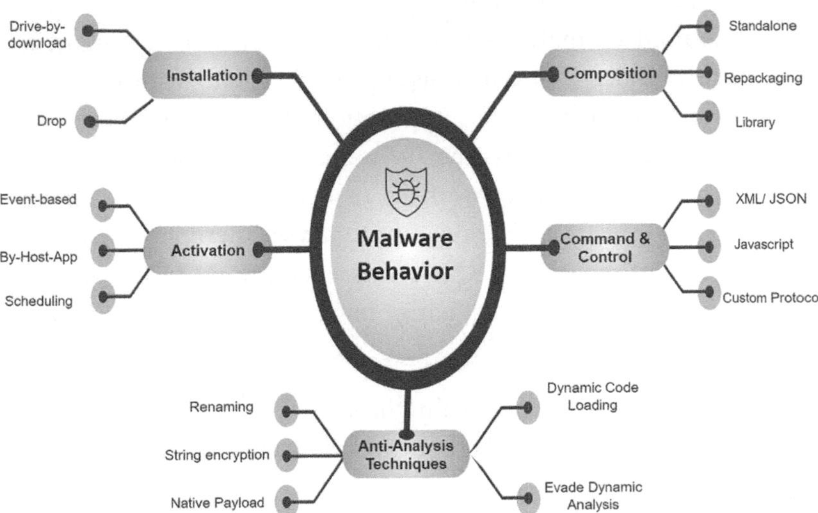

Figure 2.9 Malware behavior.

- Drive-by download (DD): Malware is downloaded and installed inadvertently onto the mobile device. A DD typically exploits an app [16], an OS, or a browser with some kind of security flaw.

2. Composition: There are three ways in which Android malware may be composed:

   - Standalone (ST): Malware is written from scratch.
   - Repackaging (RPKG): Malware is wrapped within a legitimate app.
   - Library (LIB): Malware payload is tagged on an otherwise legitimate app by an app developer unintentionally.

3. Activation: Malware activation may occur via one of three ways: event based (EV), by host app (BHA), or scheduling (SC).
4. Command and control (C&C/C2): C&C/C2 servers act as command centers from which malware-related attacks can issue special commands to launch an attack on a target or store stolen data [16]. A C&C module is composed of a message builder and a command handler. There are different ways to design the command handler, such as XML/JSON, JavaScript (JS), and custom protocol (CP).

v. Anti-analysis Techniques: This self-protection mechanism is used by malware to evade static and dynamic analysis techniques. Static analysis approaches identify the control-flow of the malicious application by analyzing the complete code, whereas dynamic analysis approaches analyze the runtime behavior of the malicious application during code execution. Various anti-analysis methods exist, including renaming (RN), string encryption (SE), dynamic code loading (DCL), native payload (NP), and evade dynamic analysis (EVA).

Subsequent chapters will explain the security comparison between Android and iOS and why Android was chosen to be the focus of this book.

3

Relevant Works and Studies Related to Android and iOS

3.1 Introduction

Android and iOS, having a global market share of ~95%, are the leading mobile platforms because of their proficiencies and popularity among users [38]. The prime focus of this chapter is on comparative analysis of Android and iOS.

Past research in the smartphone domain was based on security issues such as smartphone vulnerabilities, the impact of malware, security policies and guidelines on mobile platforms, and different mechanisms for the security and privacy of users. In [39], the authors discovered web-view vulnerabilities that caused malicious attacks on smartphones. They analyzed apps using static analysis techniques and achieved 85.00% detection accuracy. However, the authors could not analyze the execution-time/dynamic behavior of the apps. This study [40] probed the security vulnerabilities in smartphones that use SSL for secure communication, web-view technology, and HTML5. The author found that HTML5-based apps are the most vulnerable to attack. Although the work was not as comprehensive as it could have been, the limited functions used to analyze SSL vulnerabilities were still effective. In a previous study [41], researchers looked at smartphone security and the types of attacks on mobile applications that occurred between 2011 and 2017. Although the survey is not comprehensive, it provides some insight into mobile platform vulnerabilities. In [42], the authors present a complete review of smartphone security, assessing it in four categories: mobile security considerations, solutions connected to smartphone security, dangers posed by smartphone malware, and malware classification into families. The first category examines papers that conduct surveys on smartphone security. Articles regarding smartphone security issues are included in the second category. The third category

DOI: 10.1201/9781003354574-3

examines studies on malware and the dangers it causes. The final category evaluates how malware is divided into families.

Concerns about Android and iOS security are the subject of growing research. A study on the tap-wave-rub approach—a quick way to enforce permissions—was done in [43] with the aim of preventing smartphone malware. The method makes use of two mechanisms: proximity-based finger tapping, hand waving, or rubbing detection and acceleration-based phone tapping detection. According to this study, malware can be detected using the tap-wave-rub method with a low probability of false positive results. Other research ([44], [45]) has studied dangerous Android apps by examining the permissions needed by the app and categorizing them based on their maximum severity rating (MSR). After that, they looked at MSR classification user experiences. The installation of the application was then created by combining these stages. The suggested methods, however, fall short in enforcing access control mechanisms to information or resources that are covered by permission sets. This signifies that the permissions can be disregarded after obtaining root access. When root privileges are attained, Android is vulnerable due to the modified Linux kernel. Additionally, without checking the certification authority, self-signed developer certificates are included in the code-signing process used by Android [45]. As demonstrated in [46], by taking advantage of Android's code-signing system, malware can be distributed. Although a defense against this attack has been put out, it is not 100% effective. Repackaged malware remains a significant danger.

There are still some areas for improvement when it comes to the security of Android and iOS devices. In particular, more research is needed in order to get a comprehensive view of smartphone vulnerabilities and their impact on confidentiality, integrity, and availability. This chapter provides an overview of all the security aspects of Android and iOS, in order to help you make informed decisions about which platform is right for you.

3.2 Android versus iOS Battle

3.2.1 System Architecture

The core properties of Android and iOS, such as connectivity, networking, security, and runtime, are the same; however, the architectural design is different.

1. Kernel: Both Android and iOS have layered architecture, and the kernel (core of OS) lies at the lowest layer. Different layers above the kernel help in coordinating and performing the tasks with the kernel. The Android kernel is a Linux-based open-source core. The Android kernel is more secure because of its Linux-based design. On the other hand, the iOS kernel, called Darwin, is BSD derived. It provides disk access for the abstraction.
2. Hardware abstraction layer (HAL) versus core OS layer: There are two main differences between the hardware abstraction layer (HAL) in Android and the core OS layer in iOS. First, the HAL is hardware specific, and its implementation varies from vendor to vendor. Second, the core OS layer in iOS controls Bluetooth, local network authentication services, security, etc.
3. Android runtime versus media layer: The Android runtime layer lies above the HAL and consists of the Java virtual machine (JVM). This layer is responsible for managing networking and application running processes for Android applications. Conversely, in iOS, the media layer lies above the core OS layer. The media layer is made up of three different frameworks – graphic, audio, and video – and is responsible for graphics, audio, and video capabilities.
4. Virtual machine: Android consists of a special Dalvik virtual machine (DVM), which enables the execution of multiple instances of Android-based applications with high efficiency. iOS does not have any virtual machine but consists of different frameworks such as MapKit, UIKit, Gamekit, and EventKit for executing different applications.
5. Compiling layer: In Android, this layer is called the application framework and regulates the working of OS, whereas in iOS, it is known as AppKit and used to compile the libraries of iOS.

Figure 3.1 and Figure 3.2 illustrate the architecture of Android and iOS, respectively.

3.2.2 Security

Android is a mobile OS that uses the Linux kernel. Android provides a mechanism for user protection called "application sandboxing." This

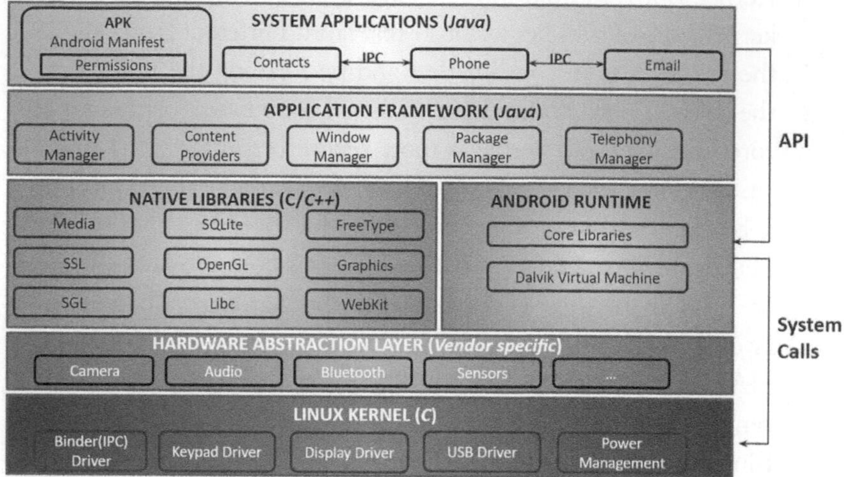

Figure 3.1 Android architecture.

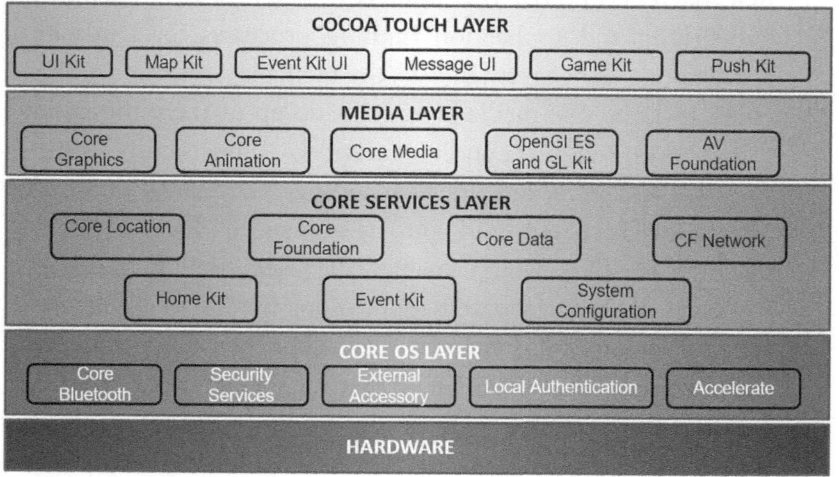

Figure 3.2 iOS architecture.

means that each Android application runs in its own process and is assigned a unique user ID. This provides isolation and security between applications and helps prevent resource exhaustion [47].

Compared to Android, iOS offers a more conservative security architecture. It's a closed system in which developers can create their applications but cannot reveal the source code. Devices include a device-level locking mechanism, such as a passcode or personal

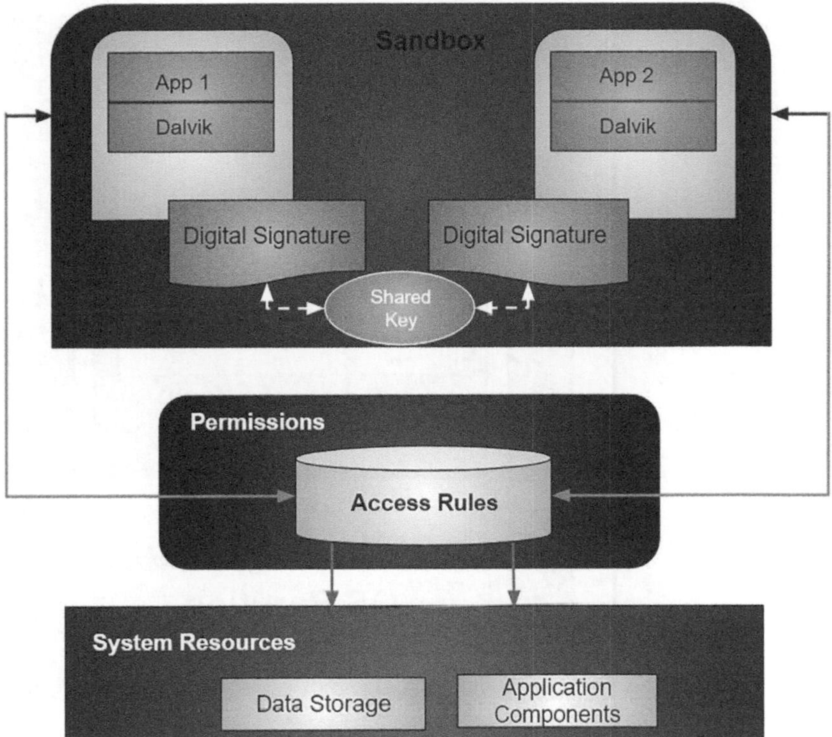

Figure 3.3 Android security model.

identification number (PIN), and may be remotely erased using MDM. System-level security, on the other hand, uses touch ID, a secure boot chain, a secure enclave, and secure software update authorization. Data-level security includes the use of hardware and software components for data protection classes and file encryption techniques. Comparatively speaking, iOS is difficult to jailbreak or hack into. This indicates that Apple Inc. is in charge of both the hardware and the software [48]. Since data encryption in iOS cannot be customized, consumers cannot turn it off. Figure 3.4. illustrates the different levels of iOS's security model.

3.2.3 Isolation Mechanism

Each application is given its own sandbox environment to use when running on the device. Applications cannot alter other applications since they run in their own environment.

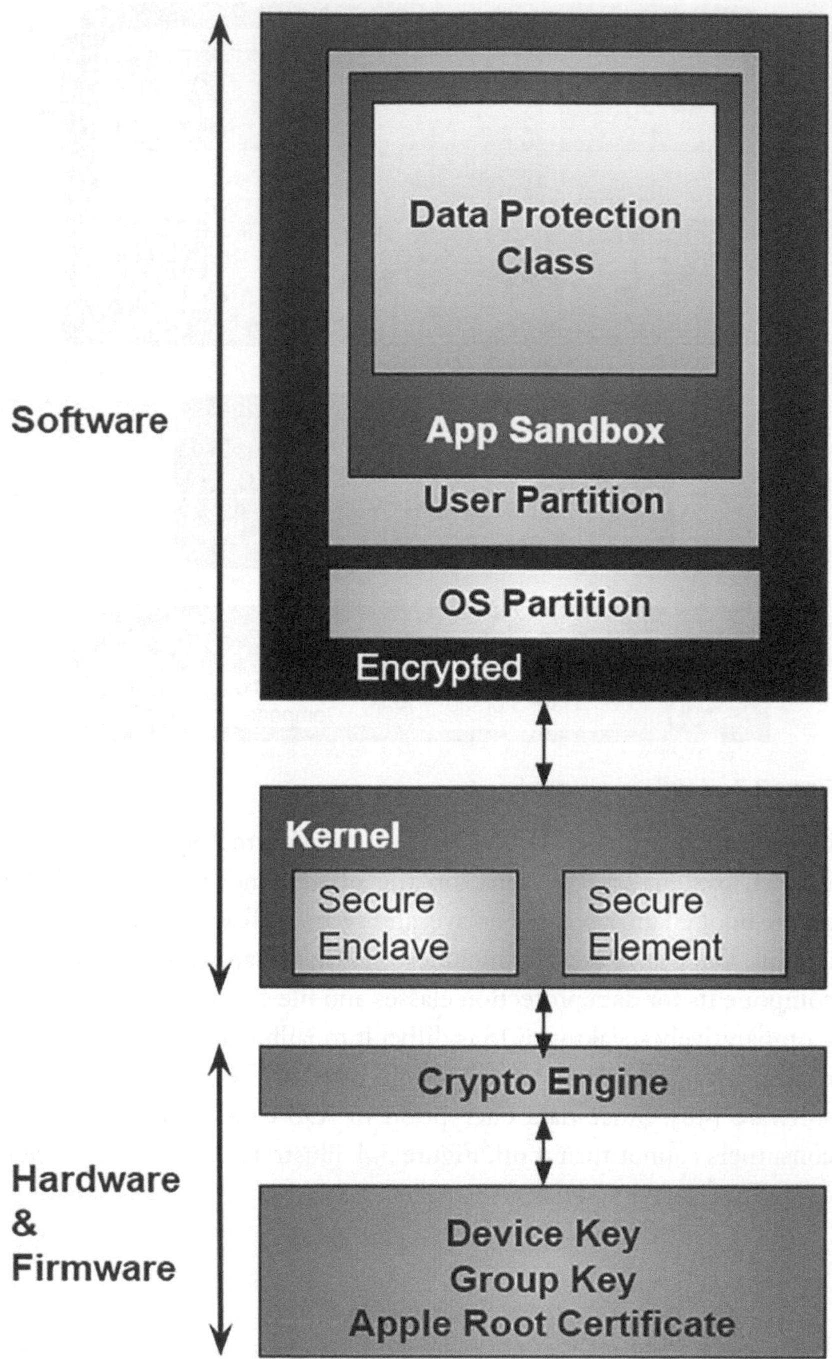

Figure 3.4 iOS security model.

The restricted access to the Android kernel reduces the potential attack surface. As a result, an attacker cannot examine or modify the logic of other apps or compromise them. Depending on the permissions they have been given, they can still carry out certain kinds of assaults and access some subsystems [49].

All applications that are running on an Android smartphone are isolated due to the security sandbox feature. This stops a single app from impacting other apps and stops third-party apps from accessing or exploiting system resources [50]. In order to separate programs from one another, iOS does not make use of this; instead, it only uses hardware-level memory protection [51]. This results in an OS that is more secure than Android's.

3.2.4 Encryption Mechanism

If data on a mobile device isn't secured, it can be easily misplaced or even stolen. To maintain safety and security, it is always preferable to encrypt the data saved on your phone. Full disc encryption is a feature available on Android phones, meaning that all the data on your phone is secured by a passphrase or password. Recently, Android 10.0 added hardware encryption, which allows for the encryption of various files with various passwords to enable independent unlocking [52], as depicted in Figure 3.5.

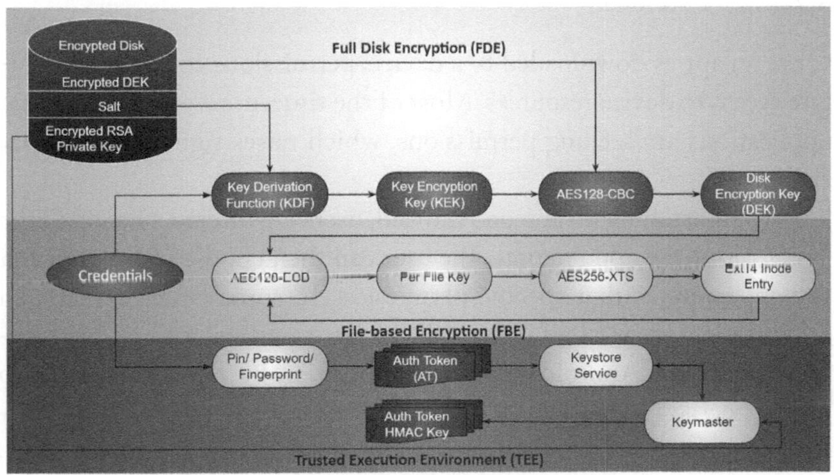

Figure 3.5 Android encryption model.

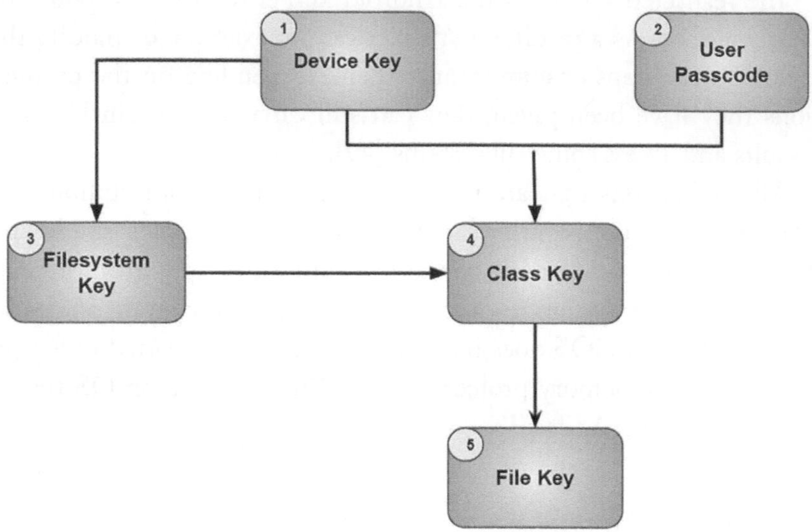

Figure 3.6 iOS encryption model.

Every file is encrypted in iOS using different hardware and software key combinations, ensuring that only offline brute-force attacks are possible. Every file has a data protection class attached to it, allowing developers to specify the conditions under which the data is accessible [53], as depicted in Figure 3.6.

3.2.5 App Permissions

Once an app is downloaded to a device, permissions control and regulate access to device resources. Most of the time, users are unaware that applications are seeking permissions, which raises significant security risks.

When installing an app on Android, users are offered a list of all the permissions the app requires. The user can then choose whether or not the app requires that specific permission. In some circumstances, an app installation will halt if the user denies it particular rights. Attackers can exploit Android's permissions system by pressuring users to grant specific rights, then stealing their sensitive data as a result. Permissions can be used to launch a variety of attacks, including data loss, data integrity, DoS, and DDoS attacks. Since security decisions are made by device users, Android's permission mechanism is ineffective.

As most users are unable to make the right decisions, this can jeopardize Android's security [54].

Users in iOS are not made aware of the permissions that an app needs to access. The majority of the device's sensitive subsystems are blocked from access because all the apps in Apple are isolated from one another. Users are not in charge of choosing any sort of security measures. Without the user's approval, iOS's isolation policy [55] grants the rights that an app needs. Users can, however, authorize usage of the device's resources in certain situations, like making an outgoing call, sending an email or SMS, receiving push notifications from the Internet, getting GPS position updates, and sending and receiving email.

3.2.6 *Auto-Erase Mechanism*

A smartphone can store a good amount of private and sensitive data. Attackers can carry out identity theft and fraud. The auto-erase [56] feature on smartphones is useful in case they are misplaced or stolen. Using the auto-erase feature, personal and sensitive information can be removed from the smartphone.

Although third-party apps can be used for auto-erase, native Android apps do not provide this feature. This feature in iOS instantly deletes all the data on the device if an attacker tries to enter an incorrect passcode ten times.

3.2.7 *Application Provenance*

Application provenance is a procedure that evaluates third-party applications for their intended functionality and security [57]. Before publishing an app to the App Store, every mobile platform provider must verify its origins and validity. The author authenticates the app, stamps it with their identity, and then uses a vendor-issued digital certificate to sign it digitally, ensuring the app is tamper resistant.

It is not obligatory for Android app developers to sign up with the Google Play store. They don't need signing certificates produced by Google. Without being monitored by Google, Android app developers can effortlessly post their products to Google Play. To have their apps certified, Google charges app developers a $25 processing fee via credit card. Google uses this procedure to associate an app with a developer's digital certificate. Since attackers can use stolen credit cards to pay the fee, there is no assurance that such a linkage will take place. The fact that the Google Play store is not the only location where the apps created by the developers are distributed presents another security concern. Developers of Android apps can make their applications available to third parties.

In contrast to Android, iOS developers are limited to distributing their apps through the official App Store. Before their apps may be distributed through the App Store, iOS developers must first register with Apple. Apple uses a screening procedure. It is a licensing agreement in which the security and privacy of every app the developer uploads are confirmed. If the app does not contravene the licensing agreement, it is digitally signed and subsequently released on the App Store. A third-party distributor or download site cannot alter the app or its developers due to the digital signing process. The vetting procedure stops hackers from attacking published apps or publishing harmful apps to the App Store. As part of the registration process with Apple and the acquisition of a signing certificate, app developers are compelled to divulge their names. This serves as yet another safeguard against any malicious behavior. The differences between Android and iOS are outlined in Table 3.1.

There are more security issues in addition to the aforementioned factors. Android is powerless over hardware vendors. Because there are many Android device manufacturers, it is challenging for Google to establish a set of uniform protocols for its affiliated OEMs. Apple has a lot tighter control over gadget makers. Android has a significant degree of device fragmentation, meaning there are many different device types and OS versions, which creates an environment for security flaws.

Android and iOS suffer from a wide range of vulnerabilities, as discussed in Section 2.3.4. This book examines the patterns of iOS and Android security flaws. CVE Details [58] is the primary source of data for this investigation. This data is gathered using the web-based scraper application Web Scraper 0.4.0 [59]. The web scraper searches for vulnerabilities with CVE IDs and pulls pertinent information. From CVE Details, a web-based scraper was able to retrieve every vulnerability in the iOS and Android categories: 7,526 CVE IDs total—2,819 for iOS and 4,707 for Android—are taken into account.

Table 3.1 Summary of Comparison between Android and iOS

FEATURES	SUB-FEATURE	ANDROID	IOS
Source model	–	Open source	Closed, but open source iOS components
Architecture	Kernel	Linux	OS X, UNIX
	Language	Dalvik (Java)	Objective C
	Layers	Kernel: control of critical system functions processing, memory, security, and networking	Hardware: contains the physical chips
		HAL: the interface used by the Android application and framework to communicate with drivers for hardware-specific devices such as cameras and Bluetooth	Core OS: manages files, networks, memory (allocation and de-allocation), etc.
		Libraries: useful for creating user interfaces, creating graphics, and accessing databases	Core services: capabilities offered by the core services include data protection, iCloud storage, file sharing, XML support, SQLite database, in-app purchases, and more
		Application framework: a database for storing data, debugging tools, and support for audio, video, and image formats, the components of the application framework	Media: in charge of the graphics, audio, and video capabilities
		Applications: apps, both native and third-party, that the user downloads, including a web browser, email, SMS messaging, etc.	Cocoa touch: offers essential frameworks for creating iOS apps and determining their aesthetic
Security	Application isolation	Each app uses its own sandbox with user's consent to access system resources	No user permission is necessary; shared sandbox for all apps
	Encryption	Later versions support TEE and FBE, whereas earlier ones support FDE	Hardware encryption with a level of data security
	App permissions	Displayed to the users	Not displayed to the users

(*Continued*)

Table 3.1 Continued

FEATURES	SUB-FEATURE	ANDROID	IOS
	Auto-erase	No	Yes
Application provenance	App distribution	Google Play store and third-party app markets	Official App Store
	Vetting process	Partial	Yes
	Digital signature	Yes	Yes

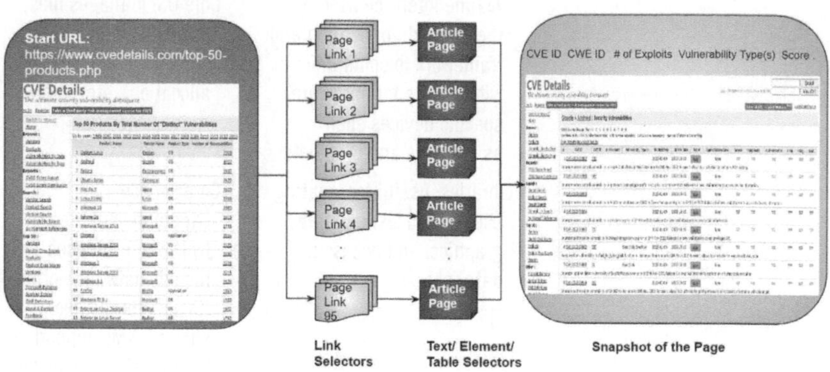

Figure 3.7 Web-based scraping process flow.

The method of web-based scraping is described in Figure 3.7. The data is pre-processed after it has been scraped, where the extraneous data components, such as the number of exploits and the update date, are eliminated.

Between 2007 and 2022, there were 4,707 and 2,819 vulnerabilities reported for Android and iOS, respectively, according to CVE Details. Figure 3.8 shows that the number of vulnerabilities increased steadily until 2017, after which there was an up-down pattern from 2018 to 2022 for both Android and iOS.

As observed in Figure 3.9, there are considerable differences in the percentage distribution of vulnerabilities for both Android and iOS. From 2007 to 2022, the percentage distribution of iOS vulnerabilities declined (from 100% to 22%), while the trend for Android increased (from 0% to 78%). The percentage distribution of Android vulnerabilities climbed significantly between 2014 and 2018 (from 9% to 83%) before declining in 2019 (to 58%) and then rising once

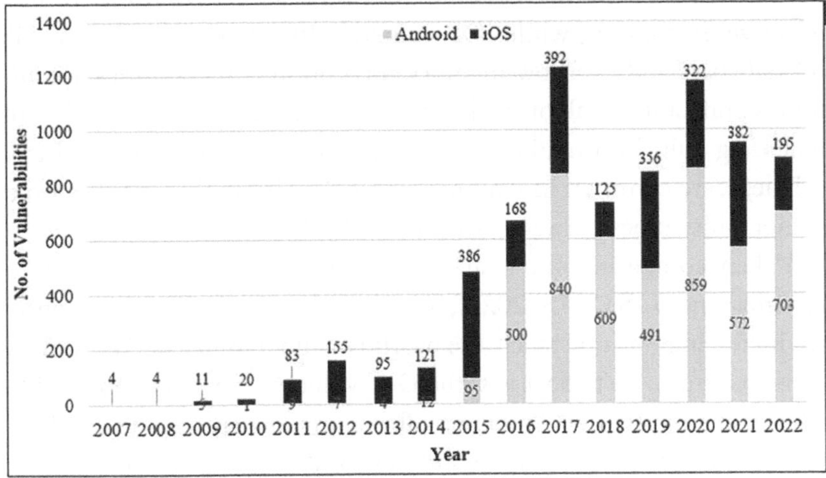

Figure 3.8 Trend of Android and iOS vulnerabilities for 2007–2022.

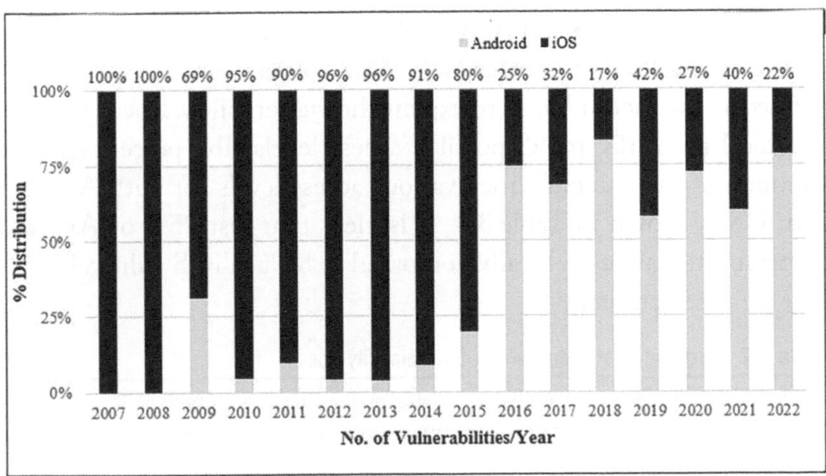

Figure 3.9 Distribution of Android and iOS vulnerabilities (in %) from 2007–2022.

more between 2020 and 2022 (73%–78%). Android became more popular among smartphone users after 2014, overtaking iOS prior to that year, increasing the number of vulnerabilities. As a result, we compare Android with iOS starting in 2015, when Android first appeared. Better detection rates employing ML and deep learning (DL) algorithms seem to be responsible for the decrease in the number of vulnerabilities [60].

Android vulnerabilities are the most prevalent, accounting for 63% of all vulnerabilities, while iOS vulnerabilities make up 37%. While iOS's bypass and overflow memory corruption vulnerabilities account for a significant chunk of the key vulnerabilities, the majority of them, including gain information, code execution, DoS, overflow, and gain privilege, are common in Android. Table 3.2 shows the distribution of vulnerability types between Android and iOS.

When comparing the year-by-year vulnerability distributions of Android and iOS (2018–2022), it is clear that Android vulnerabilities are increasing—for instance, the overflow vulnerability in Android has increased from 4% to 55% and the DoS vulnerability from 3% to 7%—while the majority of iOS vulnerabilities are decreasing. Table 3.3 displays the rise and fall of vulnerabilities for iOS and Android.

As can be seen from comparing the mean severity scores of Android and iOS, Android vulnerabilities are more severe (mean score 6.9) than iOS vulnerabilities (mean score 6.2). Figure 3.10 displays the average severity score for iOS and Android from 2018 to 2022.

The access level is another degree of comparison. Access level is defined as the method used to exploit the vulnerability. Local, remote, and local networks are all possible access levels. The percentage distribution of the vulnerabilities' various access levels for both Android and iOS is shown in Table 3.4. It is clear that just 25% of Android vulnerabilities are used locally, compared to 85% of iOS vulnerabilities that are used remotely.

Table 3.2 Distribution of Android and iOS vulnerability types.

VULNERABILITY TYPE(S)	ANDROID	IOS	TOTAL	ANDROID %	IOS %
DoS	419	104	523	80%	20%
Code Execution	755	151	906	83%	17%
Overflow	715	93	808	88%	12%
Memory Corruption	223	423	646	35%	65%
SQL Injection	19	15	34	56%	44%
Directory Traversal	20	11	31	65%	35%
Bypass Something	425	613	1,038	41%	59%
Gain Information	441	330	771	57%	43%
Gain Privileges	311	107	418	74%	26%
Others	1,379	972	2,351	59%	41%
Total	**4,707**	**2,819**	**7,526**	**63%**	**37%**

Table 3.3 Individual Vulnerability Trends for Android and iOS.

VULNERABILITY TYPE(S)	ANDROID	IOS	REMARKS
DoS	3% to 7% ↑	5% to 3% ↓	Buffer overflow in OpenJPEG 2.1.1 in Android; unhandled Java-level null pointer exceptions (NPEs) in iOS; regular software updates in Android
Code execution	12% to 14% ↑	4% to 0% ↓	Improved memory management in iOS addresses the use-after-frcc issue
Overflow	4% to 55% ↑	10% to 38% ↑	Android's open-source nature; jailbreaking in iOS
Memory Corruption	↔	0% to 46% ↑	iOS jailbreaking and limited stacking
SQL Injection	↔	0% to 1% ↑	iOS's limited allocated stacks
Directory Traversal	1% to 0% ↓	7% to 0% ↓	Improved memory management and input validation in Android and iOS
Bypass Something	5% to 6% ↑	7% to 0% ↓	Inadequate security measures in Android; enhanced iOS checks
Gain Information	2% to 3% ↑	11% to 8% ↓	Manipulated libstagefright file in Android media server applications; enhanced input validation for stack overflow in iOS
Gain Privileges	9% to 0% ↓	↔	Enhanced encryption capabilities in Android
Others	9% to 7% ↓	11% to 3% ↓	Regular iOS and Android software updates

Notes: ↑ Increase, ↓ Decrease, ↔ Constant

Another factor to consider when comparing iOS and Android vulnerabilities is access complexity. Once an attacker has acquired access to the target system, access complexity quantifies the complexity of the attack needed to exploit the vulnerability. Accessibility levels range from low to high. A low value indicates that there are no specific access conditions or extenuating circumstances, a medium value indicates that there are some specialized access conditions, and a high value indicates that there are specialized access conditions. The levels of access complexity for iOS and Android are indicated in Table 3.5. 71% of iOS vulnerabilities are moderately complicated,

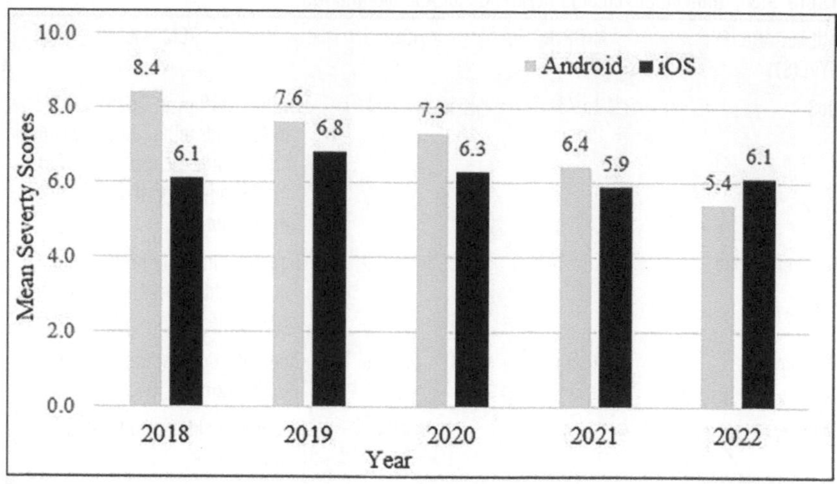

Figure 3.10 Android and iOS vulnerabilities' mean severity scores.

Table 3.4 Access Levels of Android and iOS Vulnerabilities

OS	LOCAL (%)	LOCAL NETWORK (%)	REMOTE (%)
Android	25	2	73
iOS	14	1	85

Table 3.5 Access Complexity of Android and iOS Vulnerabilities

OS	HIGH (%)	LOW (%)	MEDIUM (%)
Android	5	47	49
iOS	2	26	71

but access complexity for Android is more distributed in the extremes—high (5%) and low (47%).

The fundamental building block of information security is the CIA trinity [61]. The CIA trio is susceptible to major security flaws. The CIA trinity requires appropriate attention if a security program is to be thorough and full.

The CIA triangle is the foundation of the information security system, so it's crucial to understand how vulnerabilities affect the CIA. The effect of vulnerability scores on secrecy is seen in Table 3.6. It has been observed that 48% of the vulnerabilities in Android completely affect confidentiality, compared to 22% in iOS; iOS vulnerabilities either partially (60%) or completely (18%) affect confidentiality levels.

Table 3.6 Impact Score on Confidentiality

COMPLEXITY	COMPLETE (%)	NONE (%)	PARTIAL (%)
Android	48	11	40
iOS	22	18	60

Table 3.7 Impact Score on Integrity

COMPLEXITY	COMPLETE (%)	NONE (%)	PARTIAL (%)
Android	46	31	22
iOS	22	27	51

Table 3.8 Impact Score on Availability

COMPLEXITY	COMPLETE (%)	NONE (%)	PARTIAL (%)
Android	52	24	24
iOS	24	31	45

The effect of vulnerability scores on integrity is seen in Table 3.7. It can be noted that 51% of the vulnerabilities in iOS have a partial influence on integrity, compared to 46% of the vulnerabilities in Android.

The effect of vulnerability scores on availability is shown in Table 3.8. It is observed that 52% of Android vulnerabilities have a complete impact on availability, while 45% of iOS vulnerabilities only have a partial impact.

The number of vulnerabilities and the amount of reported malware serve as indicators of risk levels. The amount of malware represents the number of real threats that are detected, whereas the number of vulnerabilities defines the loopholes found in the platform that could possibly compromise it. A significant majority of the malware types listed in Section 2.4 target Android and iOS.

The distribution of malware types in 2022's first and second quarters (Q1 and Q2) is depicted in Figure 3.11. Ransomware has a reduction of 27.94 percentage points (pp) from Q1 in Q2, while adware outperforms Q1 by 8.36 pp in Q2. The Trojans outperform the Q1 by 5.81 pp.

According to the Kaspersky report [62], Iran led in terms of the share of infected devices in Q2 2022 with 26.91%, second was Yemen with 17.97%, and third was Saudi Arabia with 12.63%. Figure 3.12 shows the geographical distribution of the infected devices.

There won't be any crossover between Android and iOS anytime soon, and Android's market dominance will only increase. Because Android is open source and has more vulnerabilities than iOS, which

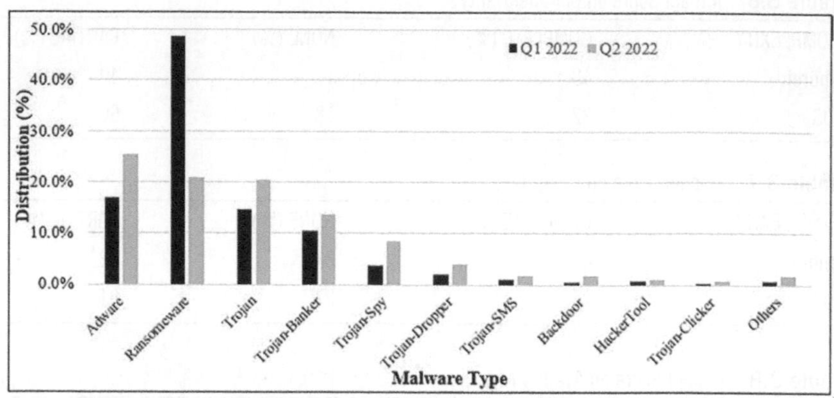

Figure 3.11 Distribution of malware types for Q1 and Q2 2022.

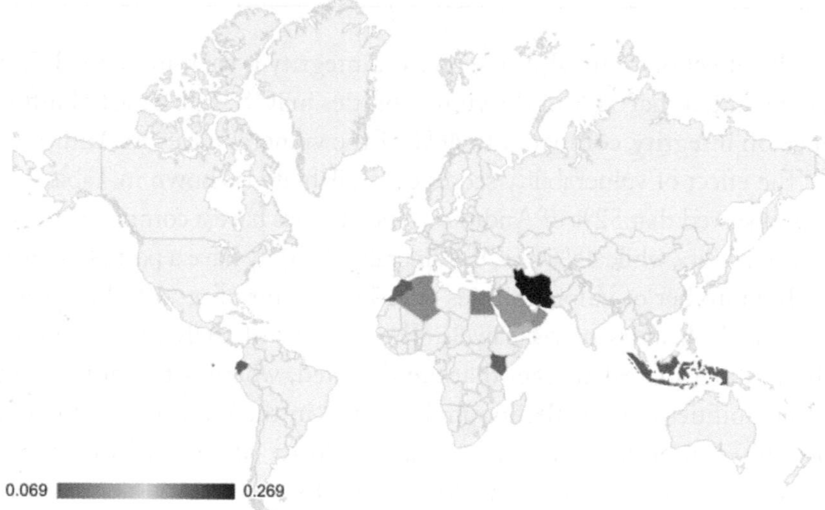

Figure 3.12 Geographical distribution of infected devices.

is closed, it has a growing market share. As a result, this book primarily concentrates on Android and the key problems it has.

3.3 Security Assessment of Android

Significant research has been carried out in the area of Android security in recent years; however, there are still many obstacles and gaps. The state-of-the-art methods used in Android security are reviewed in this part using a thorough and reliable taxonomy. This section defines the essential elements in terms of aims, analysis techniques, code representations, tools and frameworks employed, etc.; emphasizes the trends and patterns of various analysis approaches; and highlights and enumerates the research opportunities for future work. In order to conduct this study [61], a thorough systematic literature review procedure was used, and the findings of over 250 research papers were analyzed in light of various security considerations.

The contributions made to the field of mobile security since the invention of mobile phones must be recognized, examined, and understood. As far as we are aware, this study is the first of its sort to analyze Android security. No other poll focuses specifically on all the facets of Android security. The literature suggests several studies and works on Android security. Although there aren't many SLRs in the Android security space, those that do exist lack comprehensiveness and thoroughness.

Authors investigated the evolution of malware and examined 20 research projects that found mobile malware in [63]. Authors presented a survey on mobile computing that addressed privacy-related issues in another work [64]. This study included 13 privacy leak detection tools and 16 user studies on mobile privacy. Authors examined the privacy concerns raised by Android application permissions in [65].

Authors of a different survey [45] focused on Android's current security threats and security implementation options. They categorized the security features of Android into four groups: DoS attacks, information leakage, app cloning, and vulnerabilities.

Authors examined static and dynamic analysis techniques in [66]. Five categories of currently available Android security solutions were offered in their taxonomy. They came to the conclusion that the most effective method of addressing Android security issues is static analysis.

In a different study [67], authors examined works in the field of software engineering that were based on the app store. The authors discussed the technical and non-technical software repository learning behaviors. They specifically looked at previous works in seven different categories, including size and effort prediction, feature analysis, API analysis, review analysis, store ecosystem, and security.

Researchers concentrated on malware proliferation, anti-analysis methods, and malware detection methods in another survey [68]. They also commented on how malware variations can be produced via covert methods such as encryption and code manipulation. They examined static and dynamic malware detection methods.

A technical report [69] compared program analysis methods with respect to Android security on a qualitative level. After studying 336 research papers that used both static analysis and dynamic analysis techniques, the authors established a taxonomy. However, there was not much attention paid to hybrid and ML techniques that would have supplemented the traditional analysis procedures.

The contributions of various literature reviews, which focus mostly on mobile malware, are compiled in Table 3.9. These studies compared

Table 3.9 Summary of Literature Reviews

CITATION	TEMPORAL RANGE	FOCUS AREA OF REVIEW	MOBILE PLATFORM(S)	DETECTION APPROACH
[63]	2010–2013	Malware & grayware detection	Android, Windows, iOS, Blackberry	Static & dynamic
[64]	2010–2014	Privacy leaks	Android, iOS	Static, dynamic, & hybrid
[65]	2007–2019	Android application permissions and privacy issues	Android	Static, dynamic, & hybrid
[45]	2010–2015	Privilege escalation, information leaks, repackaging programs, denial-of-service attacks, and collusion	Android	Static & dynamic
[66]	2009–2014	Runtime malware detection, information leakage, elevated privileges, isolation systems	Android	Static & dynamic
[67]	2000–2015	App store analysis	Blackberry, Windows Phone, Nokia Widgets, Android, and iOS	Static & dynamic
[68]	2010–2014	Malware penetration	Android	Static analysis, dynamic analysis, behavioral analysis
[69]	2008–2016	Detection of malware, grayware, and vulnerabilities	Android	Static, dynamic, hybrid, ML (supervised & unsupervised only)

and categorized malware detection strategies using a limited set of parameters and criteria. The aims, characteristics, and technique evaluation of analyses are just a few of the crucial granular security factors that are disregarded. To the best of our knowledge, our SLR has more publications in the area of Android security than the surveys in Table 3.9 (in terms of both quantity and chronological coverage).

The fundamental parameters put forward by Kitchenham [70] served as the foundation for the research technique used to create this SLR; 250 research papers with a significant number of citations that were published in reputed journals and conferences were examined. The schematic design of the SLR is shown in Figure 3.13. Table 3.10 provides a summary of the review process used to conduct this SLR.

3.3.1 Taxonomy Construction

A taxonomy of Android security analysis methodologies was created after acquiring the pertinent papers and selecting elements from the body of current research. This taxonomy will be useful to (i) respond to the aforementioned RQs, (ii) offer a thorough evaluation of each publication, and (iii) provide a systematic basis for classifying and comparing the various approaches. Although pertinent and

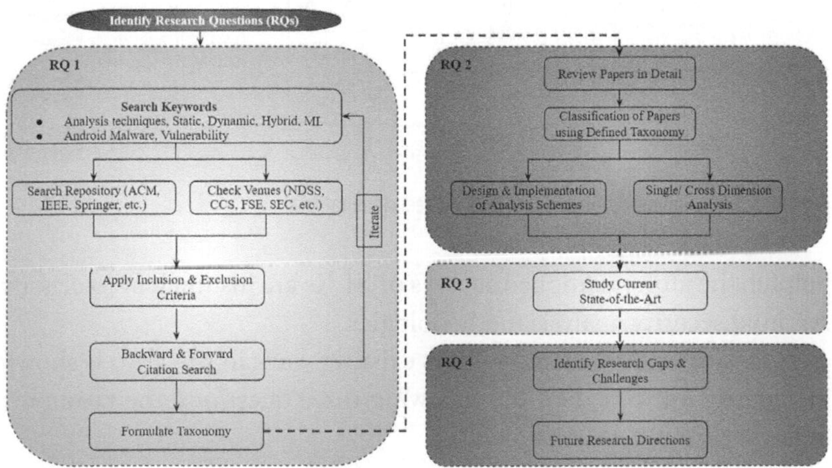

Figure 3.13 An illustration of the SLR.

Table 3.10 Review Protocol

OBJECTIVES	REVIEWING CONTEMPORARY TECHNIQUES FOR ANDROID SECURITY
Research Questions (RQs)	1. What are the various methods for analyzing Android security? 2. How are these analysis methods created and put into practice? 3. What is the state of the art in terms of Android security right now? 4. What difficulties and research gaps need to be identified and addressed?
Search Strategy	Search using keywords in databases, datasets, and repositories
Inclusion Criteria	Papers from 2013 through 2022 that were collected by IEEE, Springer, Elsevier, and ACM
Exclusion Criteria	Short papers in IEEE/ACM fewer than four pages in length, duplicate papers that were first published in conference proceedings and then in journals, and works that were published before 2013
Results	Filtered studies were examined, and a summary outlining the key ideas and findings was produced

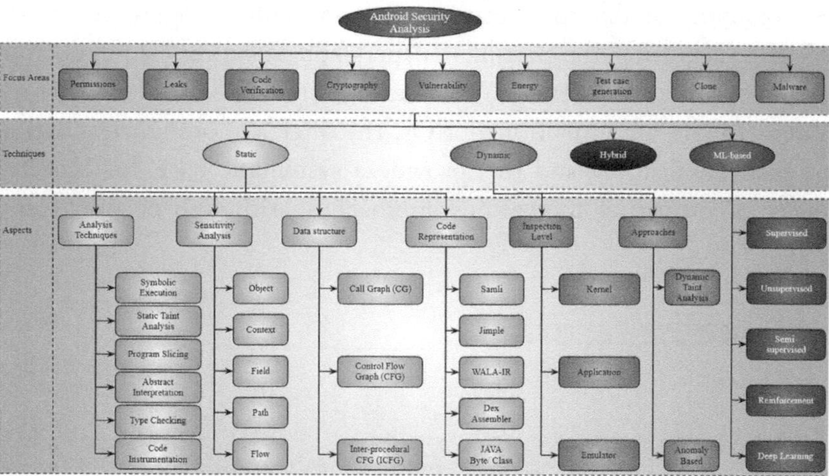

Figure 3.14 Proposed taxonomy for Android security analysis.

helpful, the aforementioned surveys or SLRs are insufficient to classify Android security analysis methodologies.

A new taxonomy that organizes existing work in this field is shown in Figure 3.14. Based on the following three questions, the taxonomy defines three dimensions:

1. Why are Android security analyses performed?
2. What are the various analytical techniques?

3. What characteristics are connected to the methods used in these analyses?

The following is a detailed discussion of each of the taxonomy hierarchy's dimensions and sub-dimensions:

1. Focus areas for Android security analysis: This dimension identifies the various goals that are the subject of analysis. These assessments address a number of security-related concerns. Some of these include issues with permission management, issues with code verification, automated test-case generation, private data leaks, clone detection, evaluating the energy efficiency of the code, etc. This SLR lists nine goals for Android security analysis methods, which are succinctly described below:

    a. Exploiting permissions: The foundation of Android design is a permission-based security approach. To access the system resources, permissions must be granted. However, since apps can make use of additional permissions that they require, there are certain inherent hazards linked to permissions [71]. Malicious apps can manage permissions and conduct a variety of attacks, including DoS and DDoS attacks, data loss attacks, and data integrity attacks.
    b. Passive content leaks: Often known as private data breaches. Researchers working on Android are quite concerned about data privacy. Phone information, Wi-Fi data, GPS location, microphone audio, and other private data leaks are examples.
    c. Code verification: Code verification is used to make sure an app is correct. There aren't many works that deal with this issue. Before installing an app, Cassandra [72] determines whether it complies with Android's privacy rules.
    d. Misuse of cryptographic methods: Security engineers are also concerned about cryptography's implementation problems. Misuse of encryption can take the form of SSL/TLS validation errors that lead to MiTM attacks that breach system authentication. A crypto misuse analyzer is used by CMA [73] to analyze misuse of cryptography.

e. Vulnerability detection: Android is plagued by a lot of security flaws. The most frequent vulnerabilities in Android are intent injection and content hijacking. By altering user data, arbitrary code is executed, resulting in intent injection. When insecure apps' exported components are used to get unauthorized access to private and protected resources, this is known as content hijacking. Static analysis is used by Epicc [74] to find inter-component vulnerabilities.
f. Energy consumption: High energy–consuming components are seen in modern cellphones with huge screens. For mobile devices, battery standby time is a crucial concern. When light colors are displayed on modern smartphones, as opposed to dark colors, more energy is used, claim the authors of [75]. They looked at whether creating web pages with dark backgrounds for mobile devices might save energy consumption by 40% and provide more effective websites.
g. Test-case generation: This includes a set of test cases that are run for automated testing that is repeatable. To verify that branches are reachable, symbolic execution is applied to the source code. One framework for testing Android apps' systems is SIG-Droid [76]. Through symbolic execution and the use of the interface model and behavior model, it automatically generates test cases. The behavior model creates the sequences of events to drive the symbolic execution, whereas the interface model identifies the values that a given app can receive.
h. App cloning: To find an Android app clone, researchers have employed a variety of analysis techniques. App cloning is often performed in mobile apps, according to [77]. The author has demonstrated in previous work [78] that the AnDarwin framework effectively identifies the cloned apps.
i. Malware detection: Malware attacks are becoming more frequent as a result of Android vulnerabilities. Malware comes in a variety of forms, including spyware, adware, Trojans, ransomware, and more, all of which have the power to adversely affect the system. As a result, malware detection has received increasing attention in recent studies.

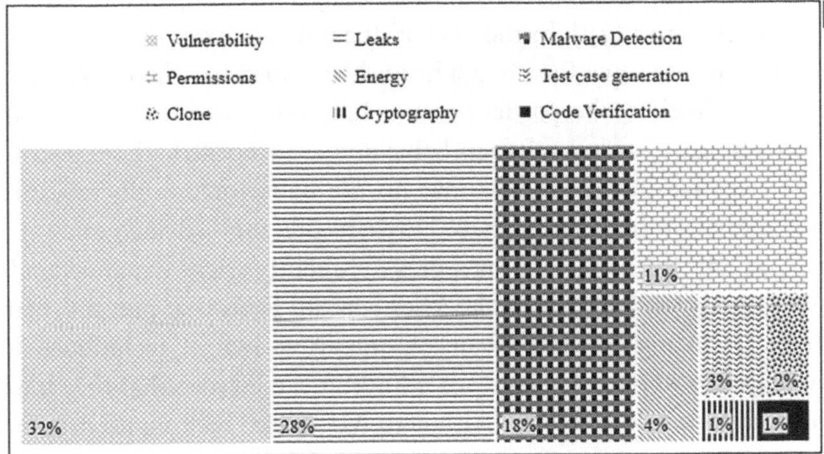

Figure 3.15 Statistics research publications addressing the main objectives.

The statistics of the articles concentrating on the aforementioned security goals are shown in Figure 3.15. The bulk of the research (32%) seem to concentrate on vulnerability detection, followed by privacy breaches (28%), and malware detection (18%).

2. Android security analysis techniques: The classification of various program analysis approaches used in Android security analysis is the focus of the taxonomy's second dimension, which aims to address RQ1. There are four of these methods: static, dynamic, hybrid, and ML based.

The potential behavior of the software structure is investigated through static analysis. These methods traverse the program paths to check the program's properties while parsing the program source code or bytecode. Dynamic analysis tracks the program's actual behavior as it is being used. In addition to pure static or dynamic techniques, there exist hybrid techniques that combine the advantages of static and dynamic techniques by employing static analysis to initially identify potential security risks and dynamic analysis to later remove the false alarms. In addition to these strategies, ML-based techniques are also employed to enhance the analysis. The supplemental techniques either get input from the program analysis or use its results.

Depending on its inherent characteristics, each technique offers advantages and disadvantages. Dynamic analysis approaches are inaccurate yet precise, whereas static analysis techniques are reliable and conservative [79]. In the case of dynamic analysis, specific occurrences are necessary for the application to function. The offered test cases are likely to be partial because it is not possible to record all events at once; as a result, app behaviors are recorded. These lead to false negatives, which means that hostile behavior or vulnerabilities are ignored in the security study. Furthermore, sophisticated malware, such as anti-taint tracking measures, frequently tricks dynamic analysis systems [80]. Hybrid approaches contain flaws that prevent them from producing flawless results. Comparing hybrid techniques to pure static and pure dynamic procedures, it can be seen that they have yielded the worst outcomes. Although ML-based techniques demand a significant amount of system resources and computational capacity because of the massive volume of data needed for training, DL can alleviate these issues.

The distribution of research papers from 2013 to 2022 is shown in Figure 3.16. It has been noted that between 2013 and 2015, static approaches received increased attention. Dynamic and hybrid procedures that are more exacting than static techniques are required because of technological innovation and bypassing mechanisms. After 2018, ML-based techniques are becoming more prevalent because they are reliable and scalable enough to be used for program analyses.

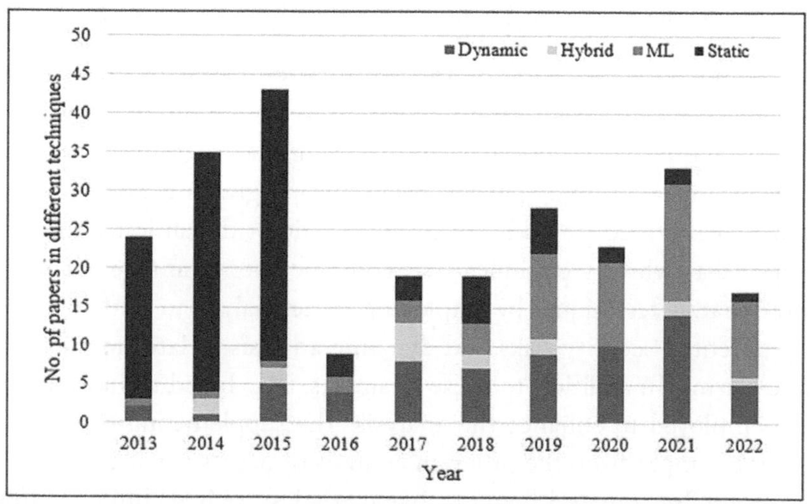

Figure 3.16 Distribution of research publications by year using various analysis methods.

3. Techniques and aspects of analysis: The third dimension discusses the various characteristics that set program analysis methodologies apart from one another. In order to address RQ2 and RQ3, which are based on the peculiarities of these approaches' design and implementation as well as the condition of Android security at the time, this dimension will attempt to provide a solution. The following discussion of seven sub-dimensions includes the first four static analytic techniques, the following two dynamic analyses, and the final ML-based technique.

Analysis methods, sensitivity analysis, data structures employed, and code representation are the static analysis aspects.

a. Analysis techniques

Six essential analysis methodologies with regard to static analysis have been looked into in this work. These are covered in the following:

i. Symbolic execution: This facilitates program analysis by identifying the various inputs that execute various software components. Symbolic values are used as inputs to propagate the program's execution; these symbolic values create variables, expressions, and constraints, which are then used to provide potential outcomes for each conditional branch. The specified path, which is thought to be impossible when no input is produced, is subsequently explored using these inputs as test cases. AppIntent [81] uses symbolic execution to construct the GUI manipulation sequences that result in data transmission. Android apps find that symbolic execution takes a long time, while AppIntent shrinks the search space without reducing code coverage.
ii. Taint analysis: This is a technique for information flow analysis in which a taint—an identifier—is applied to an object. Data-flow analysis is then used to track the compromised item. When a contaminated object flows to a sink, an exception is raised. FlowDroid [82] uses static taint analysis to find sensitive data leaks. By using taint analysis, AppSealer [83] creates patches for Android component hijacking threats.

iii. Program slicing: This is a technique for testing a group of statements in a program while keeping the program's behavior for particular test cases or conditions that might affect a value at a particular point in time. Static program slices are extensive and consider all feasible program execution paths. By performing a backward data-flow analysis, the SAAF framework, developed by authors in [84], enables program slices to follow parameter values for a specific Android method. On the other hand, by computing static program slices, CryptoLint [85] analyzes cryptographic API methods.
iv. Abstract interpretation: In general, abstract interpretation is conceived of as a partial execution of a program that takes into account the semantics of a program, including data flow, control flow, etc.
v. Type/model checking: A program's type constraints are verified using type checking. This may occur at execution time (static) or at build time (dynamic). It guarantees the type safety of a program in situations when errors could occur, such as when an integer operator is applied to strings or a float operation is applied to an integer. Model checking, on the other hand, validates the supplied specification of a finite-state system. Type checking is based on syntactic and modular style; however, model checking is based on semantic and whole-program style. As a result, type and model checking are complementary. For instance, model checking is used by COVERT [86] to confirm the security requirements of a certain program. Another illustration is the way Cassandra [72] employs type checking to ensure that Android apps are compliant with their privacy requirements even before downloading them.
vi. Code instrumentation: Static analysis can be used to locate the areas of the program where the code needed to gather runtime behavior can be inserted. As an illustration, IccTa [87] analyzes the issues caused by inter-component taint spreading using code

instrumentation in Android apps. Another application by Nyx [75] alters the backdrop color of web pages from light to dark using code instrumentation in Android web apps to make them more energy efficient. Code instrumentation is supported in Android by a number of tools and frameworks, including Soot [88] and WALA [89].

Taint analysis is found to be the technique that is most frequently used (28.6%), followed by code instrumentation (17.1%) and program slicing (12.4%). It should be mentioned that some of the publications employ simple data-flow analysis techniques. They are not classified; hence, the aggregate of percentages is less than 100%.

b. Sensitivity analysis

Techniques for static analysis must be exact and abstract. Sensitivity analysis helps improve the accuracy of static analysis. As a result, various sorts of sensitivities that are used with static analysis approaches are addressed in the sections that follow:

i. Object sensitivity: This mechanism distinguishes between method calls on various objects. To generate new instances of objects or alter existing objects, code in a method can call other methods.
ii. Context sensitivity: This method computes independent information for various calls to the same procedure while tracking the calling context of a method call.
iii. Flow sensitivity: This method takes the order of the statements into account and computes unique information for each statement.
iv. Path sensitivity: This method examines the route taken during execution and isolates the knowledge acquired from several routes.
v. Field sensitivity: Each field of each object is represented using a field-sensitive technique.

The distribution of publications by sensitivities is shown in Figure 3.17. Since Android is built on Java (an object-oriented language), in which object fields are often used to contain data, field sensitivity appears to be

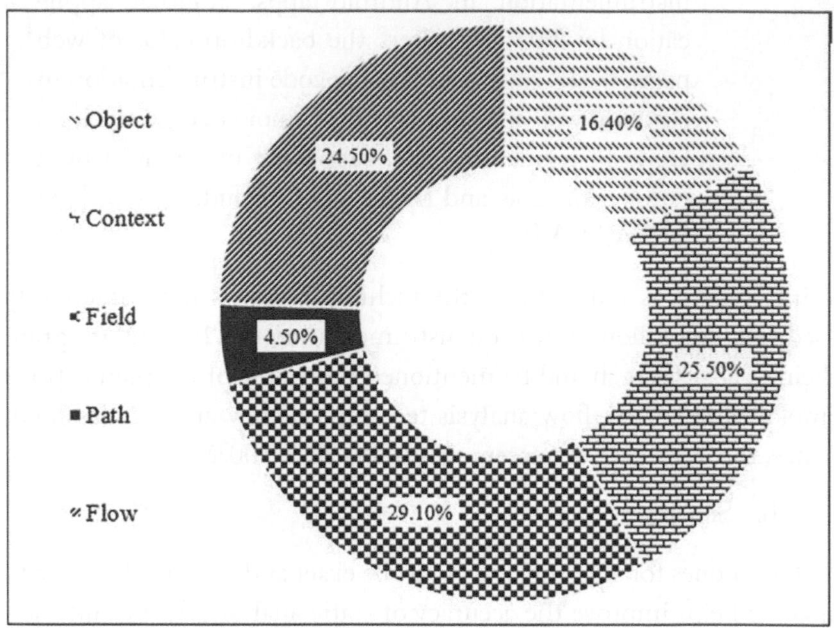

Figure 3.17 Distribution of research publications over sensitivities.

the most prevalent, with about 29% of the publications. Additionally, heavily taken into account are flow sensitivity and context sensitivity (24% and 25% of publications, respectively). Only 5% of papers take path sensitivity into account, mostly because of the scaling problems it creates. It is believed that methods that employ more sensitivities provide analysis that is more precise. They are, however, not as scalable.

c. Data structures

Well-known data structures are used by heavyweight static analysis techniques, which typically yield more accurate results, to provide an abstraction to the underlying programs. Here are some descriptions:

i. Call graph (CG): This is a directed graph in which every node denotes a method and every edge denotes the call or return to a method.
ii. Control flow graph (CFG): The basic flow of statements in a program is represented by the directed graph known as CFG. The program's nodes represent its statements, and its edges signify its control flow.

iii. Inter-procedural control flow graph (ICFG): By connecting the call from and return to edges in each program procedure, this combines the CG and CFG of all the program procedures.

A source-to-sink reachability analysis is performed using CGs (with a 38% share in existing literature), which are also used to disseminate tainted information. For instance, ContentScope [90] finds paths from public content provider interfaces to the database function APIs by navigating CG to detect database leakage. By traversing CG, PermissionFlow [91] associates Android permissions with the corresponding APIs. CG is produced by AsDroid [92] to track intent messages.

In this SLR, CFGs are used in 27% of the papers. For illustration, the constraints related to potentially hazardous pathways are extracted using CFG in ContentScope [90]. These restrictions are then used to produce inputs for potential path executions using a constraint solver.

The ICFG data structure, which links the various CFGs depending on how they refer to one another, is also built on the combination of CFG and CG. More sophisticated and thorough program analyses rely on ICFG. Tainted variables are tracked by traversing ICFG in FlowDroid [82]. To do string analysis, Epicc [74] traverses ICFG. Inter-component data leaks are found in IccTA [87] by using data-flow analysis to ICFG. Due to the complexity and potential scalability issues with the created ICFGs, there are only a few ways use them.

d. Code representation

Since Dalvik bytecode is viewed as being too complex and challenging to operate, the code is represented in an abridged version called the intermediate representation (IR), which processes and represents the original Dalvik bytecode. On-the-shelf frameworks that implement analysis on their IR of program code are used to implement static analysis methodologies. The code representations used in static analysis are listed here:

i. Smali: Apktool, a tool for Android app reverse engineering, is this IR.
ii. Jimple: Jimple is well recognized as the compact form of Java bytecode. The Soot [88] framework makes use

of it. The Dexpler [93] plugin is used by Soot to convert Dalvik bytecode to Jimple IR.

iii. WALA: T. J. Watson Libraries for Analysis is referred to as WALA. A Java/JavaScript static analysis framework is the foundation for the SSA-based representation known as WALA IR [89].
iv. Java_bytecode/class: Dex is the name of Android's unique Dalvik bytecode format. It is distinct from Java and may be executed by the virtual machine for Android (VM). Using APK-to-JAR transformers, programs such as ded [94], Dare [95], and dex2jar [96] convert Dalvik to Java bytecode prior to analysis.
v. DEX_assembler: This uses the dedexer, dexdump, and dx utilities to disassemble DEX files.

This SLR indicates that Soot (25.7%) and Jimple (29.5%) are the most widely used tools for static analysis of Android apps.

Dynamic analysis is used to track the behavior of a program's source code while it is running. The two primary facets of dynamic analysis are:

e. Inspection level

The inspection levels are used to classify dynamic analyses. The following defines them:

i. Emulator-based/virtual machine (VM) level: By altering VMs, this level examines the events that take place within the emulators. The two types of virtual machines are Dalvik and QEMU. Through enhancements to the Dalvik VM, introspection based on Android APIs keeps track of how the Android APIs are being used. Introspection using QEMU may track native code. A VM built on Dalvik is more effective than one built on QEMU. Emulators are vulnerable to emulator evasion, though [82].
ii. Kernel level: Monitoring the execution of API calls can be done by using kernel modules to collect system calls such as ltrace and strace. It enables limited native code tracing.

iii. App level: This level of monitoring is also known as method tracing, and it allows for the tracking of Java method invocation by injecting bytecode and logging statements into the original Android app or framework code.

A whopping 36.2% of the dynamic analysis techniques were examined use app-level monitoring. SIF and other libraries can be used to make app-level monitoring easier ([97], [98]). About 21% of surveyed dynamic approaches capture app behavior by monitoring system calls using kernel-level inspection, such as Andrubis, which accounts for 29.8% of the VM level [99].

f. Approaches

Dynamic taint analysis and anomaly-based dynamic analysis are the two basic methods used in dynamic analysis.

i. Dynamic taint analysis: This method is comparable to static taint analysis; however, the tainted data is monitored while the application is running. The first method to implement dynamic taint analysis was TaintDroid [98]; however, it is not addressed in this SLR.
ii. Anomaly-based: This method checks for deviations from usual behavior in the device's routine behavioral actions. This method typically costs more because it makes a lot of system calls [100].

g. Methods

Supervised learning, unsupervised learning, semi-supervised learning, reinforcement learning, and deep learning are some examples of ML-based techniques.

i. Supervised learning (SL): This group of techniques trains the model to generate predictions for a new dataset using a known set of input data and known responses to the output data. Regression and classification are two popular SL approaches. For instance, StormDroid [101] achieved an accuracy of 93.80% while using SL for malware detection over 8,000 apps with a variety of static and dynamic attributes.

ii. Unsupervised learning (UL): This family of algorithms makes deductions from the input dataset with no labels. A typical UL technique is clustering. Hidden Markov models (HMV), k-means, and k-medoids are examples of common clustering algorithms. To find Android malware, writers in [102] employed a k-means clustering approach cascaded with DT and Random Forest (RF). Using RF, they were able to reach accuracy of 91.75% for dataset 1 and 91.58% for dataset 2.
iii. Semi-supervised learning (SSL): This group of algorithms combines some labeled and unlabeled data with supervised and unsupervised learning approaches. In [103], writers employed the SSL approach for malware detection with permissions and API calls as features, and they were successful in achieving an accuracy of 93.78%.
iv. Reinforcement learning (RL): By maximizing the cumulative reward, RL algorithms give the agent the ability to learn how to accomplish a goal in a setting that may be complicated and uncertain. Deep Q network (DQN), deep deterministic policy gradient (DDPG), soft actor-critic (SAC), and others are RL examples. The authors suggested an automated GUI testing method for Android applications in [104] using DQN. Authors have determined the semantic meanings of GUI components and used them as inputs to a NN, which, during training, comes close to the application's behavioral model being tested.
v. Deep learning (DL): This is an artificial neural network (ANN)–based class of ML algorithms that mimics how the brain works. It can handle a lot of data processing. Deep neural networks (DNN), convolutional neural networks (CNN), recurrent neural networks (RNN), deep belief networks (DBN), and others are well-known DL algorithms. Using DNN, Pang et al. [105] predicted vulnerable components of Java Android applications with an accuracy of 92.87%.

The papers using ML-based methods are included in Table 3.11, together with the datasets, features, and evaluation criteria in the SLR.

Table 3.11 Publications Using ML-Based Methods

CITATION	ML-BASED TECHNIQUE	CLASSIFIER	DATASET	NO. OF APPS	FEATURES	EVALUATION
[106]	SL	DT and Adaboost	Google Play store, VirusShare, and Contagio Dump	Benign = 510 Malicious = 910	API calls, functions, and code features	Accuracy = 99.11%
[107]	UL	k-means++	Android Malware Genome Project, Google Play, alternative Chinese and Russian markets	Benign = 123,453 Malicious = 5,560	Network addresses, API calls, and permissions	Accuracy = 96.60%
[108]	DL	RF, SVM, CNNs	Microsoft Malware Classification Contest on Kaggle	Benign = 1,000 Malware samples = 10,867	–	Attack transferability rate = 88.70%
[109]	DL	DBN	Google Play, Contagio Community, Genome Project	Benign = 20,000 Malicious = 1,760	Permissions, sensitive API, dynamic behaviors	Accuracy = 96.76%
[110]	SSL	K-NN	Real-world Samsung devices	1.3 million audit logs		Learns 2,518 benign & malicious access patterns & generates 331 policy rules
[111]	DL	RF, DT, XGBoost, NN, CNN, RNN	CDAC Mohali, Malshare, VirusShare	Benign = 10,000 Malicious = 10,000	API call sequences	Accuracy = 91.79%
[112]	SL	MLP, SVM, PART, RIDOR, Ensemble Classifiers	Androzoo, AMD, Google Play, and Wandiouja	Benign = 60,000 Malicious = 24,000	Permissions, libraries, broadcast receivers, and API calls	Accuracy = 98.27%

(*Continued*)

Table 3.11 Continued

CITATION	ML-BASED TECHNIQUE	CLASSIFIER	DATASET	NO. OF APPS	FEATURES	EVALUATION
[113]	SL	SVM	APKPure, Google Play, and Amazon App Store	Benign = 28,489 Malicious= 30,113	API calls	Accuracy = 99.75%
[114]	UL	K-means	–	Event sequences = 56,800	File events, memory events, network events, registry events, and thread events are recorded during API system calls	F1 score = 0.8
[115]	DL	CNN	Cheetah Mobile	Benign = 2 Mn Malicious = 2 Mn	API calls	Accuracy = 93.00%
[103]	SSL	LLGC	Android Malware Genome Project, AndroMalShare, pandaap, gfan, hiapk, ANdrdoid, appchina, mumayi, and slideme	300,000 apks	Permissions, API calls	Accuracy = 93.78%
[116]	SL	k-NN, LR	Androtrack, Google Play	Benign = 300 Malicious = 300	Static SMS, phone, storage, contacts, location, camera, microphone dynamic close, read, get time of day, Futex, clock get time, Mprotect, Epoll_pwait, receive from, send to, Ioctl, write, Getuid intrinsic size	Accuracy = 97.50%

[117]	SL	LR, RF	TACYT	82,866 suspicious apps 259,608 malware signatures	Antivirus	F1 score = 0.84
[118]	DL	DNN	Google Play, AMD, and VirusShare	Benign = 1,901 Malicious = 1,600	API calls	Accuracy = 91.70%
[105]	DL	DNN	Java Android applications	–	Elements in source code files that are continuously repeated	Accuracy = 92.87%
[119]	SL	SVM	Comodo Cloud Security Center	Set 1 = 8,046 apps (4,729 benign; 3,317 malicious) Set 2 = 72,891 apps (40,448 benign; 32,443 malicious)	Permissions, filtered intents, API calls, new instances	Accuracy = 96.34%
[120]	DL	CNN	AMD, Drebin	100 Android instructions	Binaries	F1 score = 0.76
[121]	DL, SSL	DNN	Drebin dataset, Androzoo, ApkPure, ApkMirror	Benign = 10,000 Malicious = 8,560	Permissions, API calls	Accuracy = 99.02%
[122]	DL	ANN, LR, NB, RF, GB	Kaggle	300 applications	Permissions, API calls, command related	Accuracy = 96.75%
[123]	SL	SVM	Drebin, Asian third-party mobile markets	Benign = 123,453 Malicious = 5,560	Permissions, API calls	21% of them actually use native calls

(Continued)

Table 3.11 Continued

CITATION	ML-BASED TECHNIQUE	CLASSIFIER	DATASET	NO. OF APPS	FEATURES	EVALUATION
[101]	SL	SVM, DT, ANN, NB, k-NN, and Bagging predictor	Google Play, Contagio Mobile, MobiSec Lab	Benign = 4,350 apps Malicious = 3,620 apps	Permissions, API calls, sequences, dynamic behaviors	Accuracy = 93.80%
[124]	SL	KNN, SVM, DT, RF	Malware Genome, VirusShare database, Google Play	Benign = 683 Malicious = 923	Permissions, API calls	FNR = 0.35% when evaluating malicious apps FPR = 2.96% when evaluating benign apps
[102]	UL	k-Means cascaded with DT, RF	Dataset 1 Dataset 2	200 apps 500 apps	Permissions	Dataset 1 = 91.75% Dataset 2 = 91.58% using RF

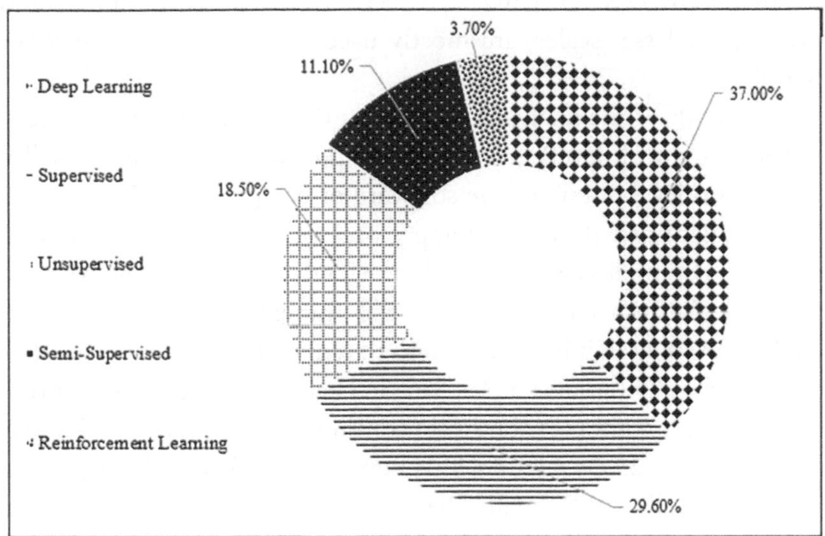

Figure 3.18 Distribution of research publications over ML-based methods.

The distribution of ML techniques used in the survey is shown in Figure 3.18.

3.3.2 Discussions and Future Research Directions

There are numerous topics of discussion when looking into the SLR. Numerous difficulties and gaps are noted in order to address the fourth research question (RQ4), after which some future study directions are provided. The numerous research gaps and difficulties are listed below:

1. Cross-Analysis

The scope of this study is further expanded to include the suggested taxonomy's various directions. Cross-analysis will be done with the intention of improving our understanding of Android security analysis. It's crucial to consider the repeated goals of Android security that program analysis tools attempt to address. It has been noted that methods for both static and dynamic analysis are employed to find data leaks and vulnerabilities. While dynamic techniques are usually used for vulnerability detection as opposed to data leaks and malware detection (58.82% vs. 41.18%), static techniques are typically employed to detect privacy data leaks (50% vs. 34.52%). While ML-based approaches are frequently used in malware detection (56%), hybrid approaches, although at lesser scales, are mostly used for vulnerability detection (19%).

The depth of the analysis approaches (i.e., at the application level or the framework level) is another component of cross-analysis. The application level examines the software of the program. Applications from unidentified third-party app stores provide a significant security risk. Potential system-level design faults and problems with the Android platform are analyzed at the framework level. For framework-level analysis, it has been found that dynamic techniques are used more frequently (around 55%). This is because by deploying runtime modules like monitors in the Android framework, dynamic techniques may observe implicit relationships between the Android permissions and system calls. Additionally, the over ten million lines of code in the Android framework make it hard for static analysis techniques to track real-time framework-level activities. So, for framework-level monitoring, dynamic approaches are typically more scalable and less expensive.

2. Challenges posed by Android specificities

Analytical methods face a number of difficulties because of Android's unique qualities. These are listed as the inter-component communications (ICC), XML file, permissions, and app component lifecycle. Callback methods for the component lifecycle, such as onStart(), onStop(), and onPause(), are independent of the apps and of one another. As a result, creating CFGs using static analysis approaches is challenging. Applications shielded in the sandbox use ICC as a message-passing mechanism. Due to a lack of encryption techniques, ICC creates a number of security vulnerabilities, such as the interception of intent messages. One of the most crucial configuration files found in any Android app is AndroidManifest.xml. The essential elements of an Android application are described, including enforced permissions. The values in the manifest file are bound to the Android app at compile time and cannot be changed at runtime. The foundation of the Android security model is permissions. An app's manifest file contains rights that allow access to a variety of resources and inter-application communication. Users can revoke permissions on Android in recent versions due to dynamic permission management. The limitations of the permission model, including the least privilege principle being violated by coarse-grained permissions [125], delegation attacks brought on by enforcing access control policies at the individual level [126], end user ignorance due to lack of permission awareness [127], and misuse of permissions [102], have been extensively discussed in a number of research publications. Since Java is used to create Android applications, there are additional difficulties that arise due to its use. These difficulties include reflection, handling dynamic code loading, multithreading, polymorphism, and native code integration.

3. Future directions

The suggested taxonomy reveals a number of research holes and problems that demand increased attention to the analysis techniques employed in Android security. To keep up with the evolving security challenges of today, the research community is given the following research recommendations:

- Combining several analytical techniques to produce more accurate and precise results: Individual procedures have inherent limitations; therefore, relying solely on them will never produce optimal results. For high-precision analysis, more dependable hybrid techniques could be used in conjunction with ML and DL, combining the benefits of both static and dynamic approaches.
- Conducting in-depth research on various coding forms: Android apps can also be written in native C/C++, Dalvik bytecode, and binaries, as well as Java. Dalvik bytecode may be accessed using dynamic code loading (DCL) [128] and reflection [129], whereas binaries can be accessed using the Java native interface (JNI) API [72]. Only a small number of cutting-edge static analysis techniques have taken DCL and JNI into account, which has led to inaccurate conclusions.
- Moving from app-level analysis of a single application to system-level analysis to reveal compositional vulnerabilities: Multiple trustworthy apps include security flaws that can be readily exploited by malware authors. However, the majority of research in the current body of literature concentrates on a single app or a single system part. As an

illustration, [100] examined the Android permission protocol to see if it met the security standards for preventing unwanted access. It is difficult to recognize such attacks, which call for thorough system analysis as opposed to examining isolated system components. In order to anticipate all potential ways to attack vulnerabilities at the system level, it is crucial to thoroughly investigate vulnerabilities.

- With a focus on repudiation: This SLR's search procedure turned up nothing regarding Android repudiation. The research community should consider the potential threats and weaknesses brought on by Android's vetting procedure. Developers can confirm the authorship of an application using the process of "vetting," which is similar to code signing. Based on a digital certificate, a user ID (UID) is given to digitally sign the application. When multiple applications are signed by the same certificate, the Android:sharedUserId key is supplied in the manifest file to allow them to share the same UID. When allocating the UID, this key may result in non-deterministic behavior [130].

The inspiration for the work was based on these observations and the knowledge gaps they revealed. Additionally, Section 3.2 provides a brief explanation of research methods.

4

A Parallel Classifier Scheme for Vulnerability Detection in Android

4.1 Introduction

Due to their open-source design and adaptability, Android smartphones are popular targets for cybercriminals. Malware attacks have increased significantly in recent years, which is concerning for Android users. Through a variety of apps, cybercriminals can insert malicious code to compromise systems or access confidential data.

In order to make Android systems more safe, numerous malware detection methodologies and approaches utilizing static, dynamic, and hybrid analysis have been introduced recently. These methods, however, take a lot of time and are unreliable and ineffective. This chapter describes how unique parallel classifiers can be applied to solve very elusive upcoming vulnerabilities and to detect zero-day Android malware.

Android distributes and installs apps using the application package kit (.apk) file type. Applications for Android are combined into a single file type called an APK, which is a JAR (Java archive). The four main parts of an Android application—activities, broadcast receivers, services, and content providers—define its general behavior. The AndroidManifest.xml file, which describes how all components communicate with one another, serves as a loose link between these components. The functions and life cycles of each component are described later in this chapter.

Services handle background processing, while activities (called by intentions) manage user interaction and the user interface (UI). The communication between Android OS and applications is controlled by broadcast receivers. Data administration and database management challenges are handled by content providers.

DOI: 10.1201/9781003354574-4

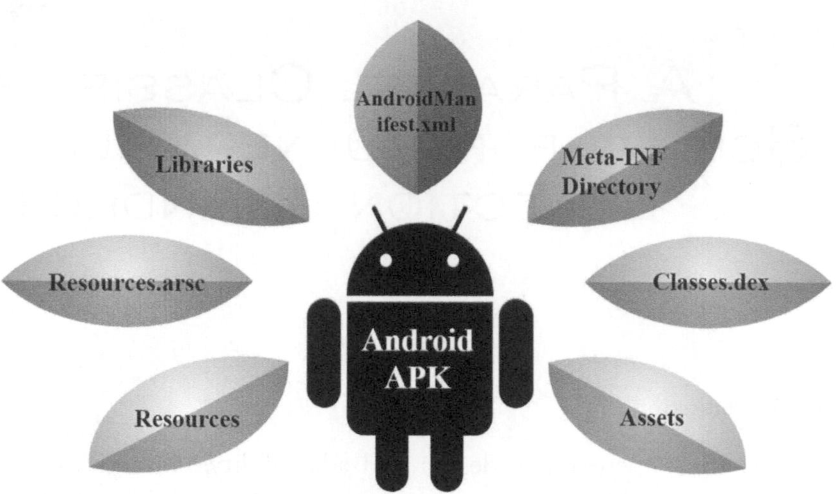

Figure 4.1 De-compilation of an APK.

Applications for Android are developed in Java. After being combined with data and resource files by the Android Software Development Kit (SDK) tools, they are archived in a file with the name "Android package" and the extension ".APK." In order to install the application, an Android smartphone uses this file. Figure 4.1 displays a few of an APK's components.

In order to identify malware, certain characteristics from APKs are extracted and used to classify an application as malicious or benign. To produce accurate results, the classification model must be properly trained. The malicious apps retrieved from benchmark datasets are used to generate these features, which are then used to train the model. Permissions, API calls, version, broadcast receivers and services, and libraries used are examples of static features that are retrieved and used in ML techniques to detect the presence or absence of malware in Android applications. These characteristics are explained as follows:

1. Permissions: In order to access the system's resources and data, Android applications should first request permissions. The system or user may grant the permission depending on the features of the application.
2. API calls: To communicate with the features of multiple devices, Android applications require API calls.

3. Version: The app's version determines whether it can operate on the current OS version or one of its older iterations.
4. Services: These carry out prolonged processes that operate in the background without requiring user intervention.
5. Libraries used: The term *Android libraries* refers to a group of distinct Java-based libraries, such as those that support database access, graphics, and application frameworks.
6. Broadcast receivers: Android OS and application communication is supervised by broadcast receivers.

Table 4.1 displays a selection of these features and how they work.

In ML, a classifier algorithm assigns a categorization to the input data. Typically, it outputs class labels based on a collection of specific extracted features. There are numerous techniques to apply ML, including SL, UL, RL, SSL, DL, and active and inductive learning. Supervised learning is the main topic of the chapter. The training dataset contains information that has been classified as either malicious or benign. Each APK's class is already known. The categorization model is built using this as its foundation. ML techniques including the pruning rule-based classification tree (PART), Ripple-Down Rule learner (RIDOR), support vector machine (SVM), and multilayer perceptron are included in our methodology (MLP). Only a few of the prior research projects had used these four methods; therefore, we chose to use them explicitly. Our method assesses the classifiers independently and concurrently. Each classifier only gains knowledge of a small portion of each subset of data. The use of a parallel classifier facilitates learning

Table 4.1 Extracted Features in a CSV

APK CHARACTERISTICS	FEATURES EXTRACTED
Name	['0d02b9d5539893efc674fbacae14944a.APK']
Permission	['Android.permission INTERNET', 'Android.permission.RECEIVE_SMS', . . . 'Android.permission.CALL_PHONE', 'Android.permission.SEND_SMS']
Version	[u'3.0']
Services	['my.app.client.Client']
Broadcast Receivers	['my.app.client.BootReceiver', 'my.app.client.AlarmListener']
Libraries	['Android.test.runner']

and, in theory, expedites classification decisions. The following is a discussion of the various classifiers.

1. Multilayer perceptron: MLP is frequently referred to as a feed-forward neural network with one or more hidden layers between the input and output layer. Data only moves forward in feed-forward systems, from the input layer to the output layer. To train the network, a back-propagation technique is used. MLP is typically used to solve datasets that cannot be separated linearly for tasks such as pattern recognition, classification, prediction, and approximation.
2. Support vector machine (SVM): This supervised ML approach can address classification and regression issues, but it's frequently applied to classification issues. Each piece of data is represented by a point in dimensional space in SVM, where is the number of features present, and a specific coordinate represents the feature value.
3. Pruning rule-based classification tree: This technique combines the separate-and-conquer and divide-and-conquer basic rule-learning methodologies. It generates decision lists, which are collections of rules in order. The greatest coverage leaf is converted into a rule as PART iteratively constructs a partial decision tree.
4. Ripple-Down Rule learner: The rule classifier RIDOR uses a separate-and-conquer strategy. In order to locate exceptions with the lowest mistake rate, it first produces a default rule. It then iteratively determines the best exception for each exception. The method used here is referred to as gradually decreased error pruning. Common laws that forecast classes other than the default make up the exceptions.

4.2 Relevant Works

Numerous methods are now being used to identify the inherent vulnerabilities in Android OS due to the exponential rise of Android malware in recent years. Static analysis, which analyzes certain code segments without running the application on a real device or an Android emulator, was the first method for finding malware on Android devices.

This technique for identifying vulnerabilities is affordable, time effective, and resource efficient. Two primary approaches to static analysis are examined:

1. Signature-based detection: AndroSimilar [131], which only detects samples of known malware, is built on this principle. The majority of the time, DroidAnalytics [132] collects, extracts, and analyzes Android APKs that have been infected with malware.
2. Permission-based detection: This methodology can identify malware samples that are unfamiliar to signature-based techniques and go undetected. Three technologies that rely on permission-based detection techniques were carefully examined. By monitoring application programming interface (API) calls, the first tool, Stowaway [133], may spot malware. The second tool may evaluate the AndroidManifest.xml file and determine the malignancy score, as suggested by R. Sato [134]. The third tool, PUMA [135], may identify malware by taking the extracted permissions into account.

The static analysis method does have one disadvantage, however: it does not support the dynamic loading of code, and code obfuscation makes pattern matching extremely difficult to identify malicious behavior in applications. In signature-based detection methods, the similarity score can falsely label benign apps as malicious, making it impossible to identify unidentified malware kinds. Permission-based detection methods have a high false-positive rate since they cannot investigate reflected calls or detect adware.

The second technique uses dynamic analysis, which aims to overcome the limitations of static analysis. In this technique, the behavior of the application in a real-time environment is monitored. This approach checks the performance of the application in the running state, which successfully resolves the issue of DCL in static analysis. In dynamic analysis, there are three key approaches:

1. Anomaly-based detection: This technique is employed by a number of mechanisms, including CrowDroid [136], Andromaly [137], and AntiMalDroid [138], among others. By starting and finishing system calls in the client-server

architecture, CrowDroid detects malware. By concentrating on and analyzing how events behave within the Android application, Andromaly can identify malware. AntiMalDroid finds malware as it is running. By logging inputs and their associated outputs in accordance with the capabilities of the application, it creates signatures.

2. Taint analysis: TaintDroid [98], which is based on the scientific method known as dynamic taint analysis, uses it notably. This technology automatically tags sensitive data, such GPS or microphone signals, and tracks the flow of tainted information.
3. Emulation-based detection: This is employed by DroidScope [139], whose functionalities rely on the examination of the OS, Dalvik Semantics, and AASandbox [140]. Working with the class.dex file, it conducts static and dynamic analysis in the sandbox. Using a monkey tool, it deconstructs the file into a format that is simple to interpret [33].

However, due to their high resource consumption, battery-operated devices are not suitable for dynamic analysis (e.g., time, memory, etc.). When a valid software makes more system calls, anomaly-based detection systems use up time and resources while fabricating erroneous findings. Taint analysis does not trace control flow, and emulation-based detection has a narrow field of detection and overlooks newly discovered malware.

The third strategy, called hybrid analysis, combines static and dynamic analytic techniques. It simultaneously extracts data and runs applications. In comparison to static and dynamic analysis, hybrid analysis yields superior findings, but it also makes the system's time complexity higher. The following is a review of the many tools used in hybrid analysis:

1. Mobile Sandbox [141] operates on the tenets of signature-based and permission-based approaches, inspecting the manifest file, user permissions, and anti-virus to detect any harmful code before examining the operation of the application while it is running.
2. Andrubis [99] performs a static analysis on byte code and the AndroidManifest.xml file and then feeds the results of that

analysis as input to a dynamic analysis that does taint tracing, method tracing, and system-level analysis as the application is being run.

3. SAMADroid [142], a three-level hybrid malware detection model, is a reliable and effective malware detection method for Android. However, because it relies on server connectivity, the malicious activity of Android APKs is detected at the peripheral location.
4. A heuristics system called DroidRanger [143] uses permission-based filtering and behavioral footprinting to find known malware samples. It only concentrates on ten permissions for each malware family, though.
5. DroidDolphin [144] employs SVM for classification and APIMonitor and APE_BOX to collect static and dynamic features. Its disadvantage is that anti-emulator techniques can readily get around it.

The maximum accuracy that either static or dynamic analysis could reach was 93.00%, while hybrid analysis was able to attain 94.00% accuracy [145] using the Malgenome dataset, proving that these techniques were unable to effectively detect malware. Hybrid analytic techniques have their own drawbacks that prevent them from delivering flawless results. For all the families, previously employed methodologies using hybrid analysis gave outcomes that were worse than the totally static situation [146].

The fourth method, known as ML, is unconventional. It is a means to accomplish certain AI objectives by letting the system learn from experience and adapt without having to explicitly program it. A comparison of the methods used to detect Android malware is presented in Table 4.2.

The methodology put forth by Suleiman et al. [146] notably contrasts with the strategy suggested in this chapter. Their strategy is restricted to using just static features such as commands, API requests, and permissions. The new approach, however, also extracts static information in addition to dynamic features. The chapter also suggests the ideal pairing of the most effective ML algorithms, improving the sensitivity, specificity, and efficacy of Android malware detection.

Table 4.2 Comparative Study of Android Malware Detection Techniques

METHODOLOGY	TECHNIQUE	TOOLS	DESCRIPTION	DRAWBACKS
Static	Signature based	AndroSimilar [131]	Used to identify only known malware samples	Malicious apps are categorized as non-harmful
		DroidAnalytics [132]	Gathers, examines, and extracts the relationship of Android APKs infected by malware	Unable to recognize unidentified malware subtypes
	Permission based	Stowaway [133]	Uses API call tracking to identify	
		Sato [134]	Estimates the malignancy score after analyzing the manifest file for an application	Produces a high rate of false positives
		PUMA [135]	Uses the extracted permissions to perform malware detection	Excludes reflected calls and adware samples from analysis
Dynamic	Anomaly based	CrowDroid [136]	Identifies vulnerabilities by starting system calls and running in client-server architecture	Consumes battery and time while producing false results
		Andromaly [137]	Concentrates on the application's actions and events	Unable to trace flow control
		AntiMalDroid [138]	Records the I/O in accordance with the functions carried out in the application to produce a signature	Coverage is insufficient, and new malware is ignored
	Taint analysis	TaintDroid [98]	Keeps track of the flow of data and its automatic tagging	
	Emulation based	DroidScope [139]	OS, Dalvik Semantic, and AASandbox all affect functionality	
Hybrid	NA	Mobile Sandbox [140]	Identifies harmful code by examining permissions and AV to test the behavior of apps while they are running	Negative results for all families compared to the totally static example

NA	Andrubis [99]	Dynamic analysis uses the results of static analysis to do system-level analysis, method tracing, and taint tracing	Mostly dependent on server communications
NA	SAMADroid [142]	High malware detection accuracy due to the combination of three techniques: static and dynamic Analysis, local and remote host, and ML intelligence	Consumes a lot of resources and concentrates on ten permissions for each malware family Anti-emulator strategies can readily circumvent it
NA	DroidRanger [143]	Using permission-based filtering and behavioral footprinting, heuristics can identify known malware samples	
NA	DroidDolphin [144]	APIMonitor and APE BOX are used to collect static and dynamic characteristics, and SVM is then used for classification. Efficiency of 86%.	

4.3 Dataset Description

As indicated in Table 4.3, malicious and non-malicious APKs (~85,000) were gathered from four benchmark datasets: Google Play [147], Wandoujia [148], AMD [149], and Androzoo [150].

AMD comprises ~25,000 samples spanning the years 2010 to 2016. These are divided into 135 different subcategories by 71 malware families. There are three source files for the data (.csv). A single comma-separated values (CSV) file containing all the datasets is built. In order to generate a performance matrix, the ML algorithms will use this CSV file as a training dataset. The following list of steps describes how to download and retrieve the datasets:

1. We used APKPure.com, an online APK downloader, to obtain an APK from the Wandoujia app market and Google Play [151].
2. To access the dataset from Androzoo [152], we used the following command to download a safe APK using a web browser (such as Firefox, Chrome, etc.): *https://androzoo.uni.lu/api/download?apikey=**${APIKEY}**&sha256=**${SHA256}***.
3. The AMD dataset includes almost 25,000 malicious APK samples from 2010 to 2016. These are divided into 135 different subcategories by 71 malware families. Figures 4.2 and 4.3 display, respectively, the distribution of malware families with the formation year and the discovery year.
4. To access the AMD dataset: In accordance with the access policy, AMD shares an SSH key to enable APK downloads on local machines [153].
5. There are six characteristics for each APK file: SHA256, SHA1, MD5, APK size, market, and certificate. You can find the code samples in [154].

Table 4.3 Datasets

DATA SOURCE	APKS (IN NOS.)	MALICIOUS/BENIGN
Google Play, Wandoujia (3rd Party)	800	Malicious + Benign
AMD	24,650	Malicious
Androzoo	60,000	Benign

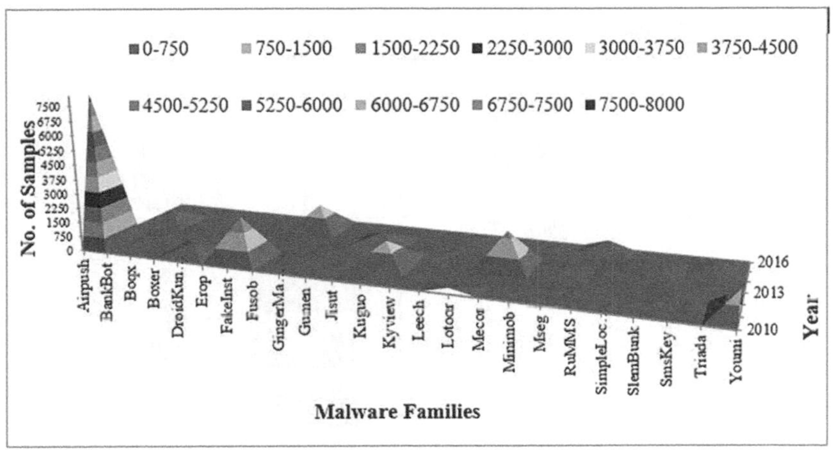

Figure 4.2 Malware families' surface distribution and genesis year.

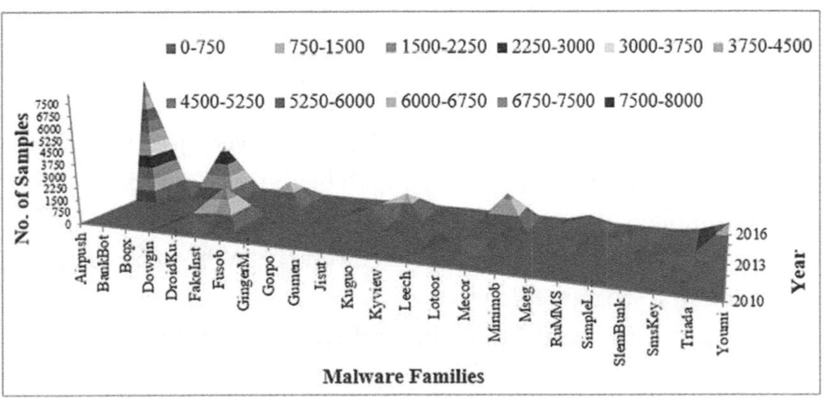

Figure 4.3 Malware families' surface distribution and detection year.

4.4 Proposed Methodology

The process for combining the different ML parallel classifiers is described in Figure 4.4. Each algorithm is given access to one CPU core, which is then forced to run simultaneously in order to increase accuracy by generating a single categorization decision. This is done to find malware as quickly and accurately as feasible. Following the parallel classifier scheme is decision fusion, which combines the outputs from various classifiers to produce estimates of higher quality than those obtained from any one of the individual sources alone. In other words,

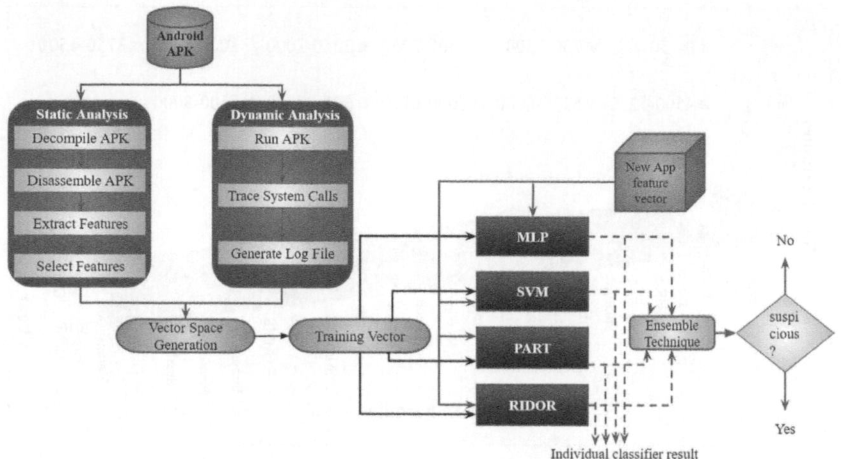

Figure 4.4 Parallel classifier scheme.

it enhances the ability of individual classifiers to generalize. A quick summary of how the ML classifiers operate is provided next.

The process includes these three crucial steps:

1. Input pre-processing: Benchmark datasets were used to gather ~85,000 Android applications, both benign and malicious. We decompiled the input from APKs using the Apktool [155]. Following decompilation, we received the APKs' component parts in a separate folder.
2. Feature extraction: From the gathered dataset, we extracted the static and dynamic features for feature extraction.

    a. Static analysis: Android applications are available in the form of an APK archive, or Android package. The manifest, Gradle, resources, and other directories are all included in the APK archive. We reverse engineered the APK files using the Apktool to extract the features that were of interest to us. The decompiled directories were parsed by the custom Python script, which also extracted the necessary static features from the AndroidManifest.xml and Apktool.yml files.

There are 135 permissions available for Android in total. The features that were extracted were used to build a binary feature vector. This feature vector is $E = e_1, e_2, \ldots, e_n)$, where

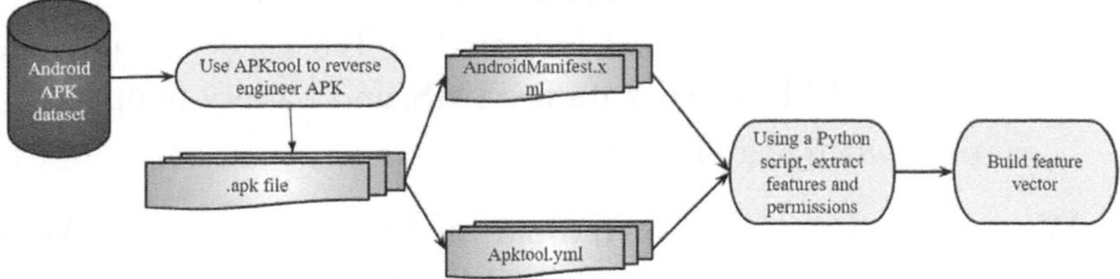

Figure 4.5 Scheme for extracting static features.

$$e_i = \begin{cases} 1, if\ i^{th}\ permission is\ present \\ 0, else \end{cases}$$

The procedure for static feature extraction is shown in Figure 4.5.

Bit 1 indicates the presence of the permission, while bit 0 indicates its absence. A second variable, D, is also introduced, with the values D denoting harmful or benign applications. $D = 1$ denotes a benign application, whereas $D = -1$ denotes a malicious application. Equations (4.1) and (4.2), respectively, denote the benign and malicious APK vectors. Here, the variables E_{Benign} and $E_{\alpha\beta Benign}$ stand for benign and malicious vectors, respectively, where α and β stand for row and column:

$$E_{\alpha\beta\ Benign} = \begin{pmatrix} 0&0&0&0&0&0&0&1&0&0&0&0&0&0&0&0&0&0&0 \\ 0&0&0&0&0&0&0&0&0&0&0&0&0&0&0&0&0&0&0 \\ 0&0&0&0&0&1&0&0&0&0&0&0&0&0&0&0&0&0&0 \\ 0&0&0&0&0&1&0&0&0&0&0&0&0&0&0&0&0&0&0 \\ 0&0&0&0&1&0&0&0&0&0&0&0&0&0&0&0&0&0&0 \end{pmatrix} \quad (4.1)$$

$$E_{\alpha\beta\ Malicious} = \begin{pmatrix} 0&0&0&0&0&0&0&1&0&0&0&0&0&0&0&0&0&0&0 \\ 0&0&0&0&0&0&0&0&0&0&0&0&0&0&0&0&0&0&0 \\ 0&0&0&0&0&-1&0&0&0&0&0&0&0&0&0&0&0&0&0 \\ 0&0&0&0&0&1&0&0&0&0&0&0&0&0&0&0&0&0&0 \\ 0&0&0&0&-1&0&0&0&0&0&0&0&0&0&0&0&0&0&0 \end{pmatrix} \quad (4.2)$$

b. Dynamic analysis: System calls, which we extracted through dynamic analysis, are the means by which an

Android application interacts with the OS. Dynamic features were extracted as indicated in Table 4.4, including CPU, RAM, network traffic, SMS, and battery temperature (when charging).

We connected the built-in Android Studio emulator to the ADB shell for dynamic analysis (a command-line tool). It produces n random events (UI interactions), such as clicks, touches, etc., and sends them to the system or a program that records system calls. We used the monitoring program Strace [156] to log system calls. The dynamic feature extraction technique is shown in Figure 4.6.

The set of potential system calls available in the Android OS is denoted by $C=(c_1,c_2,\ldots,c_n)$. The number of instances of system call c_j is thus indicated by element j in the system call feature vector. The

Table 4.4 Dynamic Features Extracted

DYNAMIC FEATURE	FEATURE DESCRIPTION (WITH MEASUREMENT UNIT)
BattIsCharging	Battery amount on charging (Percentage)
BattTemperature	Battery temperature while charging (Degrees Celsius)
Network traffic	Receive packet, transmission packet (Bytes)
Memory	Allocated, free, shared (Bytes)
CPU	Usage of CPU (Percentage)
SMS	Send SMS, receive SMS (Bytes)

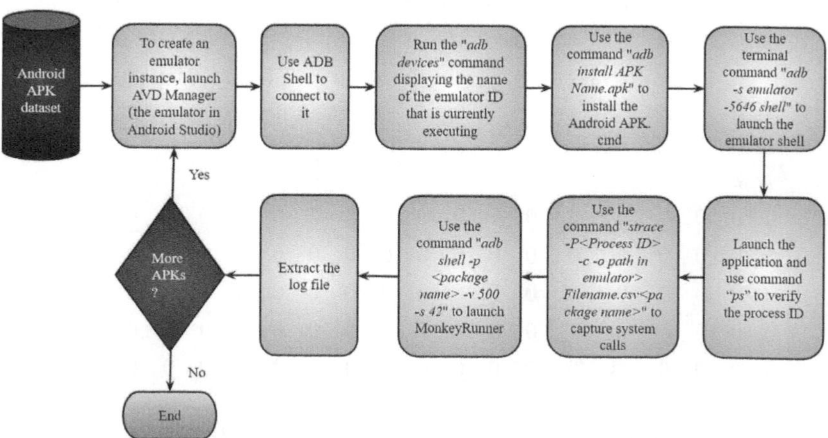

Figure 4.6 Scheme for extracting dynamic features.

parameter Υ is an n-length sequence that represents the frequency of system calls for each application as recorded in a log file.

Let $s_i \in C$ be the ith observed system calls in the log file, and let $\Upsilon = (s_1, s_2, \ldots, s_n)$. The previously obtained feature vector is subsequently forwarded to the next stage of feature extraction. Every attribute in the feature vector in this case indicates how frequently system calls appear in the strace log. The feature vector $x = [x_1, x_2, \ldots, x_{|c|}]$ is defined using this sequence Υ, where x_i denotes the frequency of system call $x_i \in \Upsilon$. In Equations. (4.3) and (4.4), the feature vector for system calls is determined for both legitimate and malicious applications.

$$E_{\alpha\beta\ Benign} = \begin{pmatrix} 0 & 0 & 0 & 0 & 2500 & 0 & 0 & 1 & 0 & 0 & 0 & 1500 & 0 & 0 & 0 & 0 & 1 & 0 & 32 \\ 0 & 0 & 36 & 0 & 0 & 0 & 0 & 0 & 753 & 0 & 0 & 0 & 0 & 1 & 0 & 0 & 90 & 0 & 56 \\ 0 & 150 & 0 & 0 & 110 & 1 & 0 & 0 & 0 & 0 & 0 & 1 & 0 & 0 & 0 & 0 & 0 & 0 & 0 \\ 0 & 0 & 0 & 55 & 0 & 1 & 0 & 0 & 0 & 0 & 0 & 0 & 0 & 87 & 0 & 0 & 0 & 1 & 0 \\ 0 & 0 & 0 & 0 & 1 & 0 & 0 & 0 & 65 & 0 & 0 & 425 & 0 & 0 & 0 & 0 & 1 & 0 & 0 \end{pmatrix} \quad (4.3)$$

$$E_{\alpha\beta\ Malicious} = \begin{pmatrix} 0 & 0 & 0 & 0 & 500 & 0 & 0 & 1 & 0 & 0 & 0 & 1500 & 0 & 0 & 0 & 0 & 1 & 0 & 32 \\ 0 & 0 & 86 & 0 & 0 & 0 & 0 & 0 & 653 & 0 & 0 & 0 & 0 & 1 & 0 & 0 & 90 & 0 & 56 \\ 0 & 150 & 0 & 0 & 110 & -1 & 0 & 0 & 0 & 0 & 0 & 1 & 0 & 0 & 0 & 0 & 0 & 0 & 0 \\ 0 & 0 & 0 & 55 & 0 & 0 & 0 & 0 & 0 & 0 & 0 & 0 & 0 & 887 & 0 & 0 & 0 & 1 & 0 \\ 2238 & 0 & 0 & 0 & 1 & 0 & 0 & 0 & 65 & 0 & 0 & 425 & 0 & 0 & 0 & 0 & 1 & 0 & -1 \end{pmatrix} \quad (4.4)$$

c. Model evaluation: The performance of the classifiers in various parallel combination approaches was assessed using ten-fold cross-validation. The dataset was divided into ten equal and distinct (or mutually exclusive) partitions here, numbered part1, part2, . . . , part10. One partition was used as the testing data for the assessment process at each level, while the remaining nine partitions were intended to apply the training model. Ten-fold cross-validation was considered because it offers a good balance between low computational cost and low bias in a model performance estimate. To provide each classifier a unique value for its performance metric, the arithmetic mean of the output was calculated. This method guarantees the detection of unidentified malicious applications.

Table 4.5 lists the various performance measurement measures.

Table 4.5 Confusion Matrix

		PREDICTED		
		Positive	Negative	Total
Observed	Positive	TP (a)	FN (b)	a + b
	Negative	FP (c)	TN (d)	c + d
	Total	a + c	b + d	a + b + c + d

- True positive ratio (TPR)/sensitivity: The ratio of accurately identified malicious APKs to all harmful APKs in the dataset.

$$TPR = \frac{a}{(a+b)} \tag{4.5}$$

- True negative ratio (TNR)/specificity: Proportion of correctly categorized non-harmful APKs divided by all non-harmful APKs in the collection.

$$TNR = \frac{d}{(c+d)} \tag{4.6}$$

- False positive ratio (FPR): The ratio of non-harmful APKs in the dataset that were wrongly identified as harmful.

$$FPR = 1 - TNR = 1 - Specificity \tag{4.7}$$

$$FPR = \frac{c}{(c+d)} \tag{4.8}$$

- False negative ratio (FNR): The ratio of harmful apps that were wrongly classified in the dataset to all harmful apps.

$$FNR = \frac{b}{(a+b)} \tag{4.9}$$

- Accuracy (Acc): The ratio of correct predictions to all other predictions in a dataset.

$$Acc = \frac{(a+d)}{(a+b+c+d)} \tag{4.10}$$

- Error ratio (Err): The ratio of inaccurate predictions to all other predictions in a dataset.

$$Err = 1 - Acc \tag{4.11}$$

4.5 System Configuration and Experimental Setup

Table 4.6 displays the system configurations for the host and guest machines.

4.6 Results

The results for Android malware detection using several ML classifiers are summarized in the paragraph that follows:

4.6.1 Individual Classifiers

To achieve a standard result for the suggested approach to Android malware detection, the first phase of the research was carried out using each of the unique classification algorithms that were listed and explained in the previous section. An aggregated outcome of these individual classifiers is shown in Table 4.7. Before the model is trained, the parameters are tuned (learning rate [0.25 for training MLP, regularization constant] and kernel type [linear] in SVM). In this case,

Table 4.6 System Configurations

	HOST MACHINE
Model	HP ProBook
Processor	Intel(R) Core™ i7–7500U CPU @ 2.70 GHz 2.29 GHz
RAM	8.0 GB
System Type	64-bit operating system
Operating System	Windows 10
	GUEST MACHINE
OS Image	Ubuntu 14.04 LTS
Memory	226.0 GB
System type	32-bit
	ANDROID EMULATOR CONFIGURATION
Platform	Android Studio 1.5.1
Device	Nexus 7
Target	Android 4.2.2 – API level 17
CPU/ABI	Intel Atom (x86)
RAM	512 MiB
SD Card	200 MiB

Table 4.7 Performance Indicators for each Classifier (in %)

ALGORITHM	TPR	TNR	FPR	FNR	ACC	ERR
MLP	96.11	95.67	4.33	3.89	95.89	4.11
SVM	93.29	94.81	5.19	6.71	94.05	5.95
PART	95.36	96.59	3.41	4.64	95.87	4.03
RIDOR	95.68	94.37	5.63	4.32	95.02	4.98

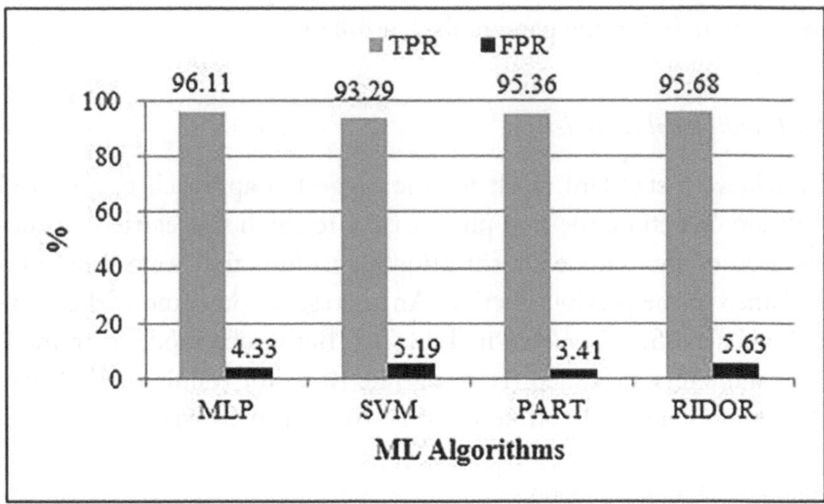

Figure 4.7 Comparative analysis of various individual classifiers.

we employed the grid-search technique, which selects a grid of hyperparameter values and assesses each one individually.

MLP proved to be the most accurate classifier of the four, as shown in Table 4.7. According to Figure 4.7, TPR, or the detection rate of MLP, was 96.11%, with the lowest FPR of 4.33%. As demonstrated in Figure 4.8(a), MLP surpassed all with an accuracy of 95.89% while SVM had the lowest accuracy of the four at 94.05%. In Figure 4.8(b), the ROC curve for MLP (AUC = 0.9589) is displayed.

4.6.2 Parallel Classifiers

The composite model was used for the research's second phase, which involved parallel execution of the results from 4.5.1. To assess the effectiveness of the cumulative technique, four parameters—majority voting, maximum probability, average probability, and product of

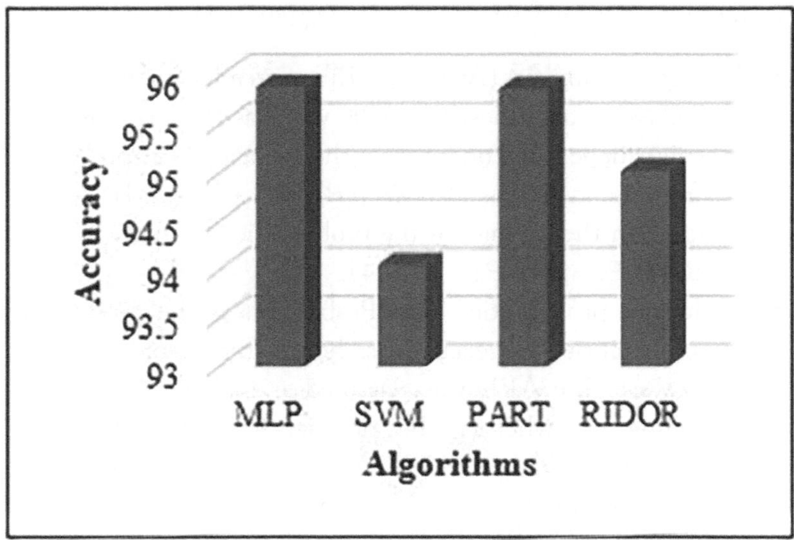

Figure 4.8(a)

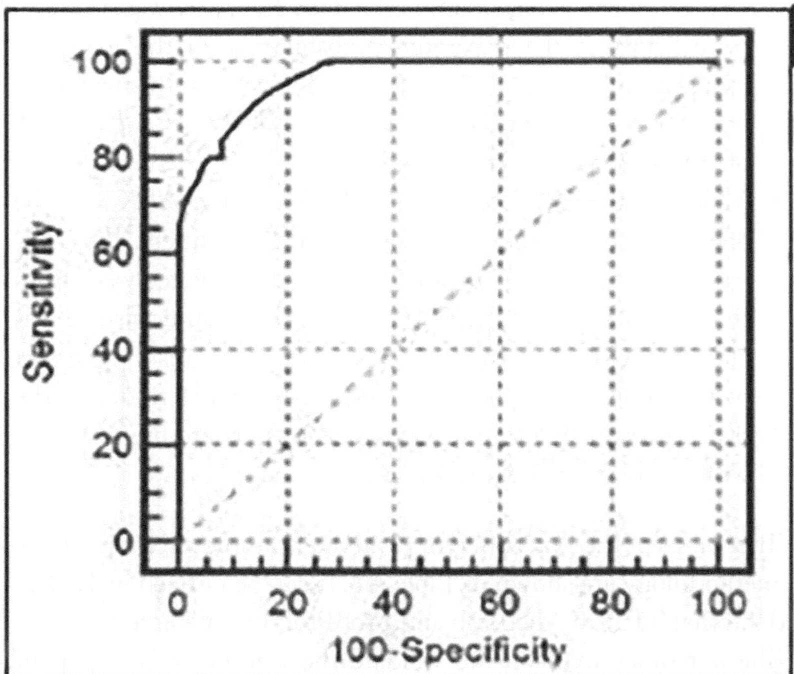

Figure 4.8(b)

Figure 4.8 Accuracy and ROC for different individual classifiers.

probabilities—were taken into account. The individual classifiers provided these probabilities. There were two classes: malignant (*Mal*) and benign (*Ben*).

- Average probabilities (AvgProb): This term refers to the average of all class probabilities. The APK was classified as malicious or benign, depending on whether the average of the probabilities from the malicious $classMal[(P1+P2+P3+P4)/4]$ was higher than the average of the probabilities from the benign $classBen\,[(P1+P2+P3+P4)/4]$.
- Product of probabilities (ProdProb): This is the product of the probabilities for each class: hence, the term *product of probabilities*. The APK was classified as malicious or benign depending on whether the product of the probabilities from the malicious $classMal(P1\times P2\times P3\times P4)$ was greater than the product of the probabilities from the benign $classBen(P1\times P2\times P3\times P4)$.
- Maximum probability (MaxProb): The highest probability for each class is known as maximum probability. The APK was classified as malicious if the maximum probability from the malicious $classMax[Mal(P1,P2,P3,P4)]$ was higher than the maximum probability from the benign $classMax[Ben(P1,P2,P3,P4)]$; otherwise, it was classified as benign.
- Majority vote (MVote): The final class of the APK was the one that received the most votes from all classifiers. The APK was classified as malicious if the majority of votes were from the classifier $MVote(C1,C2,C3,C4)=Mal$; otherwise, it was classified as benign. If there was a tie, it was resolved either by randomly assigning the unidentified instance to one of the tied classes or by using class proportions, where the tied class with the highest proportion wins.

The results of the four different parameters employed in the suggested methodology are shown in Table 4.8. It can be noticed in Tables 4.7 and 4.8 that TPR in MaxProb and ProdProb has increased.

The outcomes in Table 4.8 validate the viability of using parallel ML classifiers. It is clear that our method significantly closes the gaps and overcomes the shortcomings of existing methods, improving the detection of Android malware.

Table 4.8 Performance Indicators for Parallel Classifiers (in %)

ENSEMBLE TECHNIQUE	TPR	TNR	FPR	FNR	ACC	ERR
MaxProb	98.79	97.75	2.25	1.21	98.27	1.73
ProdProb	96.02	95.81	4.19	3.98	95.91	4.09
AvgProb	95.82	93.63	6.37	4.18	94.72	5.28
MVote	92.06	93.13	6.87	7.94	92.59	7.41

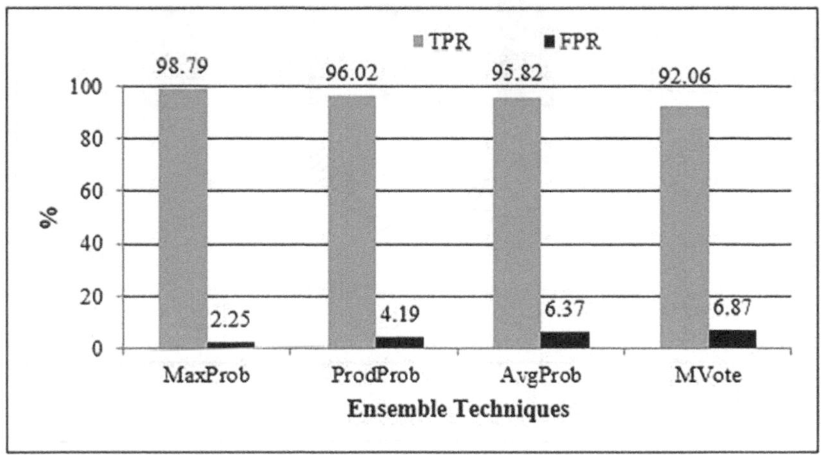

Figure 4.9 Comparison of different parallel classifiers.

Overall, as shown in Figure 4.9, the highest detection rate (TPR = 98.79%) was attained by using the largest number of probabilities (AUC = 0.9827). Individual classifiers couldn't compete with the parallel classifier scheme's TPR. Figure 4.10(a) displays the accuracy for various algorithm configurations. Figure 4.10(b) displays the ROC curve for maximum probability (0.9827).

4.7 Conclusion and Future Directions

Android mobile platforms are vulnerable to malware attacks, and while researchers have previously handled such malware identification and categorization, the accuracy of their approaches might be improved. This chapter shows how to effectively detect and classify malware as malicious or benign in Android applications. Both static and dynamic features, including battery temperature, battery charging percentage, network traffic, SMS sent and received, CPU and memory usage, etc., were tracked and assessed. Examples of static features tracked and

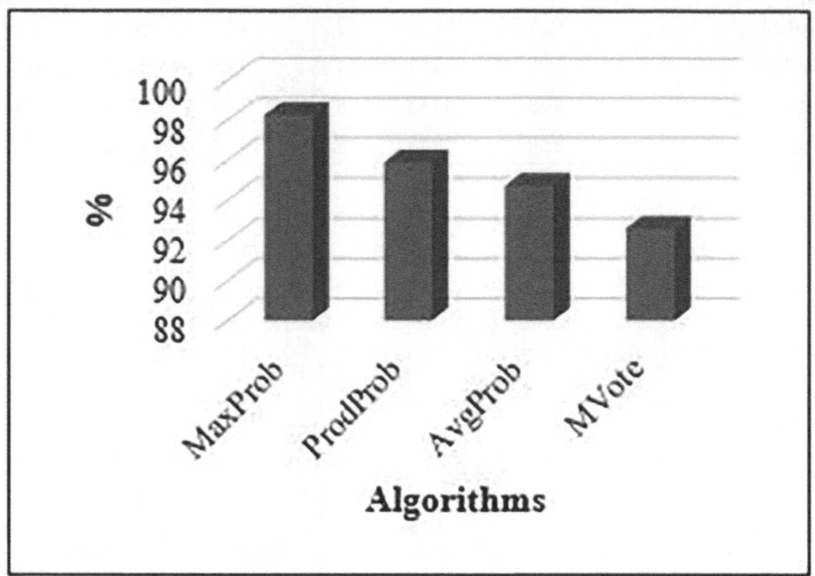

Figure 4.10(a)

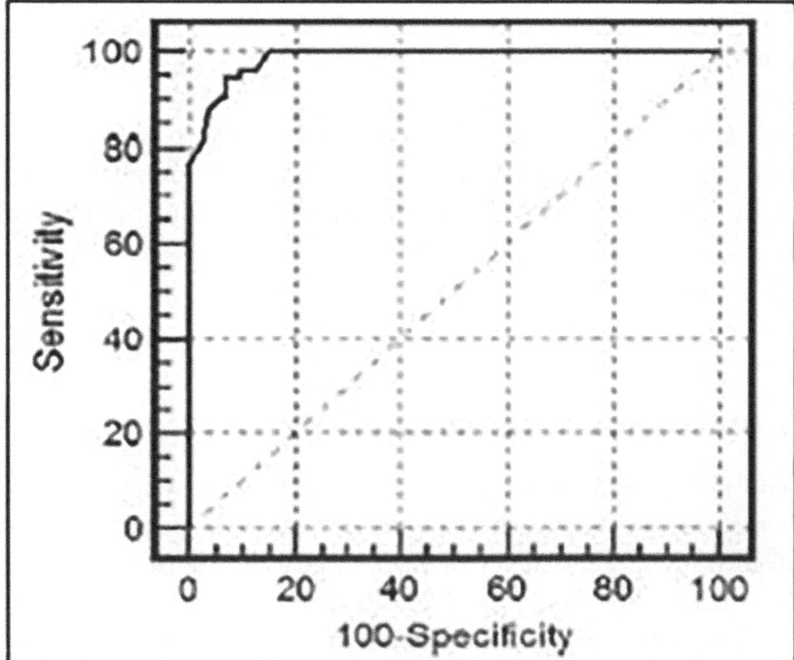

Figure 4.10(b)

Figure 4.10 Accuracy and ROC for different parallel classifiers.

evaluated include permissions, API calls, version, receiver broadcast, services, and libraries used. The methodology outlined in this chapter leverages a combination of MLP, SVM, PART, and RIDOR individual classifiers to produce a solution that is both accurate and effective. This solution fixes the flaws and restrictions of the earlier methods while also accurately detecting malware in the Android OS with a 98.27% accuracy rate. This methodology reduces the impact of each classifier's limitations while maximizing its strengths and advantages. As a result, the approach as a whole is reliable and less error prone.

We intend to build additional parallel classifiers in our upcoming work by combining fresh sets of separate classifiers. Using DL models on a sizable real-world dataset, our objective is also to identify and forecast vulnerabilities and infections. There is a strong theory that the malware that is now in existence may be grouped into different families and that by using sophisticated ML models, useful patterns can be extracted from them. In the next chapter, we classify Android malware using a parallel classifier scheme.

5

Classification of Android Malware Using Ensemble Classifiers

5.1 Introduction

The adaptability and open-source nature of Android makes it widely used. These factors raise security concerns because hackers may misuse users' private information or compromise their systems. In order to address this issue, a number of malware detection and classification techniques have been developed. While ML algorithms such as NB, DTs, and others appear to have produced better results than static and dynamic analysis, they are still not completely reliable in terms of cost and efficiency. This chapter describes a method for classifying zero-day Android malware by combining four distinct parallel classifiers with various features.

The classification of a malware sample into known families is crucial after detection. Malware belonging to the same family will have comparable traits and behaviors. The payload for an attack can be inserted using the same package names. A malware family's signature is defined by its common malicious behavior, traits, and usage of package names. In order to overcome these challenges, an ensemble classifier technique for malware classification is proposed, in which features are extracted from quick and expandable, precise, and obfuscation-resistant APKs. This technique selects four ML algorithms based on their distinct qualities: MLP, SVM, PART, and RIDOR. A blend of these algorithms is then run in parallel to increase accuracy and efficiency.

5.2 Relevant Works

An information flow analysis method was suggested by authors in [157] to uncover mobile malware. Their strategy emphasized on the design of the intricate flows, patterns, and actions of both good and

DOI: 10.1201/9781003354574-5

bad apps. Here, native code was not examined; hence, the method was unable to identify any harmful behavior.

RevealDroid is a framework for detecting and identifying families of Android malware, as described in [158]. ML algorithms under supervision were employed to identify malware families. They succeeded in identifying malware families with a 95.00% accuracy rate. However, external validity was threatened by the dataset that RevealDroid used.

A tool called DroidCat was created and put into use by the authors of [159] to identify and classify Android malware using systematic dynamic profiling and supervised ML techniques. Out of the 122 behavioral measures they identified, 70 showed a significant difference between benign and malicious apps. By using random forests, DroidCat's accuracy was 92.00%.

In another study, researchers used ML algorithms to analyze harmful Android apps in static form [160]. First, using the BoW feature-extraction algorithm, APKs were decompiled to extract static features. Then a feature vector was acquired. They used a permissions-based strategy and source code analysis. For categorization based on permission, an F-measure of 89% was attained. However, because APKs had to be decompiled before analysis, it turned out to be more computationally expensive.

A technique for automatically classifying Android malware called FalDroid [161] demonstrated the shared behavior of malware from the same families via a lot of subgraphs. Researchers used a TF-IDF–like approach to assign various weights to various critical APIs after filtering program semantics into a representation of a function call graph. Native code was not taken into account here. Although it attained an accuracy of 94.50%, it was unable to defeat sophisticated obfuscation techniques like encryption and reflection.

5.3 Proposed Methodology

The classification of malware involves several phases, as shown in Figure 5.1.

The following are the steps for malware classification:

1. Identifying and removing harmful Android APKs: Identifying and removing harmful APKs from the combined dataset is the initial step in categorization. In the separation process,

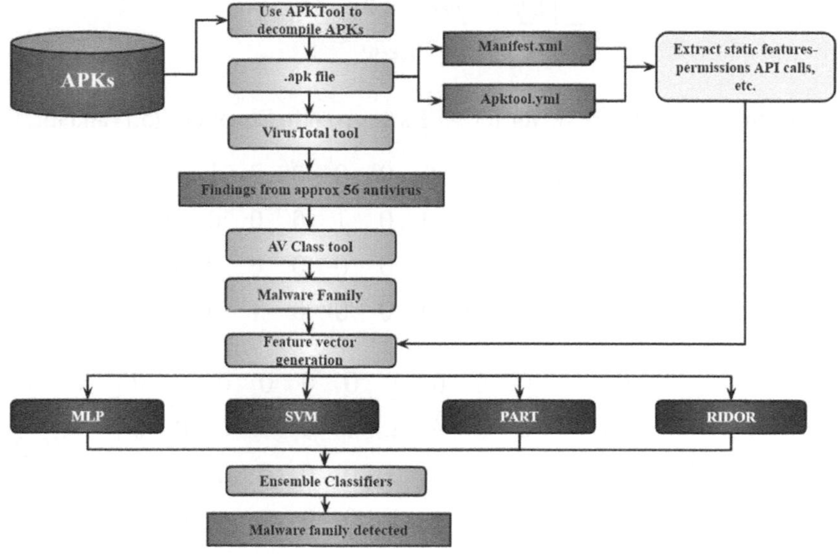

Figure 5.1 Illustration of an Android classification scheme.

the APKs' MD5 hashes are created in order to send them to VirusTotalAPI [162]. The results are then obtained for each APK that has been uploaded. The API offers the evaluation results for roughly 56 antiviruses. It keeps track of how many antiviruses have flagged the APK as harmful. Each APK maintains its JSON response in a separate location that will be used for additional processing.

2. Identifying the malware family: Following the separation of malicious APKs, the AVClass tool [163] is launched, which accepts the JSON results from step 1 as input. A malware family that was created is mentioned.
3. Extracting the features: APK contains a number of features, including permissions, version information, the library that was used, and API calls. APKTool is reverse engineered to extract the static features. Both Manifest.xml and APKtool.yml files are produced by this process. The required features are then extracted using a custom Python script. The binary feature vector, $e = (e_1, e_2, \ldots)$ for the 216 permissions that were retrieved from the APKs has been created.

$$e_i = \begin{cases} 1, if\ i^{th}\ permission\ is\ present \\ 0, else \end{cases}$$

For example, the feature vector for APKs is given in Equations (5.1) and (5.2).

$$e_{airpush} = \begin{pmatrix} 0 & 1 & 1 & 0 & 0 & 0 & 0 & 0 & 0 & 1 & 0 & 0 \\ 0 & 0 & 0 & 0 & 0 & 0 & 1 & 0 & 0 & 0 & 0 & 0 \\ 0 & 0 & 0 & 0 & 0 & 0 & 0 & 0 & 0 & 0 & 0 & 0 \\ 0 & 1 & 0 & 0 & 0 & 0 & 0 & 0 & 1 & 0 & 0 & 0 \end{pmatrix} \quad (5.1)$$

$$e_{aples} = \begin{pmatrix} 1 & 1 & 0 & 0 & 0 & 1 & 0 & 0 & 0 & 0 & 0 & 0 \\ 0 & 0 & 0 & 0 & 0 & 1 & 1 & 0 & 1 & 0 & 0 & 0 \\ 1 & 0 & 0 & 0 & 0 & 0 & 0 & 0 & 0 & 0 & 1 & 0 \\ 0 & 0 & 1 & 1 & 1 & 1 & 0 & 0 & 0 & 0 & 0 & 0 \end{pmatrix} \quad (5.2)$$

4. Training and evaluating the model: During this stage, the dataset created by feature extraction and family identification is divided into two halves, one for training and the other for testing several ML algorithms, including SVM, RIDOR, MLP, and PART. Comparisons and plots are made between the outcomes of the four algorithms' separate classifications. Ensemble approaches are utilized to increase efficiency even more. The algorithms are compared using a variety of accuracy metrics (Equations 4.5–4.11).

5.4 Setting Up the Data

The steps for data collection, filtering, and pre-processing are described in this section.

1. Collecting and pre-processing the data: Google Play [147], Wandoujia [149], AMD [149], and Androzoo [150] are just a few of the sources from which APKs are gathered. To build the dataset required for training and testing, these gathered APKs are processed and decompiled.
2. Filtering the data: Only harmful APKs are needed for additional processing and implementation in order to identify and categorize malware families. The steps are as follows:

- Create a CSV file with the names of various APKs.
- Use a Python script to generate MD5 hashes for each APK contained in the CSV file.
- Upload the APKs using the VirusTotalAPI.
- Use the Python script to receive the results. The API returns results for 56 antiviruses. A count of antiviruses is kept for malicious APKs. After that, each APK's JSON response is saved in a separate file for later processing.

3. Classifying the data: The AVClass tool uses the results from VirusTotal to determine the malware family for each APK. The APKs are divided into 71 malware families according to VirusTotal's identification. The families that VirusTotal discovers serve as a class that can be predicted using supervised ML. The static characteristics that are taken from the APK make up the feature vector that will be used to train the model.
4. ML approaches: In ML, a classifier algorithm converts the input data into a category. Our study focuses on supervised learning, in which training is performed with a labeled dataset. Our methodology uses the ML algorithms MLP, SVM, PART, and RIDOR. These four algorithms were selected since they are diverse in nature and have few applications in previous studies. Additionally, no one has ever classified Android malware using MLP, SVM, PART, and RIDOR together. Prior ML-based methods for detecting Android malware were put out, but they were not very effective or scalable [164]. These issues call for more effective malware detection mechanisms to slow the spread of Android malware. For this reason, the chapter suggests a strategy for detecting and categorizing Android malware at an early stage using the parallel ML classifiers' different characteristics. Since different classifiers pose different properties like rule based, function based, etc., with advantages such as ease of quick classification of new instances and large coverage of these combined classifiers, the goal of selecting only these particular classifiers is an achievement of maximum accuracy. By allocating one core to each algorithm, the algorithms are executed simultaneously,

increasing accuracy. Additionally, running several threads concurrently on several cores may aid in generating quicker results.

5.5 Results

The following are the outcomes of the application of several ML approaches:

1. Grouping malware into different families: The distribution of the APKs into 71 malware families, obtained via the aforementioned methods, served as the class label for our ML algorithms. It was also used to train and test the model. Figure 5.2 displays the classification of the dataset into several malware families.
2. Individual classifier results: All the algorithms were evaluated separately in the initial phase. The necessary representations were constructed, and the outcomes of each algorithm's execution were recorded. The 71 malware families into which the APKs were divided were then used to determine the precision and recall for each family, and graphs were presented to illustrate the findings. The outcomes of each algorithm are compiled in the section that follows.

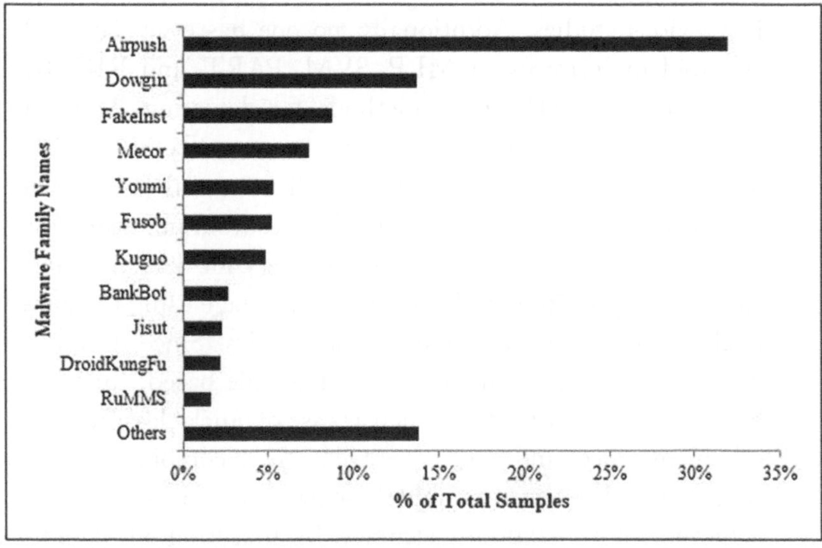

Figure 5.2 A representative fraction of malware families.

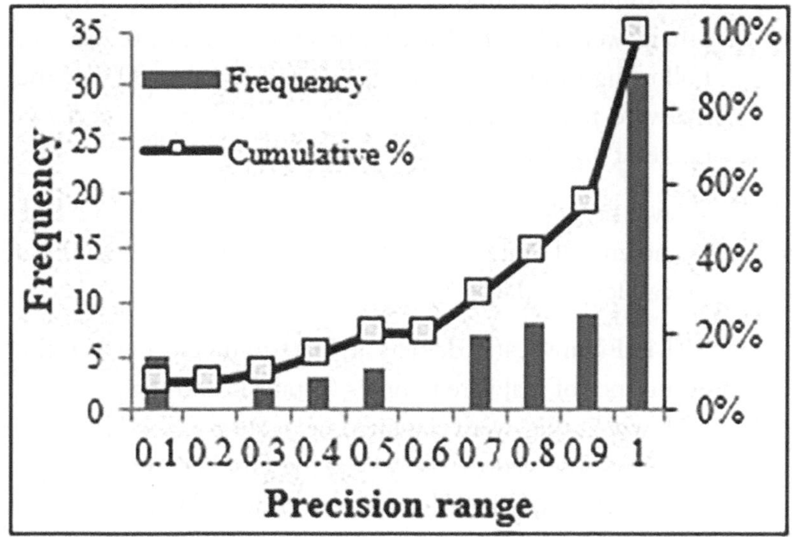

Figure 5.3(a) Precision

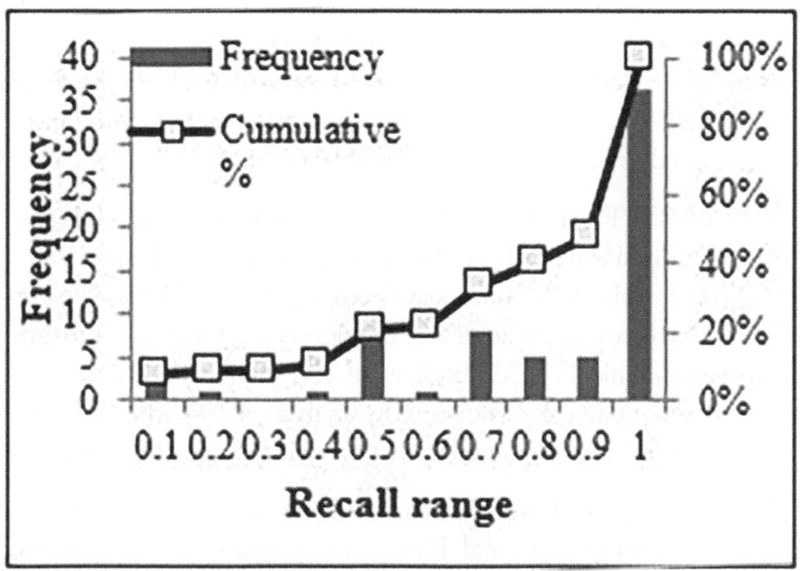

Figure 5.3(b) Recall

Figure 5.3 Histogram for different malware families for MLP.

- MLP: Figure 5.3(a) depicts a histogram of malware families (a total of 71) and the precision with which they were identified using the MLP classifier. The cumulative percentage of families falling inside various precision ranges is shown by the black boxed line. Approximately 45% of all families, including SimpleLocker, FakeInst, Vidro, and others, were identified with a precision level of 0.9 to 1.0. Following investigation, it was discovered that 80% of the malware families had been categorized with a precision range of 0.7–1.0.

A recall level of 0.8–1.0 was attained for approximately 52% of all families, as shown in Figure 5.3(b). Eighty percent of the families fell under the recall level of 0.5 to 1.0.

- SVM: Figure 5.4(a) depicts a histogram plotted for the occurrence of malware families (total 71) and the precision with which they were classified using an SVM classifier. It has been observed that ~75% of the families in total (e.g., Airpush, Cova, FakeAV, etc.) were classified with a 0.9–1.0 precision level. Post analysis, it is seen that ~80% of the malware families were classified with a precision range of 0.8–1.0.

In addition, as shown in Figure 5.4(b), a recall level of 0.8–1.0 was obtained for 67% of the families in total. Eighty percent of all families were classified as having a recall level of 0.6–1.0.

- PART: Figure 5.5(a) depicts a histogram plotted for the occurrence of malware families (total 71) and the precision with which they were classified using the PART classifier. It was discovered that 38% of the families in total (e.g., Finspy, Slembunk, FakeAV, etc.) were classified with a precision level of 0.0–0.1. Following the analysis, 45% of the malware families were classified with a precision range of 0.7–1.0.

Figure 5.5(b) also shows that a recall level of 0.0–0.1 was obtained for 38% of the families in total. Fifty-seven percent of all families were classified as having a recall level of 0.5–1.0.

- RIDOR: In Figure 5.6(a), a histogram is plotted for the occurrence of malware families (total 71), and the precision with which they were classified using the RIDOR classifier is shown. Seventy-five percent of the families in total (e.g., AndroRAT, DroidKungFu, GoldDream, etc.)

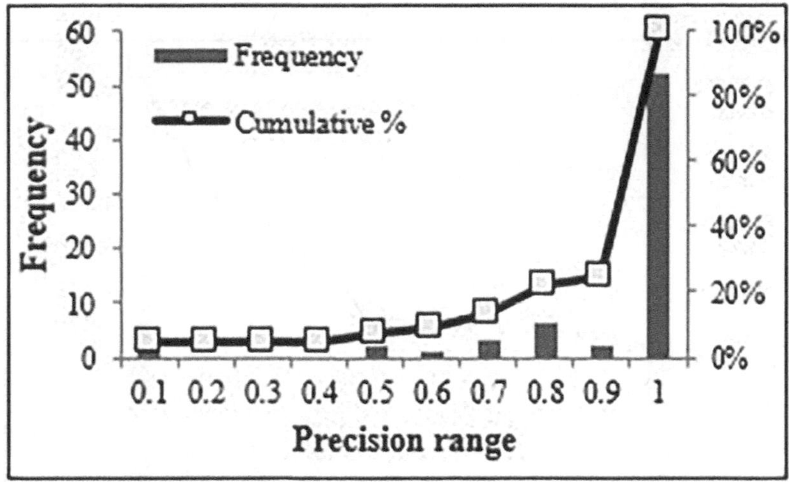

Figure 5.4(a) Precision

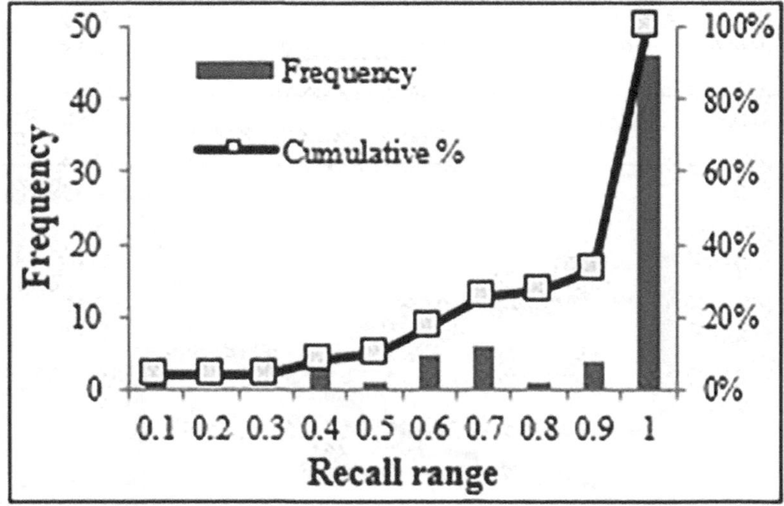

Figure 5.4(b) Recall

Figure 5.4 Histogram for different malware families for SVM.

were classified with 0.9–1.0 precision levels. Following the analysis, 78% of the malware families were classified with a precision range of 0.8–1.0.

Also, it can been seen in Figure 5.6(b) that a recall level of 0.9–1.0 was obtained for ~67% of the families in total. Eighty percent of all families were classified as having a recall level of 0.6–1.0.

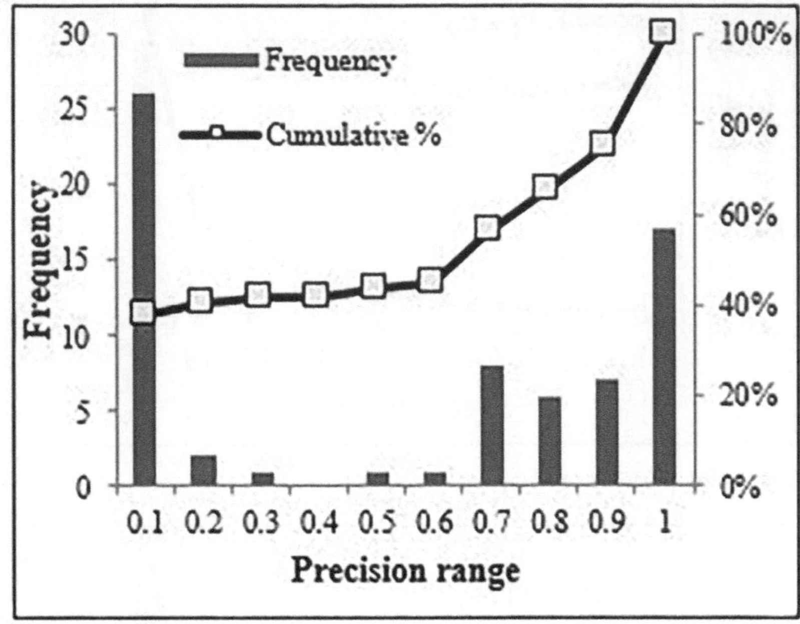

Figure 5.5(a) Precision

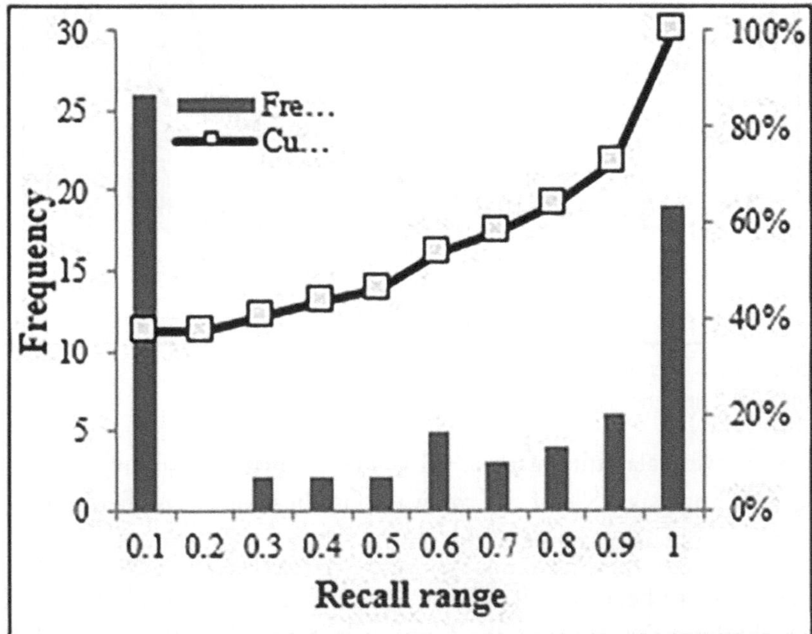

Figure 5.5(b) Recall

Figure 5.5 Histogram for different malware families for PART.

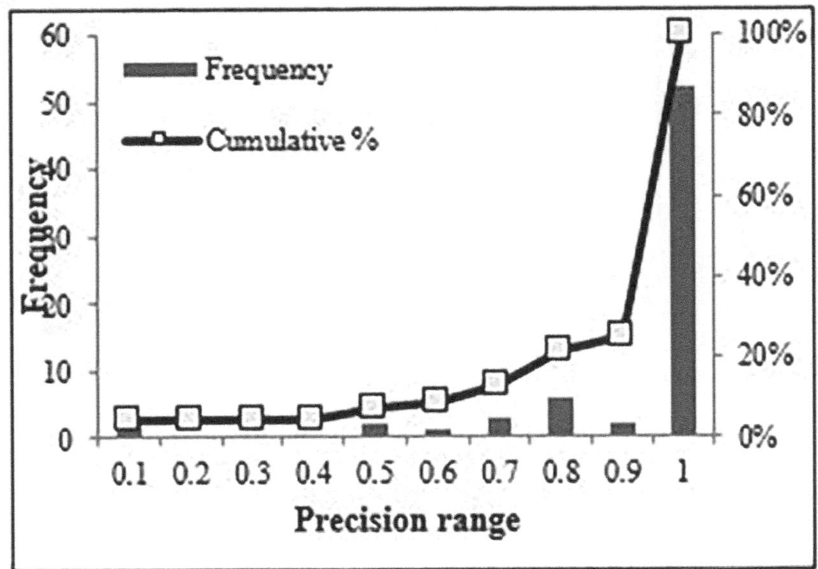

Figure 5.6(a) Precision

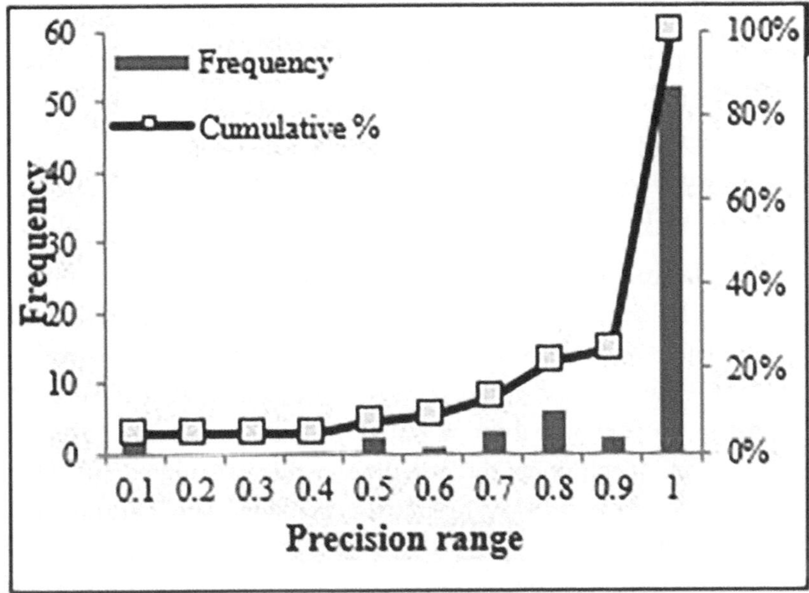

Figure 5.6(b) Recall

Figure 5.6 Histogram for different malware families for RIDOR.

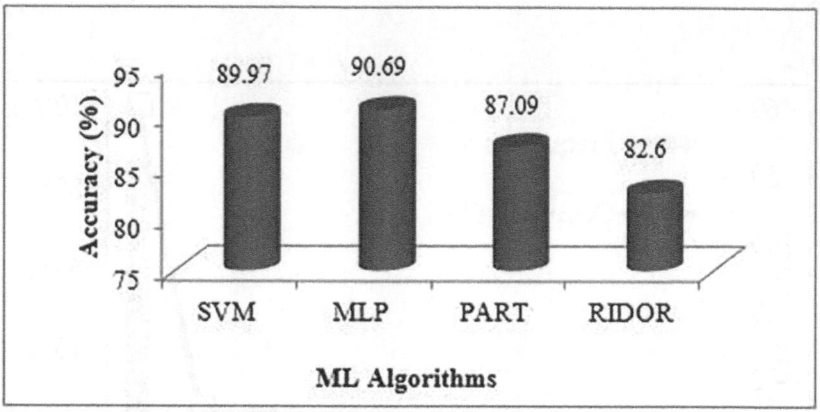

Figure 5.7 Accuracy of individual classifiers.

According to the results, MLP has the highest accuracy of 90.69% for the dataset while RIDOR has the lowest accuracy of 82.61%. Figure 5.7 depicts the accuracy of various individual classifiers.

3. Parallel classifier results: The results (obtained from individual classification) were executed using several ensemble techniques using the parallel model. Since it is a multiclass classification problem, the effectiveness of the ensemble approach was evaluated using only two parameters: maximum voting and averaging probability. The individual classifiers provided these probabilities. Seventy-one malware families were discovered. Here are the two ensemble approaches that were employed:

    - Maximum vote (MaxVote): The maximum vote ensemble technique determines the predicted class by averaging the votes of several prediction classifiers, and the class with the highest mode value is chosen as the final predicted class.
    - Averaging probabilities (AvgProb): In the averaging ensemble technique, the outcome of the ensemble approach is anticipated by averaging the predicted probabilities of the classifiers.

As shown in Figure 5.8, the results of employing various ensemble strategies indicate that the MVote ensemble strategy is more accurate, with an accuracy of 93.90%, and the AvgProb ensemble technique has an accuracy of 80.63%.

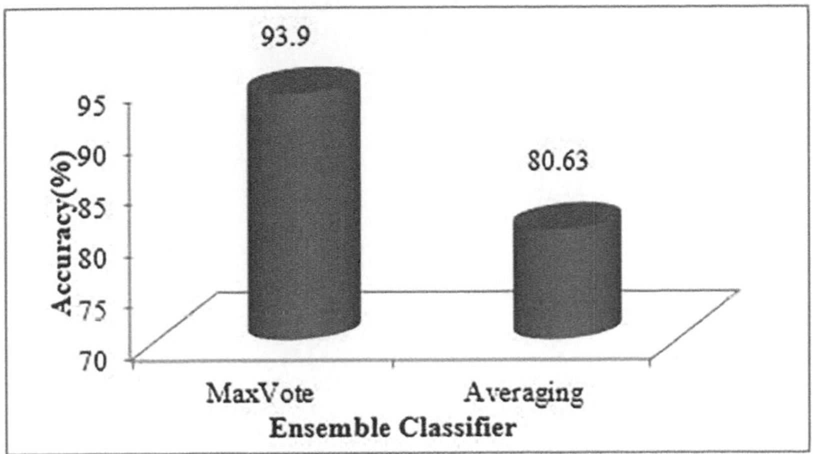

Figure 5.8 Accuracy for ensemble classifiers.

5.6 Conclusion and Future Directions

Ensemble parallel classifiers in ML are used to categorize Android malware. The work outlined in this chapter produces vectors that include the permissions, libraries utilized, services, broadcast receivers, and version number features of the APK. The class of malware family that must be predicted for a specific APK is added to the dataset in addition to the static features. Comparing the suggested methodology in this chapter to individual classifiers, it is more accurate in classifying Android malware (93.90%).

The proposed mapping between discovered and categorized malware and exploited vulnerabilities appears in the next chapter. In order for Android practitioners and developers to create more secure coding techniques, it is crucial to examine vulnerabilities at the CIA level of Android architecture using this mapping.

6

Text Processing–Based Malware-to-Vulnerability Mapping for Android

6.1 Introduction

The Android OS is targeted by more than 90% of mobile malware. The detection and analysis of Android malware has made use of numerous ML and DL techniques; however, there is a many-to-many mapping between malware and vulnerability. This implies that a single malware can exploit many security flaws, whether they are known or undiscovered, and that multiple forms of malware can exploit a single vulnerability. Therefore, it's crucial to examine malware behavior in order to identify and minimize vulnerabilities. No ML/DL or other technique has yet been used to analyze malware behavior in order to find and patch vulnerabilities. This chapter proposes a novel framework, M2VMapper, that uses a 2D matrix to map malware and potential vulnerabilities. The many-to-many mapping matrix is produced by fusing NLP techniques like BoW that take advantage of n-gram probability construction with supervised ML classifiers such as MLP, SVM, RIDOR, and PART. To achieve even more effective outcomes, we further enhance M2VMapper to make use of DL models such as multilayer perceptron (MLP), recurrent neural network (RNN), and textual convolutional neural network (TextCNN) that integrate transfer learning with pretrained language models such as BERT and XLNET. Using this malware-to-vulnerability mapping throughout the early stages of application development will allow security analysts to gauge the severity of malware and unknown vulnerabilities. This ground-breaking analysis takes into account 150 malware families from various datasets, including AMD [149], Androzoo [150], and CICInvesAndMal2019 [165], with a total of 48,907 malware samples and nine Android vulnerability classes.

DOI: 10.1201/9781003354574-6

6.2 Relevant Works

Numerous research projects, such as those on malware detection, vulnerability patching, malware classification, etc., are focused on Android vulnerabilities and malware. With an emphasis on feature selection and malware behavior analysis using ML/DL techniques, this section concentrates on the most pertinent and scientifically noteworthy papers.

In order to map bugs with potential vulnerabilities for Android applications, Bajwa et al. [166] created a matrix. They obtained many-to-many mapping between bugs and vulnerabilities using severity and probability mapping. To find bugs, static analysis techniques viz., Lint [167] and FindBug [168] were employed. The list of defects discovered in each application, together with the severity or bug rank, was produced by the static analysis. Each bug was given a score between 1 and 20 and placed into one of four categories: scariest (bug ranks 1 to 4), scary (ranks 5 to 9), disturbing (ranks 10 to 14), and of concern (15 to 20). They carried out this mapping on 230 apps, which were grouped into six functional areas (general, money, gaming, weather, online shopping, and education), as well as four key permissions (Internet, location access, storage, and SMS). The mapping in the study was manual and required a lot of human intervention, which we strive to reduce by using ML techniques. Nevertheless, the study is closely related to our approach.

In another study [169], NLP and ML techniques were used to identify ransomware outbreaks. The authors used various supervised ML techniques to analyze the ransomware at various levels, including the dynamic link library, function call, and assembly instruction levels. Using LR classifiers for generated TF-IDFs trigrams at integrated multilevels, they were able to identify ransomware assaults with a detection rate of 98.59%.

The MalDy framework was suggested by the authors in [170] for malware detection, leveraging supervised ML and advanced NLP. Using NLP and ML techniques, MalDy behavioral reports were converted into word sequences to automatically engineer the necessary security measures. MalDy was able to produce positive findings, but it was hampered by its inability to assess the behavioral reports' level of accuracy.

In a different study [171], dynamic analysis was used to create the fingerprints of Android malware. For fingerprinting Android malware's dynamic behavior, the authors suggested a novel technique dubbed DySign. Using dynamic analysis in relation to already-known malware, they created a digest of a malware sample. Although DySign used dynamic analysis and served as the initial line of security against Android malware threats, it had a number of drawbacks. First off, DySign was found to be non-deterministic since various fingerprints were produced by different DySign executions. Second, DySign failed to identify fresh malware families.

The text semantics of network traffic were used by the authors of [172] to identify Android malware. They viewed each HTTP transaction produced by mobile apps as a text document, processing it by using NLP to extract text-level information. The development of a powerful virus detection algorithm took advantage of the text-semantic aspects of network traffic. They employed 5,258 harmful flows and 31,706 benign flows for evaluation. Despite achieving an accuracy of 99.15%, they had significant shortcomings. First off, some malicious actions required effective user inputs to be completely activated. The approach was also successful in identifying unknown samples that had some traits with the malware samples in the training dataset using gram features.

For Android malware categorization and detection, researchers have employed MLP. Unlike conventional ML models, MLP can recognize intricate patterns in Android malware. MLP was used by the authors in [173] to identify Android malware. The Android Asset Packaging Tool (AAPT) was used by the authors to extract the permissions. Later, the one-hot encoding approach was used to vectorize the string features. For several hyper-parameters, including batch size, number of epochs, dropout rate, number of neurons, optimizer, and weight constraint, they optimized MLP using the grid search technique. On 48,643 Android apps, they achieved an accuracy (detection) of 95% and F1 scores of 93%.

In order to assess the performance, authors in [174] retrieved features from 129,000 Android apps. Through the use of one-hot encoding, the features were changed. Their F1 score was 65%, their precision was 66%, and their recall was 65%.

Maldozer, a tool developed by the authors in [175], automatically identified Android malware and assigned malware families using CNN with the input of API calls. To vectorize API sequences, the authors used word2vec [176] and GolVe [177]. On 70,693 apps, they found malware with an F1 score of 99% and a false positive rate (FPR) of 2%.

The methodologies listed here concentrate on malicious intentions, and many tools based on static and dynamic analysis have been developed to find Android malware. None of the studies, however, discuss the risks brought on by malware. Therefore, it's important to comprehend the extent of Android malware so that quick action may be taken to prevent malware attacks. To the best of our knowledge, this study is the first of its type to link malware to Android security flaws.

6.3 Malware-to-Vulnerability Mapping

Malware is a result of flaws in the stages of software development that are frequently overlooked by a software developer or are purposefully inserted by an attacker. Malware can take advantage of a variety of security flaws, both known and unknown, and several types of malware can take advantage of the same flaw, creating a many-to-many mapping as depicted in Figure 6.1. A 2D mapping matrix between

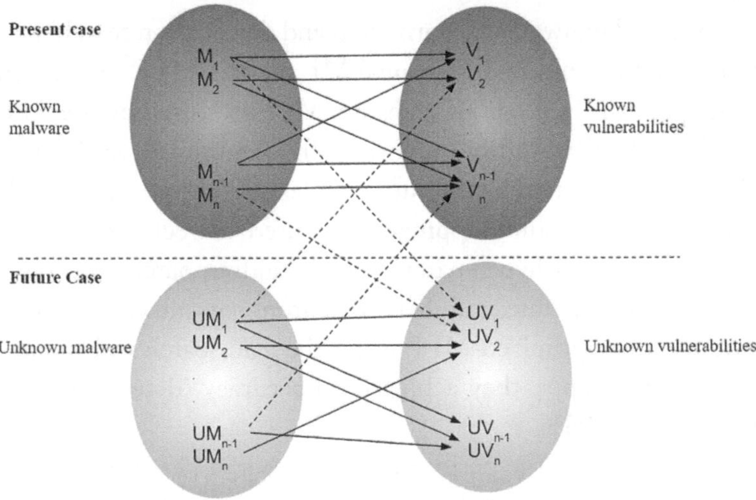

Figure 6.1 Malware-to-vulnerability mapping.

malware and potential vulnerabilities is what this chapter seeks to create. Static analysis, dynamic analysis, hybrid approaches, and ML algorithms are just a few of the methods that may be used to detect malware in Android applications. These methods can also be used to provide an empirical list of an app's vulnerabilities.

The vulnerability set V is written as $V=\{v_1,\ldots.,v_y\}$ while the malware set M is represented as $M=\{m_1,m_2,\ldots.,m_3\}$. Because $f(m)$ is multi-valued and this mapping produces numerous values of v for each value of m, the mapping function $f(m)=v$ is also known as $f:m\rightarrow v$, where $m\in M$ and $v\in V$. It maps malware in M to the vulnerabilities in V.

Malware-to-vulnerability mapping has the following characteristics:

1. A set A of ordered pairs (m,v) s.t. $m\in M$, $v\in V$ and $\forall m\in M$; $m\in\{A_i,A_j\}$ is the first component of at least one ordered pair in A defining a mapping function $f(m)$ from a set M to a set V. Alternatively, $\forall m\in M$, $\exists\ v$, s.t. $(m,v)\in\{X,Y\}$, where $\{X,Y\}$ define for $f:X\rightarrow Y$.
2. It is not recommended to unmap any malware found in the descriptive report. To ensure that the mapping of malware to vulnerabilities is always rich, use $\forall m\exists v$ s.t. $f(m)\in\{v_1,v_2,\ldots.,v_y\}$. Consequently, $f(m)\neq\phi$ holds true for mapping to be complete (generate all those mappings that hold) and sound (produce just those mappings that genuinely hold).
3. Assuming that the vulnerability sets are not mutually exclusive and that $v_i\in V'$ and $v_j\in V''$, where V'' and V'' are two vulnerability datasets with i and j number of vulnerabilities, respectively, then $v_i\cap v_j=\phi$ and $V'\cup V''=V'+V''-(V'\cap V'')$. This stipulation still applies to upgrading the vulnerability dataset in order to prevent any redundant mapping.

6.4 Proposed Methodology

The overall M2VMapper methodology is presented in this section. The M2VMapper is shown in Figure 6.2 with traditional NLP methods, such as BoW and grams, together with supervised ML models.

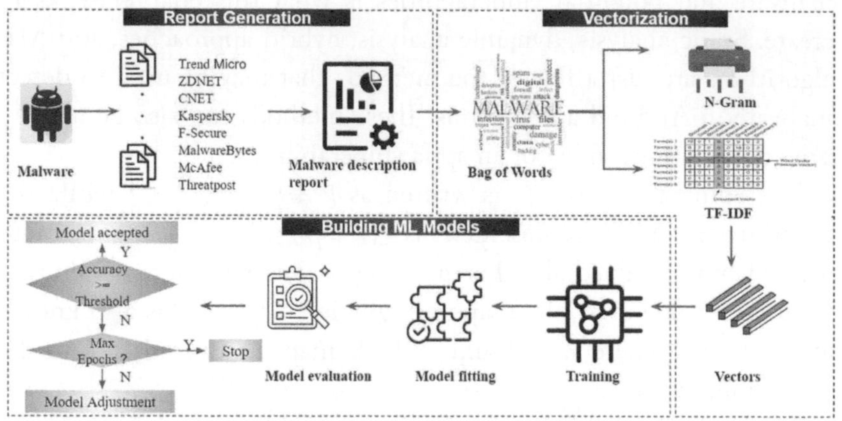

Figure 6.2 M2VMapper with BoW and conventional ML models.

Table 6.1 Information about Data Collection

DATASETS	MALWARE FAMILIES	MALWARE SAMPLES
AMD	71	24,553
CICInvesAndMal2019	42	4,354
AndroZoo	37	20,000
Total	150	48,907

The following is a description of the steps in Figure 6.2:

1. Data gathering and creation of malware reports

Benchmark datasets such as AMD [149], with 24,553 malicious APK samples from 2010 to 2016, are used. They contain a dataset of 150 malware families that have been discovered across numerous apps. These are divided into 135 different subcategories by 71 malware families. The specifics of this data are reported in [154]. Table 6.1 lists the 37 remaining malware families with 20,000 malware samples from AndroZoo [152] and the 42 distinct malware families with 4,354 malware samples grouped into Adware, Spyware, Ransomware, and SMS malware from CICInvesAndMal2019 [165].

Cybersecurity firms such as Trend Micro [178], Kaspersky [179], F-secure [180], Malware Bytes [181], CNet [182], ZDNet [183], Checkpoint [184], and New Jersey Cybersecurity and Communications Integration Cell (NJCCIC) [185] have all published reports and blogs that contain the ground truth in the form of training

ALGORITHM 6.1 MALWARE DESCRIPTION REPORT GENERATION AND UPDATION

Input: *mal _ dataset*: known/detected malware information from cybersecurity solutions (CSS) as text file (.txt)

Output: *Malware description report* in CSV file (.csv)

while true, **do**

if <*Apex–Italic*> ∃ *new_malware*, **then**

Add *new_malware* to *mal_dataset*;

for <*Apex – Italic*> $M_i \in$ *mal_dataset* </*Apex – Italic*>, **do**

Report ← collectDescription (*M*);

wordBag ← getwordBag (*Report*);

saveReport (*wordbag*);

corpora related to these malware. Nine categories of vulnerabilities from the NVD [21] and CVE details [59] are presented in order to map a malware with the vulnerability it exploits. These are directory traversal, code execution, DoS, overflow, memory corruption, gain information, gain privileges, bypass something, and DoS. The processes for creating and updating a malware description report are presented in Algorithm 6.1.

2. NLP-based vectorization techniques

This section provides a solution to the problem of modelling terms in the malware corpus to fit into classifications. Prior approaches relied on manual examination of malware features from various sources. Since generating fresh reports on a regular basis necessitates a significant amount of revision, this method is labor intensive and not scalable. Therefore, feature engineering must be automated so that features (expressed as words) can map vulnerabilities. The BoW [186] NLP model is used by M2VMapper in conjunction with gram generation, probability [187], and TF-IDF [188]. The BoW keeps the count statistics of each word that appears in the document while converting text into structured features. As described in Algorithm 6.2, this method uses word frequencies to construct fixed-length vectors from the corpus. In order to create classification models, the reports are transformed into feature vectors.

a. *n*-gram: An gram is an extension of BoW that takes into account word order. An *n*-gram is a contiguous group of *n* words in a text corpus (malware description). The malware description corpus's sequence of words can be predicted by using an *n*-gram model.
   i. *n*-gram generator: The size of *n* can be any positive integer and depends on the type of dataset and issue domain. The analysis of malware-vulnerability mapping uses *n* values ranging from 1 to 4. The value of *n* can be used to produce potential *n*-gram sequences.
   ii. *n*-gram probability scoring: The probability scoring component receives the *n*-gram sequences produced in step 1 as input. When the Markov assumption is used, it simply takes into account the word length of the first *n* -1 words, as indicated in equation 6.1.

$$P(t_i \mid t_1, \ldots, t_{i-1}) = P(t_i \mid t_{i-n+1}, \ldots, t_{i-1}) \tag{6.1}$$

Unigram, bigram, and trigram are represented as:
Unigram: P(t_i); bigram: $P(t_i \mid t_{i-1})$; trigram: $P(t_i \mid t_{i-2}, t_{i-1})$.
According to Equation 6.2, relative frequency counts on a training corpus can be used to estimate *n*-gram probabilities.

$$P(t_b \mid t_a) = c(t_a, t_b) / c(t_a) \tag{6.2}$$

where *c* represents the number of word sequences in the training corpus.

The study took into account *n*-gram sequences for vulnerability names like "steal information," "gain privileges," "DoS," "bypass information," etc. The probability scores were then kept in a feature database for each *n* gram sequence.

b. TF-IDF: Term frequency (TF) and inverse document frequency (IDF) are combined to form TF-IDF (IDF).

Equation 6.3 provides the term frequency, which is the frequency of a particular n-gram sequence appearing in a malware description.

$$tf(x,d) = \frac{n_{x,d}}{\sum_k n_{x,d}} \tag{6.3}$$

whereas the IDF is given as

$$Idf(x) = 1 + log\left(\frac{N}{dN}\right). \tag{6.4}$$

Therefore, TF-IDF is computed as

$$tfidf = tf(x,d) \times idf(x) \tag{6.5}$$

where x = word; d = document (set of words); N = corpus count; *corpus* = total document set.

ALGORITHM 6.2 MAPPING ALGORITHM

Input: *Report*: malware report

Output: *M*: Mapping Decision

$M_{malware} \leftarrow M^1_{malware}$

$V_{vulnerability} \leftarrow \left\{V^2_{vulnerabilityI}, \ldots, V^Y_{vulnerabilityK}\right\}$

$x \leftarrow$ vectorize (*Report*);

$malware\_result \leftarrow M_{malware}(x)$

if $malware_{result} < 0$, **then**

$malware\_result;$

for $V_i \in V_{vulnerability}$, **do**

$map\_result \leftarrow V_{vulnerabilityK}(x)$

<*Apex – Italic*> *malware_result, map_result;*</*Apex – Italic*>

3. NLP-based vectorization techniques

According to Algorithm 6.3, the M2VMapper framework builds malware-to-vulnerability mapping models using supervised ML. The multi-labeled dataset cannot be used directly for supervised classification techniques. Consequently, the binary relevance (BR) technique is used to alter the target variable (multi-label binarizer in this case). Additionally, each ML algorithm's classification performance is automatically adjusted by a variety of hyper-parameters (different for each algorithm, such as the learning rate and momentum of the neural network, training set size, kernel preference in SVM, etc.). In M2VMapper, various ML classifiers including MLP, SVM, RIDOR, and PART are applied. These algorithms were selected because they have effective public implementations and acceptable findings from prior studies [112].

Notations:

$Y = \{Y_{build}, Y_{test}\}$: For constructing and presenting the performance of M2VMapper in the various tasks, global dataset 'Y' is used. For training and fine-tuning M2VMapper model hyper-parameters, use Y_{build}. A test set called Y_{test} is used to gauge M2VMapper's ultimate performance. Y_{build} (70%) and Y_{test} (30%) are split using a stratified random split on Y.

$Y_{build} = \{Y_{build}, Y_{test}\}$: Y_{build} is used to create M2VMapper models and consists of training and validation sets.

$Y_{train} = \{(y_0, z_0), (y_1, z_1), \ldots, (y_t, z_t)\}$: The training set for the ML models used by M2VMapper is called Y_{train}.

$Y_{valid} = \{(y_0, z_0), (y_1, z_1), \ldots, (y_v, z_v)\}$: The validation set known as Y_{valid} is used to fine-tune the training models. The best results on the validation set are achieved by tuning hyper-parameters.

(y_i, z_i): A single record in Y is made up of the variable y_i and its label $z_i \in \{V_1, V_2, \ldots, V_n\}$, where z_i is multi-label with the set of vulnerabilities.

$Y_{test} = \{(y_0, z_0), (y_1, z_1), \ldots, (y_x, z_x)\}$: The final performance results are computed and reported back using Y_{test}.

M2VMapper is further enhanced using advanced DL models such as MLP, RNN, and TextCNN that combine transfer learning with

ALGORITHM 6.3 BUILDING MACHINE LEARNING MODELS

Input: Y_{build}: Building set

Output: Op: Optimal models

<*Apex – Italic*> Y_{test}, Y_{valid} <*Apex – Italic*> $\leftarrow Y_{build}$

$V_{vulnerability} \leftarrow \left\{V^{2}_{vulnerabilityI}, \ldots, V^{Y}_{vulnerabilityK}\right\}$

for $ml \in MLalgorithms$, **do**

$score \leftarrow 0$ **for** p in $ml.p\_array$, **do**

$model \leftarrow \text{train}\left(algo, Y_{train}, p\right)$;

$t, u \leftarrow \text{validate } \left(model, Y_{valid}\right)$;

if $t > score$, **then**

$mla \leftarrow < ml, u, p >$;

Op.add (mla);

Op

pretrained language models such as BERT and XLNET. Figure 6.3 illustrates enhanced M2VMapper.

The steps shown in Figure 6.3 are as follows:

1. Data gathering and creation of malware reports: This step, mentioned in Section 6.3, is the same as those using conventional ML models with NLP.
2. Modelling with dynamic word embeddings: M2VMapper uses dynamic word embeddings such as BERT and XLNET to record the distinctive features of malware samples. The beneficial information that can be quantified by these word embeddings can be used as training data for classification models. Various DLs are used in Figure 6.4 to illustrate the use of word embeddings.

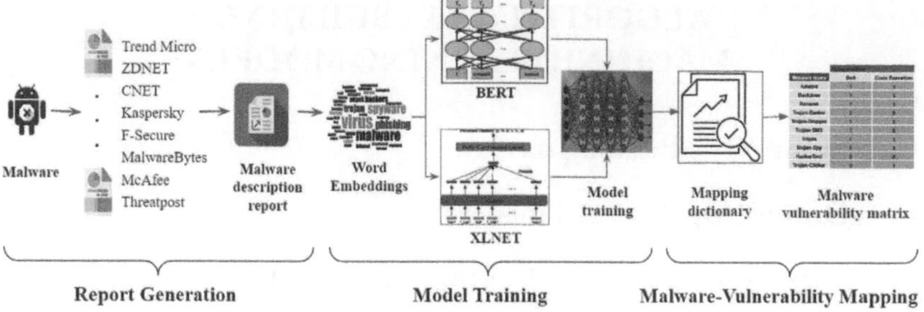

Figure 6.3 M2VMapper with advanced DL and pretrained models.

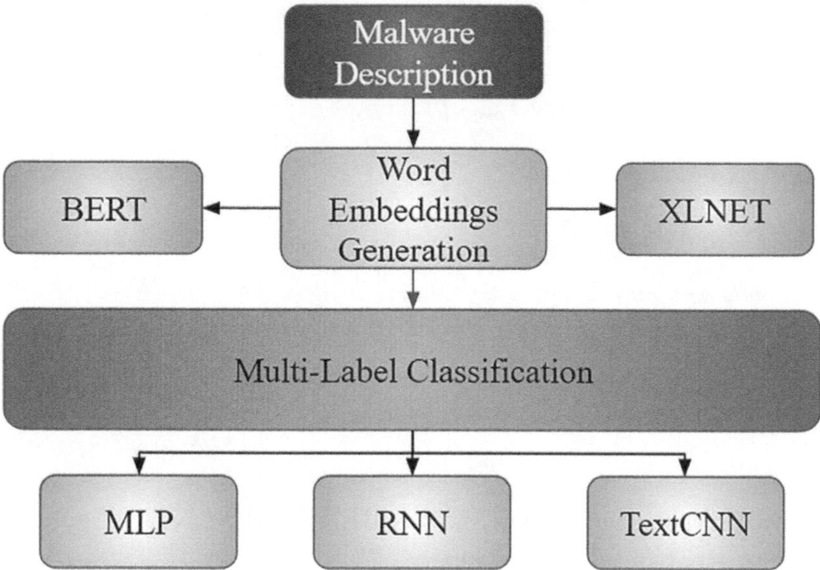

Figure 6.4 Generation of word embeddings.

a. BERT: This transformer-based model trains in two directions using next sentence prediction (NSP) and masked language model (MLM) training tasks. A [MASK] token is used to randomly mask 15% of the input sentence tokens. The BERT is then taught to forecast the tokens that are hidden. The input sentence is marked at the beginning and the conclusion with [CLS] and [SEP] tokens, respectively. The token [CLS] records all the data pertaining to the malware sample. This data is necessary for language-processing operations like NSP, and it can also be used to map malware to vulnerabilities.

b. XLNET: This is a generalized auto-regressive (AR) pre-training technique. The context word is used by the AR language model to predict the subsequent word. In this case, the context word is restricted in two directions: either forward or backward. In the pretraining stage, XLNet concentrates on the permutation operation. Sharing of the model parameters across all permuted factorization orders is possible with this permutation of language modelling.

As illustrated in Equation 6.6, we created the malware-vulnerability mapping model:

$$\hat{U} = f(\sigma, \alpha) \tag{6.6}$$

where α denotes "input characteristics" taken from the malware description; σ denotes modelling parameter; f denotes the predictive function that the model defines, and $\hat{U}$ depicts the predicted mapping probability in the range [0, 1].

The dataset for mapping prediction is referred to as P,Q, where $P = \left[p^{(1)}, p^{(2)}, \ldots, p^{(x)}\right]$; $p^{(i)}$ is the ith malware description; and x is the number of vulnerabilities in P. In line with this, $G = \left[g^{(1)}, g^{(2)}, \ldots, g^{(x)}\right]$ denotes the ground truth label vector, and $g \in \{1,0\}$ depicts whether or not the ith vulnerability is present.

For the purpose of mapping prediction, P is transformed into a feature matrix $M = \left[m^{(1)}, m^{(2)}, \ldots, m^{(x)}\right]$ where $m^{(i)} \in D^n$ signifies the extracted feature from $p^{(i)}$, and n is the feature dimension. In accordance with Equation. 6.6, the expected output for M is given as $= \acute{U} = f(\sigma, P)$, where $\acute{U} = \left[\hat{U}^{(1)}, \hat{U}^{(2)}, \ldots, \hat{U}^{(x)}\right]$; $\hat{U}^{(i)}$ is the predicted mapping probability for $m^{(i)}$.

3. Building DL models

To create malware-to-vulnerability mapping, the M2VMapper framework leverages DL models. The DL classifiers MLP, RNN, and TextCNN are among those employed in M2VMapper. These algorithms were chosen because they offer a great deal of flexibility, have effective public implementations, and have produced reasonable results in previous studies [187].

a. MLP: We deployed the basic MLP as in the case of conventional ML models. Similar to a single-layer perceptron, MLP is trained using a gradient descent approach (such as error backpropagation).
b. RNN: This is a different kind of feed-forward network (FFN) with an additional self-recurrent connection that transmits data from one time-step to the others. Let $s(t)$ be the state vector at time instance t, where $t = \overline{1, Y}$, and let $H(t)$ with $(h_1, h_2, \ldots, h_n)$ components denote the input vector at time instance t. Let V_i, V_r, a, V_j, a_{out} represent the input, recurrent weight matrix, bias, output weight matrix, and bias for the hidden layer, respectively. Let the hidden layer and output layer's activation functions be β and μ, respectively. For the hidden layer and the output, we used *tanh* and *softmax* Equations (6.7) and (6.8) explain the recurrent models:

$$s(t) = \beta \times (V_i \times H(t) + V_r \times s(t-1) + a) \tag{6.7}$$

$$\acute{U}(t) = \mu \times (V_j \times s(t) + a_j) \tag{6.8}$$

This RNN model predicts the corresponding class label $\acute{U}(t)$ for the malware based on equations (6.7) and (6.8).

c. TextCNN: The n-word sentence is transformed into a d-dimensional word representation vector, indicated as $(t) = \{w_1, w_2, \ldots, w_n\}(w \in R_d)$. Here, we used convolution operations to generate n-grams, which were used as the features for classification, using different kernel sizes $(2,3,\ldots,y)$. When words $w_x, w_{x+1}, \ldots, w_{x+m-1}$ are concatenated, n-grams are created. The d-dimension of feature vectors is determined by the quantity of convolution filters; $p_{\overline{1:N}} \in R_d$, where N is the total number of n-grams, is the notation used to identify n-gram features.

Equation (6.9) shows the calculation for the feature vector $p_{\overline{1:T}}$:

$$p_{\overline{1:T}} = Y_m \cdot w_{x+m-1} + o_m \tag{6.9}$$

where, $Y_m \in R_d$ and, $o_m \in R_d$ are convolution operation parameters.

The main difficulty with text classification is the varied length of the input sentences. The phrase vector X produced by the max-pooling layer, which integrates the n-gram features, is d-dimensional and is specified by equation 6.10:

$$X = \max\left[p_{\overline{1:T}}\right] \tag{6.10}$$

To obtain a score $s \in R$ over the target categories, the sentence vector X was next input into a fully linked layer. According to equations 6.11 and 6.12, the final output q represents the probability distribution $q \in R$ on the target categories:

$$s = P.X + c \tag{6.11}$$

$$p[x] = \frac{exp(s[x])}{\sum_{y=1} exp(s[y])}$$

where P and c are fully-connected layer parameters. The architecture of TextCNN is shown in Figure 6.5.

6.5 Evaluation and Results

The evaluation findings for M2VMapper are presented in this section.

As indicated in Table 6.2, the various malware varieties were matched to the vulnerabilities. Here, indicates that the vulnerability is there, and indicates that it is not. The mapping of malware to vulnerabilities is shown in Table 6.3. Due to space restrictions, only a portion

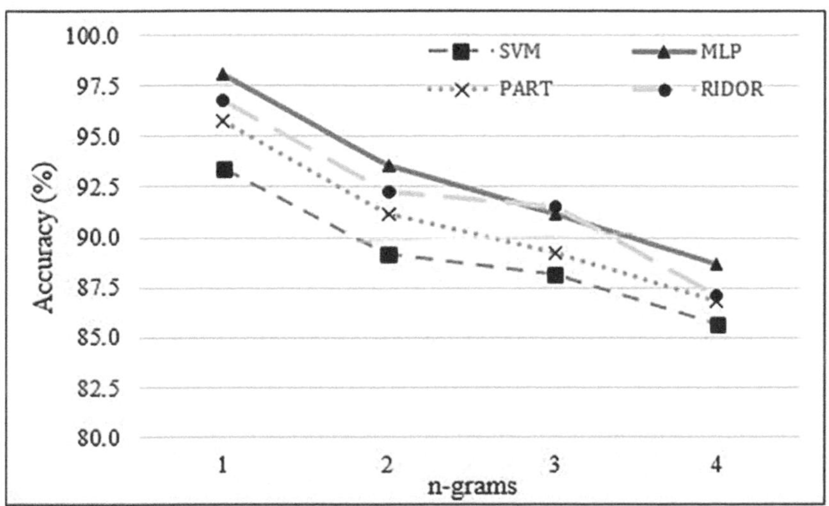

Figure 6.5 Accuracies of ML algorithms for n-gram probabilities.

Table 6.2 Mapping Malware Types to Vulnerabilities

MALWARE TYPES	BYPASS SOMETHING	CODE EXECUTION	DIRECTORY TRAVERSAL	DOS	GAIN INFORMATION	GAIN PRIVILEGES	MEMORY CORRUPTION	OVERFLOW	SQL INJECTION
Adware	1	1	0	1	1	1	0	0	0
Backdoor	1	1	0	1	1	1	0	1	0
HackerTool	1	1	0	1	1	1	1	0	0
Ransom	1	1	0	1	1	1	0	1	0
Trojan	0	1	1	1	1	1	0	0	0
Trojan-Banker	1	0	0	1	1	1	0	0	0
Trojan-Clicker	1	0	0	0	1	1	1	0	0
Trojan-Dropper	1	0	0	0	1	1	0	0	1
Trojan-SMS	1	1	0	0	1	0	0	0	0
Trojan-Spy	1	1	0	0	1	1	0	1	0

Table 6.3 Mapping Malware to Vulnerabilities

MALWARE TYPES	MALWARE	BYPASS SOMETHING	CODE EXECUTION	DIRECTORY TRAVERSAL	DOS	GAIN INFORMATION	GAIN PRIVILEGES	MEMORY CORRUPTION	OVERFLOW	SQL INJECTION
Adware	AdDown	1	1	0	0	1	1	0	0	0
Adware	Chamois	0	1	0	0	1	0	0	0	0
Backdoor	Androrat	1	0	0	1	1	1	0	0	0
Backdoor	Dendroid	1	1	0	0	1	0	0	0	0
Hackertool	Lotoor	1	0	0	0	0	0	1	0	0
Ransom-ware	Fusob	0	1	0	0	1	1	0	0	1
Trojan-Dropper	Boqx	0	0	1	0	0	0	0	0	0
Trojan-SMS	Gumen	0	0	0	0	1	1	0	0	0
Trojan	Xiny	0	0	0	1	1	1	0	0	0
Trojan-Spy	Triout	0	0	0	0	1	0	0	0	0
.	.	.	.	.	.	.	.	.	.	.
.	.	.	.		.	.	.	.	.	.
.	.	.	.	.		.	.	.	.	.

of Table 6.3 is shown. This link[1] will take you to the full table. This link[2] will take you to the M2VMapper Python scripts.

1. Accuracy evaluation for *n*-gram probabilities

In M2VMapper, ML classifiers are assessed using a ten-fold cross-validation method. This was chosen because it offers a good balance between minimal computational expense and low bias in a model performance estimate. The accuracy of several ML classifiers is assessed with *n* values ranging from 1 to 4.

At $n = 1$, MLP has the maximum accuracy 98.04% (unigram). Each word in a unigram is thought to occur independently of the word that came before it, so each word becomes a feature in this sentence. RIDOR exhibits the second-best performance with 96.81% accuracy at $n = 1$. As illustrated in Figure 6.5, it is evident that as the value of *n* increases, the accuracy of ML classifiers decreases.

2. Comparison of performance of ML/DL models used in M2VMapper

On the basis of different measures, including true positive rate (TPR), true negative rate (TNR), false positive rate (FPR), false negative rate (FNR), accuracy (Acc), and error (Err) [29], ML and DL models employed in MalVulDroid are compared in Figures 6.6(a), 6.6(b), 6.6(c), and 6.6(d). Table 6.4 presents the comparative performance of DL models used in M2VMapper (%).

Figure 6.6(a) demonstrates that, in comparison to other ML algorithms, MLP has a reasonable TPR, TNR, and accuracy. However, as seen in Figure 6.6(b), SVM has the highest error rate, followed by PART and RIDOR.

Figure 6.6(c) makes it clear that when compared to other DL methods, XLNET with TextCNN has a respectable TPR rate, TNR rate, and accuracy. Additionally, Figure 6.6(d) illustrates that the largest error rate is produced by BERT when paired with MLP.

3. Performance of M2VMapper

With hyper-parameters, the effectiveness of M2VMapper is evaluated for several ML/DL models. The architecture of the neural network model is defined by hyper-parameters. In order to create a

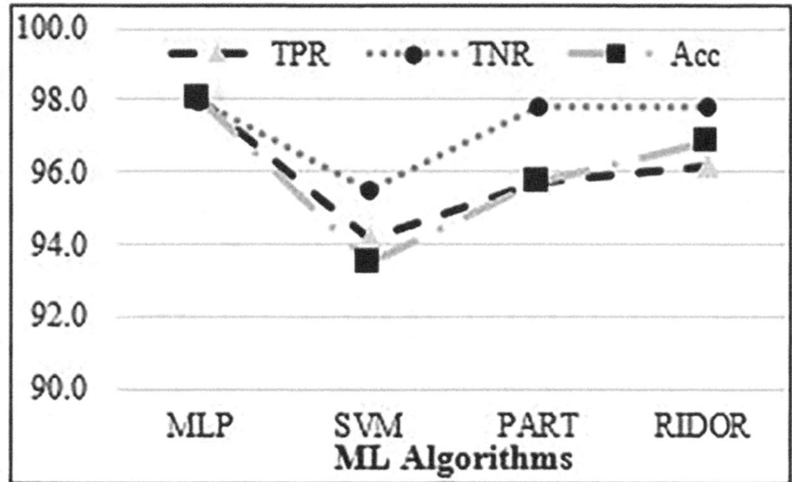

Figure 6.6(a) TPR, TNR, Accuracy

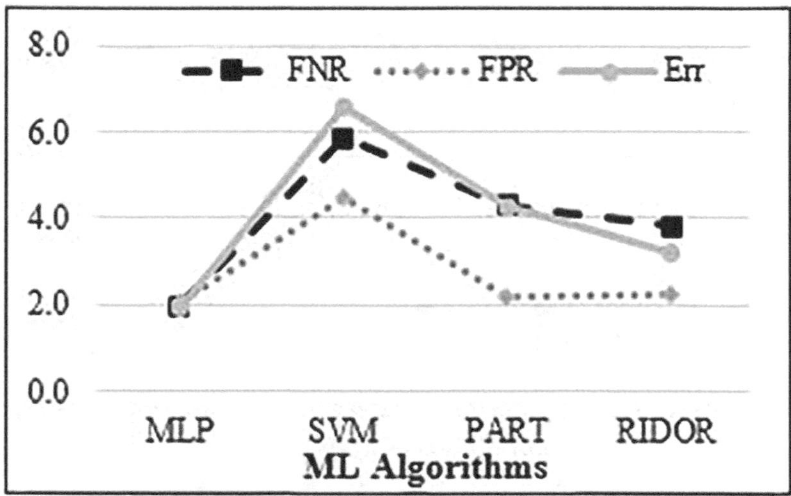

Figure 6.6(b) FNR, FPR, Error

high-quality model, it is imperative to obtain the ideal hyper-parameter values. The grid search algorithm has been used to identify the ideal hyper-parameter combinations.

With customized hyper-parameters, such as learning rate for training MLP (0.3 in this case), momentum (0.2), number of hidden layers (2), and number of epochs (450), the effectiveness of M2VMapper is assessed for various ML techniques.

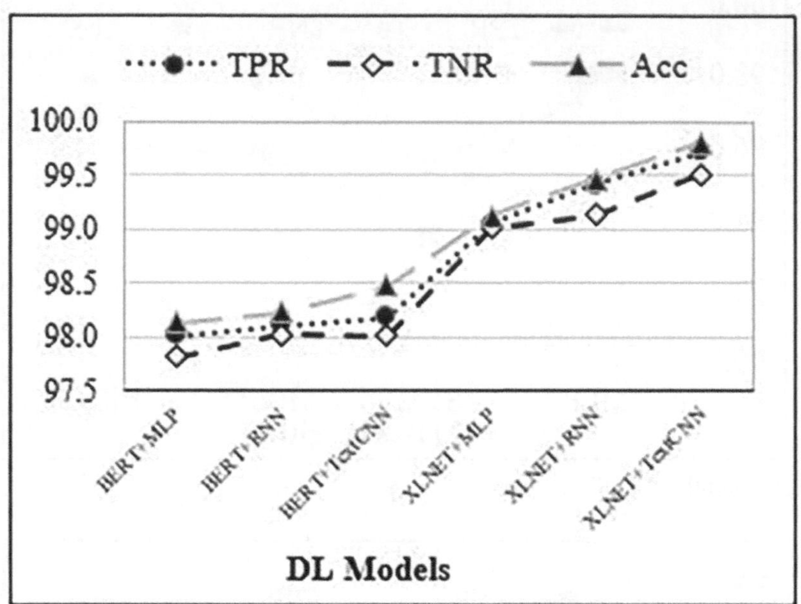

Figure 6.6(c) TPR, TNR, Accuracy

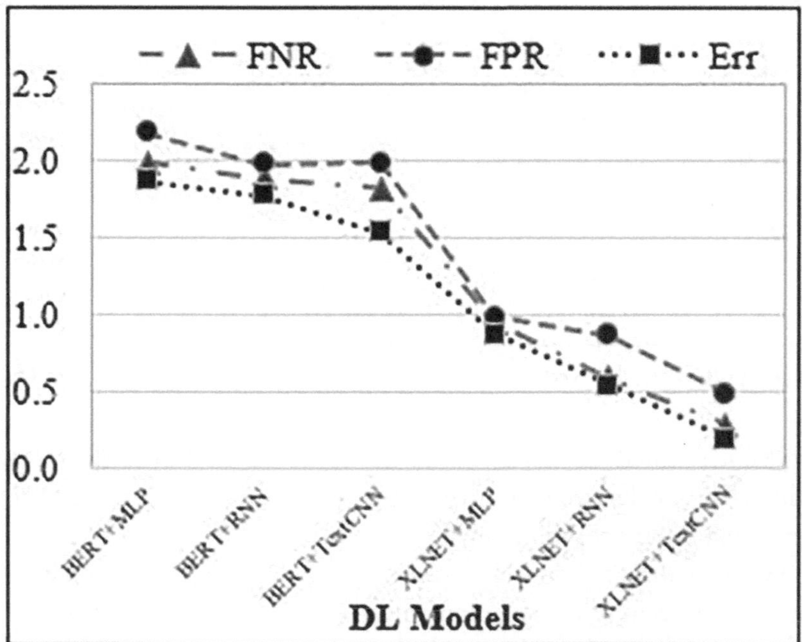

Figure 6.6(d) FNR, FPR, Error

Figure 6.6 Comparison of ML/ DL algorithms based on different metrics.

Table 6.4 Comparison of Performance of DL Models Used in M2VMapper (%)

DL MODELS	ACCURACY	PRECISION	RECALL	F1 SCORE
BERT+MLP	98.13	98.01	97.82	97.91
BERT+RNN	98.23	98.11	98.02	98.15
BERT+TextCNN	98.47	98.18	98.01	98.23
XLNET+MLP	99.12	99.05	99.01	98.89
XLNET+RNN	99.46	99.41	99.13	99.12
XLNET+TextCNN	99.81	99.72	99.51	99.32

Table 6.5 Hyper-Parameters Used in DL Models

HYPER-PARAMETERS	MLP	RNN	TEXTCNN
Learning rate	0.25	0.30	0.35
Momentum	0.9	0.5	0.99
Decay rate	0.0001	0.0001	0.001
Optimizer	AdaGrad	Adam	AdaGrad
xFilter	–	–	2 × 2
Kernel	3 × 3	3 × 3	3 × 3
Max-pooling	2 × 2	2 × 2	2 × 2

F1 score: In most cases, M2VMapper achieves an F1 score of 90% as shown in Table 6.6.

The various hyper-parameter combinations used for DL models are shown in Table 6.5.

Table 6.6 demonstrates that all ensemble models attain a respectable F1 score, with MLP achieving the highest.

Additionally, as can be observed from Figure 6.7, TextCNN achieves the highest F1 scores when all XLNET models are merged with DL models.

4. Efficiency of M2VMapper

The efficacy of M2VMapper is measured in terms of the typical investigation time for behavioral reports. Pre-processing and mapping time together make up the M2VMapper runtime (comprising training and prediction time). All ML/DL methods have the same pre-processing time; however, the mapping times differ. Figure 6.8(a) makes clear that MLP is expensive in terms of training and prediction time. In case of DL, Figure 6.8(b) makes clear that using XLNET in combination with TextCNN results in expensive training and prediction times. On an Intel(R) Core TM is–7500U CPU @

Table 6.6 F1 Score (%) of ML Algorithms after Hyper-Parameter Tuning

		BASELINE	TUNED	ENSEMBLE
SVM	Mean	86.666	90.697	94.428
	SD	7.354	7.555	6.867
	Min	69.629	73.854	77.685
	25%	83.807	89.075	91.375
	50%	85.723	89.801	96.726
	75%	92.164	96.835	92.164
	Max	93.209	98.225	93.209
MLP	Mean	89.761	94.091	97.664
	SD	5.978	5.719	5.200
	Min	78.006	82.341	85.354
	25%	85.930	89.960	98.135
	50%	91.971	97.209	99.932
	75%	92.823	97.036	92.823
	Max	93.512	97.983	93.512
PART	Mean	89.025	93.558	97.607
	SD	5.654	5.096	5.517
	Min	78.688	83.908	85.906
	25%	85.427	89.693	96.737
	50%	91.679	96.507	91.679
	75%	92.797	97.475	92.797
	Max	93.306	98.042	93.306
RIDOR	Mean	81.116	85.390	88.890
	SD	7.091	6.621	6.362
	Min	70.004	74.459	77.691
	25%	76.019	81.052	85.456
	50%	84.458	89.549	91.943
	75%	86.884	89.125	93.482
	Max	86.263	90.416	94.128

2.70 GHz 2.90 GHz system with a quad-core processor, the effectiveness of M2VMapper is assessed.

The malware-to-vulnerability mapping results of the M2VMapper framework are very encouraging. The mapping effectiveness of M2VMapper can be enhanced, nevertheless, by taking into account more reliable virus description reports. The mapping findings grow

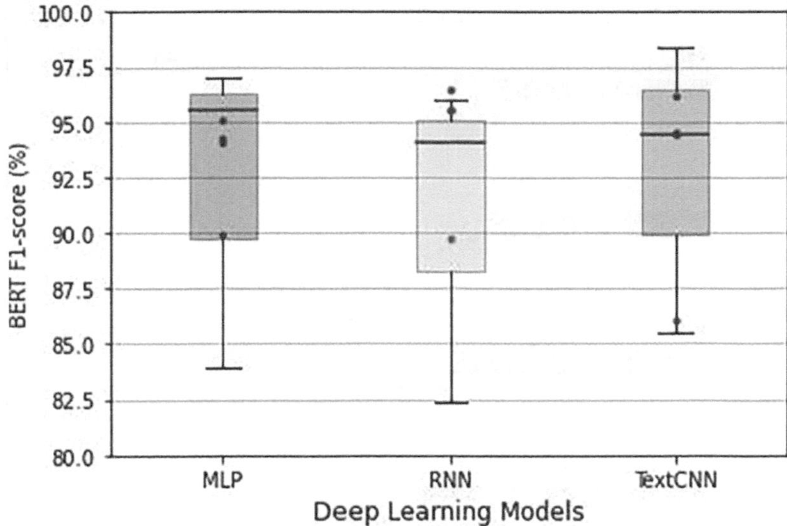

Figure 6.7(a) BERT

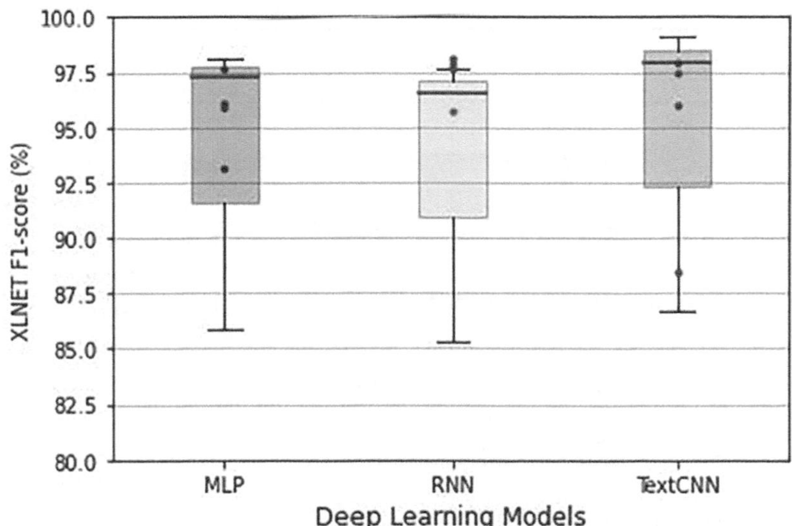

Figure 6.7(b) XLNET

Figure 6.7 F1 scores of BERT and XLNET for DL models.

wider and more precise the more enriched the malware reports are. Multiple vulnerabilities can be linked to the same malware family, according the evaluation's findings. However, a malware family may have a number of variants. For instance, the AMD dataset counts the DroidKungFu malware family as one family. However, this family has a number of variations, including DroidKungFu1, DroidKungFu2,

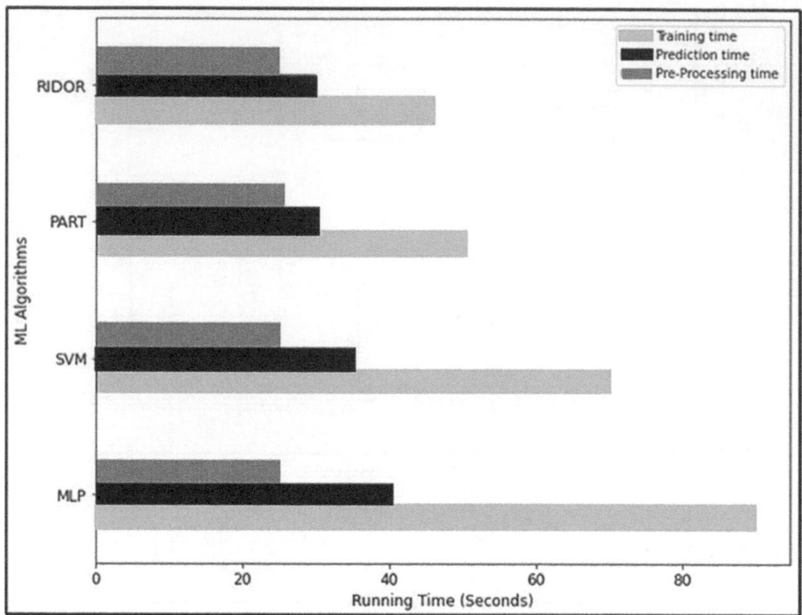

Figure 6.8(a) using ML models

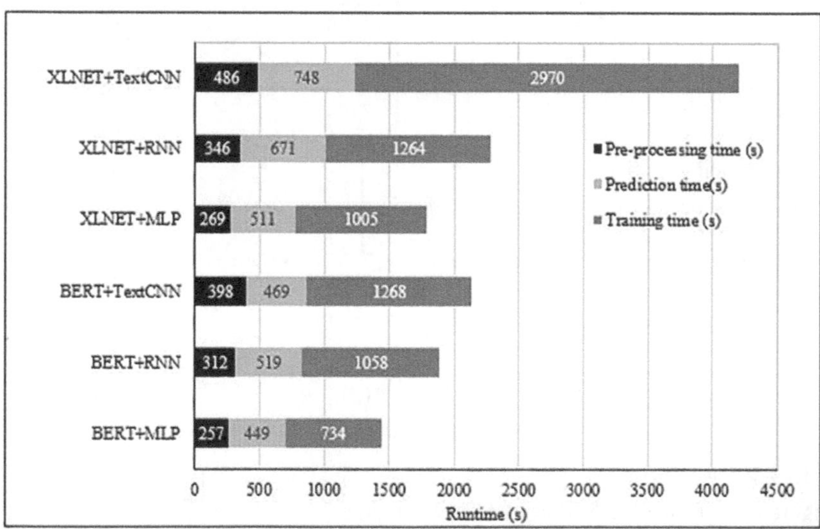

Figure 6.8(b) using DL models

Figure 6.8 Average runtime of M2VMapper.

and DroidKungFu4. The common primary vulnerabilities that this virus exploits are matched to these variations. By mapping malware categories like Trojan, adware, spyware, ransomware, etc. to vulnerabilities, a more comprehensive picture can be produced.

It is not possible to compare this study to any previous work because it is the first of its kind, and there is not much research being done in this area. The closest piece of research to ours was done in 2015 by authors in [166], who linked vulnerabilities with unintended Android bugs. Our method differs considerably from that used by authors in [166] in terms of the dataset of malware samples and the text-processing strategy we used to map malware to vulnerabilities.

The set theory principles on which M2VMapper is based enables it to map malware and vulnerabilities to a great extent. This study is the first of its type in the field of Android security, where word embeddings are used to map malware and vulnerabilities. Security experts, Android researchers, and developers can use it directly to improve Android security even while it is being developed.

6.6 Conclusion and Future Directions

Security experts are worried about the malware that targets Android, which is multiplying exponentially. To understand the main reason for an attack, it is crucial to look at the malicious behavior of malware. A novel M2VMapper framework is presented in this chapter, which also offers methodical mapping between malware and vulnerabilities.

In order to create ensemble ML models, M2VMapper uses NLP and ML approaches to model the malware description reports using BoW. M2VMapper uses MLP to attain an accuracy of 98.04%. The findings are promising; thus, it is critical to look into this mainly untapped area even more. In addition to DL approaches, M2VMapper models malware description reports using semantic modelling methods like BERT and XLNET. M2VMapper uses XLNET and TextCNN to attain an accuracy of 99.81%. The findings are promising; thus, it is critical to look into this mainly untapped area even more.

The caliber of the malware description report affects M2VMapper's performance. The current M2VMapper design gives investigators the freedom to select alternative malware reports while unable to assess the caliber of the description report. Future studies can take this aspect into consideration. Additionally, more advanced pretrained models with active learning can be applied.

The impact analysis of the identified vulnerabilities on the Android OS stack is the goal of the next chapter.

Notes

1 https://docs.google.com/spreadsheets/d/1gocjQfJ8Ukryif3rCZHUuiWa1ONkLtuOIxXVidtzKvo/edit?usp=sharing
2 https://drive.google.com/drive/folders/1NLsX7mCaLREmWITlanACQKmBeCwyhElj?usp=sharing

7

Android Vulnerabilities Impact Analysis on the Confidentiality, Integrity, and Availability Triad at the Architectural Level

7.1 Introduction

Malware attacks on the Android mobile OS have been ongoing and varied, although historical malware trends only provide a partial picture. Since 2018, the malware situation for Android has improved slightly, according to the AV-Test security report [189]. The use of Android malware increased dramatically in 2016 and 2017; however, in 2018 and 2019, cybersecurity advancements and OS upgrades resulted in a considerable drop in the use of straightforward and easily replicated Android malware [60].

The Android mobile environment is still very vulnerable, despite a number of security upgrades. Malware has adapted new techniques such code obfuscation, wrappers, modified versions of older malware, packers, etc. to attack underlying system flaws with the same objective of gaining access to sensitive data and acquiring privileges. Android malware has developed into a persistent intrusive resident on users' devices that can access and steal private data. The Android threat landscape is challenging to comprehend because of the sophisticated strategies used in malware [190].

This research is an essential component of the field of Android malware research. Using the parallel ensemble classifier technique, we were able to identify malicious applications in Chapter 4 with an accuracy of 98.27% [112]. Then, with an accuracy of 93.90% [191], we classified malware into 71 known families in Chapter 5. Additionally, in Chapter 6, text processing techniques were used to match the

DOI: 10.1201/9781003354574-7

classified malware to the known vulnerabilities. Finally, the impact of the mapped vulnerabilities on the various levels and components of the Android OS is evaluated in the current chapter.

It's critical to research fundamental vulnerabilities in order to comprehend the Android threat landscape. This chapter seeks to present a research study that examines Android OS vulnerabilities. The main emphasis is placed on the many layers and subsystems of the Android OS that are vulnerable, as well as how these vulnerabilities affect the CIA trinity. Such analysis can assist Android developers in concentrating on validating and verifying security flaws and redesigning the development processes of the underlying platform and Android apps to make them safer.

7.2 Relevant Works

The majority of earlier research focused on Android vulnerabilities in specific components. In [192], writers found six undiscovered flaws in the application framework layer's location manager, activity manager, and mount service subsystems. Android has application framework layer stroke vulnerabilities that can lead to DoS attacks and soft reboots, according to the authors of [193]. The authors examined the input validation techniques utilized in the application framework in another work [194]. Researchers examined privilege escalation flaws that took advantage of inter-application connections in [195]. The authors in [196] examined a number of security issues brought on by third-party libraries.

A group of 28 code smells relating to the security of Android apps were categorized in another study [197] into five categories: inadequate attack defense, security invalidation, broken access control, exposed sensitive data, and weak input validation. By examining 42 vulnerabilities from the CVE database, the authors of [198] were able to pinpoint complex function calls that led to vulnerabilities in Android components. In [199], the authors examined 660 Android OS flaws in terms of their viability as well as the afflicted subsystems/layers and components.

The aforementioned methods examined vulnerabilities at various layers and parts of Android; however, this study is all inclusive because it concentrates on the entire Android OS stack.

7.3 Design Approach

The investigation of Android vulnerabilities identified between 2009 and 2021 was the goal of the study [200]. From CVE details [58], a vulnerability repository that processes extensible markup language (XML) feeds delivered by the NVD [21], we mined 4,707 vulnerabilities. The following research questions (RQs) were addressed by this study:

- RQ1: Which Android layers are most vulnerable? In order for Android researchers and app developers to provide better verification and validation tools for secure coding, this question focuses on the various Android subsystems that are impacted by the vulnerabilities.
- RQ2: How do these flaws affect the CIA trinity of the Android OS? The impact (full, partial, or none) on Android devices is indicated by the response to this question.

Vulnerability extraction and impact analysis were the first two parts of the study.

7.3.1 *Vulnerability Extraction*

The three major procedures for extracting Android vulnerabilities from the vulnerability database are depicted in Figure 7.1.

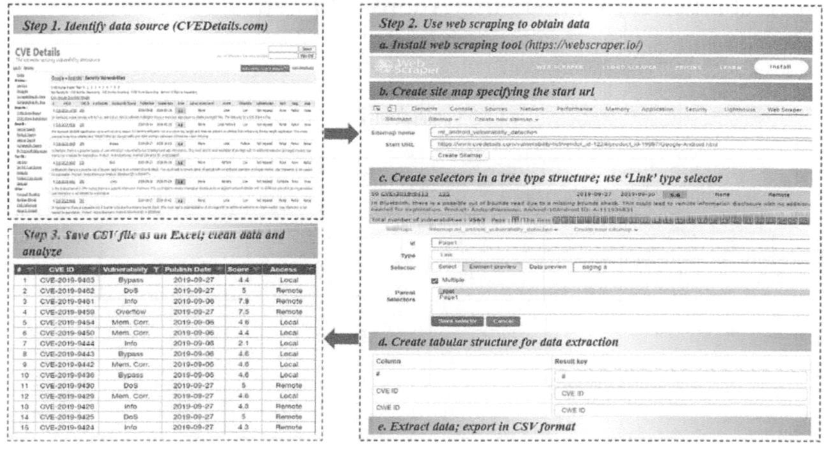

Figure 7.1 Vulnerability extraction.

1. Identifying the data source: CVE details is where vulnerability info is extracted. Between 2009 and 2021, 4,707 vulnerabilities were mined from the database.
2. Installing a web-scraping tool: To mine vulnerability data from CVE details, a web-based scraper program called Web Scraper 0.4.0 [59] is employed. The development of the sitemap, which is designated with a start URL, initiates the web-scraping process. The "Link" selector is then entered when the data is chosen as a tree-like structure. Following this, a tabular structure for data extraction is provided, and data scraping is started. The exported CSV file contains the scraped data.
3. Saving the scraped data: After being cleaned and preprocessed, the data is then saved for later study.

The vulnerability type according to the CWE is automatically inferred using a keyword-based approach in CVE details. This automated procedure can produce inaccurate data and is prone to mistakes. As a result, a hierarchy is built and then examined for each vulnerability category, as shown in Figure 7.2.

7.3.2 Impact Analysis

Using the Android issue tracker NVD and CVE details, it is possible to manually identify the layers and subsystems of Android that are vulnerable to various flaws to fix RQ1 [201]. The distribution of vulnerabilities throughout the Android OS stack is revealed by the manual examination.

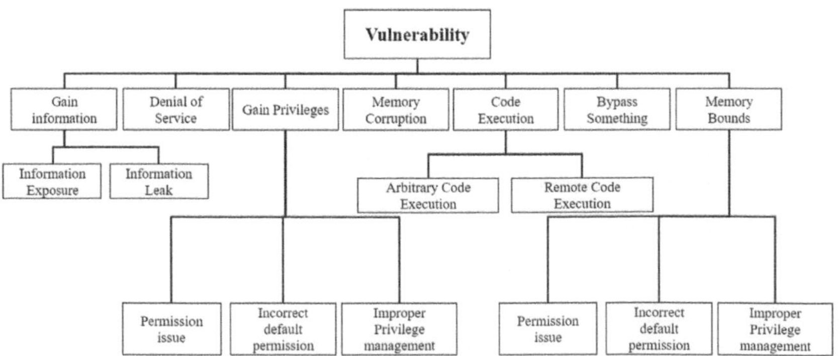

Figure 7.2 Types of vulnerabilities in order of severity.

By examining CVSS [202] vectors such severity scores, access levels, attack complexity, and impact on CIA for various vulnerabilities, RQ2 was addressed. In order to examine these vectors, CVSS 2.0 was referenced. Confidentiality is the defense of private data against unauthorized access. Integrity guarantees that data has not been altered by a third party, and availability guarantees that users can easily access all system resources and network services.

7.4 Results

Based on the RQs, this section presents the quantitative and qualitative findings (defined in Section 7.2). By referencing the CVE IDs of the vulnerabilities, quantitative data is supplemented with qualitative examples (e.g., CVE-2016–2439).

In order to answer RQ1 (Which Android layers are most vulnerable?), the heat map in Figure 7.3 shows how vulnerabilities are distributed throughout various Android layers and subsystems and the severity impact in different Android layers/components (internal boxes) in each layer.

With 53.3% of vulnerabilities, it is clear that the Linux kernel is the layer most adversely affected. This is backed by the fact that the Android Open-Source Project (AOSP) has incorporated the majority of the modifications made to enable mobile capabilities into the main

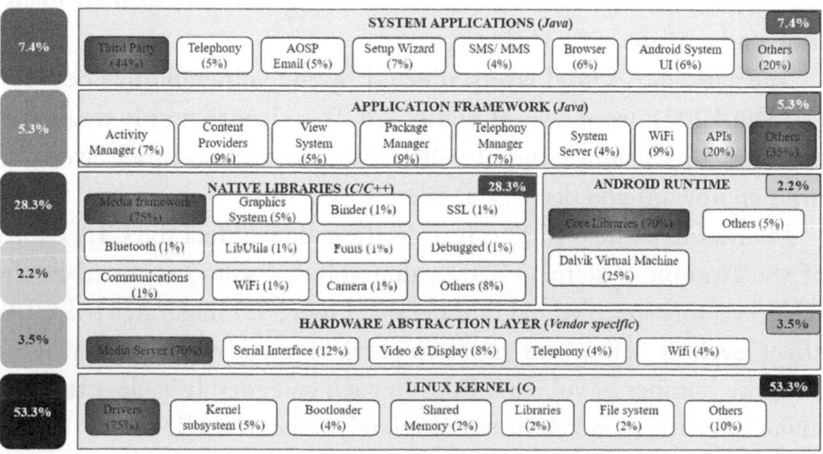

Figure 7.3 Vulnerability distribution across levels and subsystems of Android.

kernel. Drivers created by OEMs are affected by 75% of the vulnerabilities at this layer, including memory corruption, buffer overflow, and privilege escalation, followed by the kernel subsystem (5%) and the bootloader (4%).

Native library, with a 28.3% impact, is the second most affected layer. Seventy-five percent of the vulnerabilities are attributable to the *libstagefright* library, which is part of the media framework. Buffer overflow, information gain, and code execution have all been identified as media framework flaws.

With 7.4% of the vulnerabilities, the system applications layer is the third most affected Android layer, with the majority of the vulnerabilities (44%) in third-party applications. The apps are designed in Java. This layer is vulnerable to DoS attacks, information gathering, privilege escalation, and circumvention.

The application framework, which has 5.3% vulnerabilities in 2020 and 7.26% in 2018, is the next layer to be vulnerable. The vulnerabilities, including memory corruption, buffer overflows, privilege escalation, and DoS, usually affect application frameworks.

The hardware abstraction layer (HAL), which has 3.5% vulnerabilities, is the next impacted layer. The media server is responsible for 70% of the vulnerabilities. Code execution, memory corruption, and denial-of-service vulnerabilities affect HAL.

Android runtime has the remaining 2.2% of the vulnerabilities (ART). Core libraries contain 70% of these flaws, which include the ability to escalate access, obtain information, get around security measures, and corrupt memory.

The various Android layers affected by the vulnerabilities between 2018 and 2021 are shown in Figure 7.4. It is clear that only the kernel layer has a persistent trend of vulnerabilities, whereas other layers exhibit an upward and decrease tendency over time.

In order to address RQ2 (How do these flaws affect the CIA trinity of the Android system?), 4,707 vulnerabilities were examined in the CVSS vectors specified in CVE details. Figure 7.5 illustrates the CIA's effect levels as a complete impact, a partial impact, or no impact, along with the number of vulnerabilities in each category. It is clear that the majority of the vulnerabilities completely affect the CIA.

The CIA impact on the Android OS stack was also examined. The effect of vulnerabilities on secrecy at various Android layers is depicted

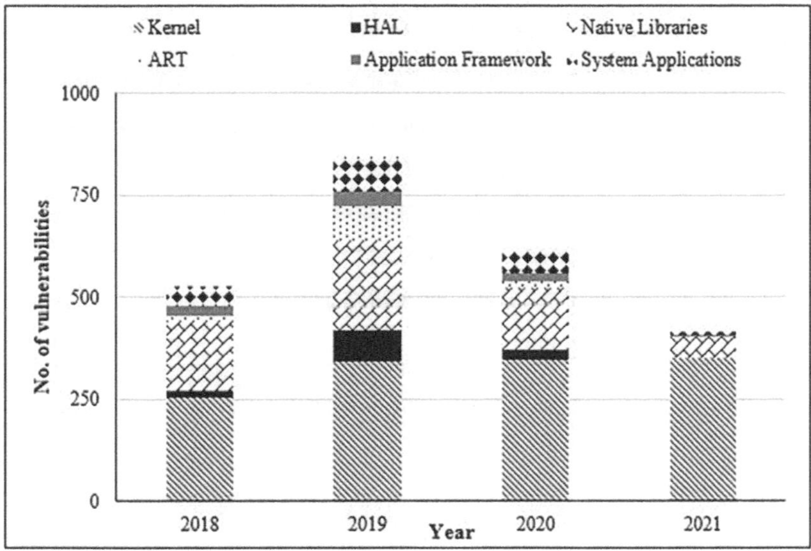

Figure 7.4 Android layers impacted by vulnerabilities from 2018 through 2021.

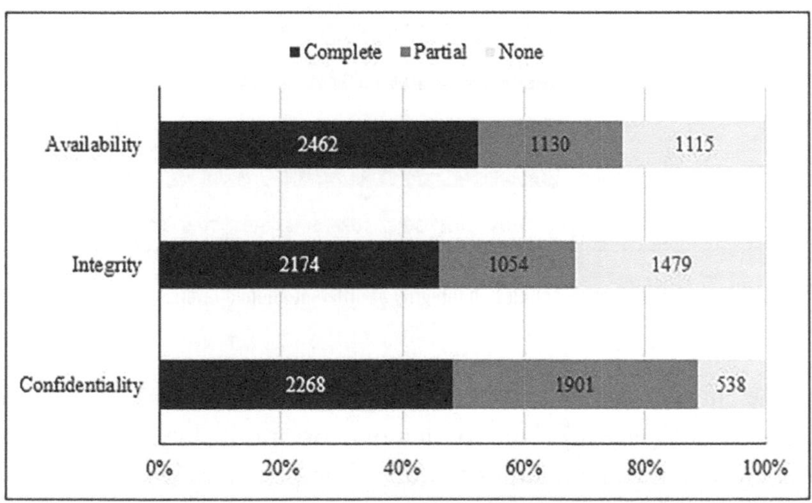

Figure 7.5 Number of vulnerabilities impacting the levels of CIA.

in Figure 7.6. It should be highlighted that the layers having the greatest impact on confidentiality are the kernel (47.4%) and native libraries (52.2%). The main reason is that the AOSP's kernel is a fork of the original Linux kernel. The Linux kernel is modified in every way relevant to Android in order to enable mobile functionality.

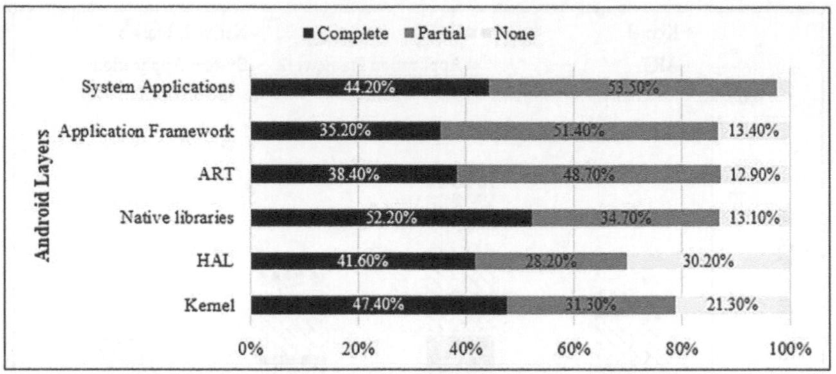

Figure 7.6 Impact of vulnerabilities on confidentiality at different Android layers.

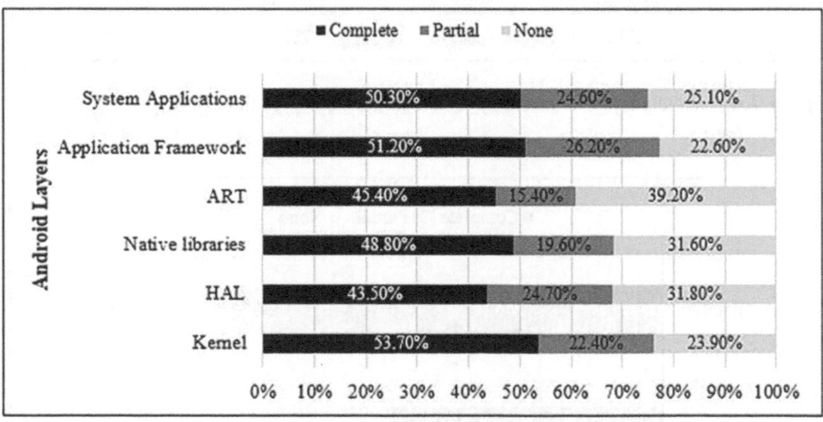

Figure 7.7 Impact of vulnerabilities on integrity at different Android layers.

The effect of vulnerabilities on integrity at various Android layers is depicted in Figure 6.7. Due to memory corruption, bypass, and privilege escalation vulnerabilities as well as complete information leakage, the kernel (53.7%), application framework (51.2%), and system applications (50.3%) have a complete impact on integrity.

The effect of vulnerabilities on availability is depicted in Figure 7.8. The layers that have the greatest overall impact are the kernel (62.3%), native libraries (57.7%), and application framework (55.5%), all of which include DoS vulnerabilities that prevent intended users from accessing the services and resources.

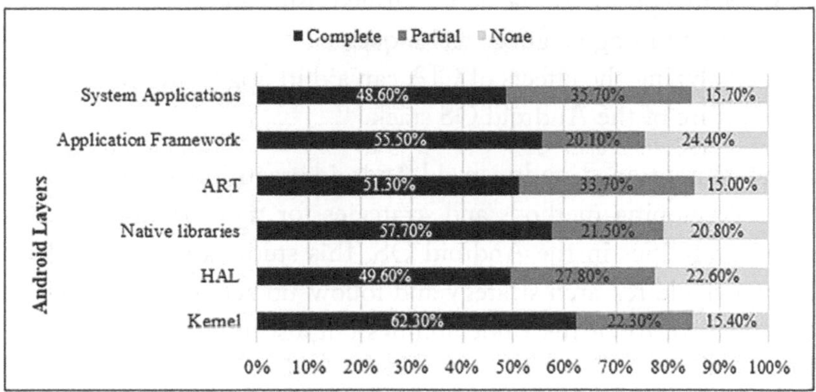

Figure 7.8 Impact of vulnerabilities on availability at different Android layers.

7.5 Conclusion and Future Directions

On various layers and components of Android, we examined the effects of 4,707 vulnerabilities. The layers of Android that are most impacted are the kernel and native libraries, it can be concluded. Additionally, the elements most adversely affected in these layers are the drivers in the kernel layer and the media framework of native libraries (inference from answering RQ1).

Answering RQ2 reveals that the majority of vulnerabilities result in the complete disclosure of information (confidentiality), complete access for the attacker to alter or tamper with any information (integrity), and complete shutdown of the system's services and resources (availability).

The aforementioned study can assist researchers and Android developers in the early detection of vulnerable OS stack components. There have been a lot of studies done in the past to find application-level vulnerabilities, but relatively few works have been done to find OS-level vulnerabilities. Based on the foregoing conclusions, we offer the following solutions:

1. To address vulnerabilities, code changes can be used, such as pre-condition checks for buffer overflows and managing permissions in the manifest file for privilege escalations.
2. The most vulnerable parts of the kernel layer are third-party hardware drivers; hence, more stringent validation and verification requirements should be put in place.

3. Secure coding can be accomplished using more sophisticated programming language techniques.
4. Analyzing the effects of CIA can aid in upgrading the architecture of the Android OS stack.

The aforementioned study can aid Android practitioners and researchers in developing methods and strategies for the early identification of vulnerabilities in the Android OS. This study is unique in that it offers a viable research strategy and follow-up activities to lessen not only the severity of the vulnerabilities but also their influence on the Android OS.

This study does have certain restrictions, though. First, subjectivity results from the manual analysis of vulnerability categories using keyword-based procedures. To address this problem, cross-validation requires a significant amount of manual work. Second, vulnerability persistence in the subsystem or Android component, or how long a specific vulnerability lasts, is not taken into account.

8
Conclusion and Future Directions

8.1 Introduction

Applications for software are used in a variety of industries, including finance, education, healthcare, and transportation, and a wide range of smart devices such as smartphones and tablets. Due to their convenience, mobile applications have become widely used. Smart gadgets commonly use the Android mobile OS as their mobile platform. Concerns about security in smart devices have grown along with the app market's expansion. Over time, samples of malicious software or malware have increased dramatically. Every day, new malware varieties are created to conduct nefarious tasks including stealing personal information, causing data leaks, etc.

Therefore, it is essential to suggest reliable, scalable, and effective methods that can address the following three issues: malware detection involves distinguishing malicious from legitimate applications; malware family classification involves categorizing malware samples into known families; and malware vulnerability mapping involves connecting malware to exploited flaws and evaluating those flaws at the architectural level of the Android OS.

In this book, a unique method for identifying and categorizing Android malware is proposed. Additionally, we suggest a system for mapping malware to vulnerabilities using supervised ML classifiers and NLP. The fundamental approaches and strategies put forth in this book are contrasted with the cutting-edge options accessible at the time this book was being written. Figure 8.1 depicts the various chapters' contributions in pictures.

In this book, we have explicitly highlighted the following contributions:

DOI: 10.1201/9781003354574-8

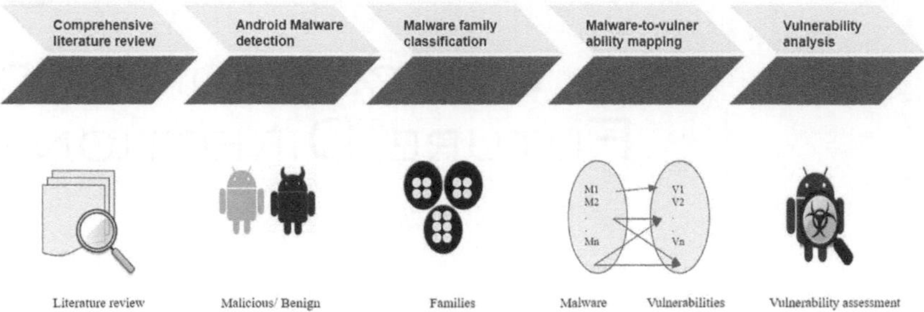

Figure 8.1 Different steps in Android malware study.

- A Parallel Classifier Scheme for Vulnerability Detection in Android (Chapter 4): This chapter shows how to distinguish between harmful and good Android apps using binary classification and a parallel ensemble technique. A feature vector was created by testing and correlating a number of static and dynamic features. The methodology combines individual classifiers, including MLP, SVM, PART, and RIDOR, to provide a more accurate and effective result. This methodology not only outperforms the shortcomings and restrictions of the earlier approaches, such as the use of either static or dynamic characteristics, large computational complexity, poor detection accuracy, etc., but also identifies malware in the Android OS with an accuracy of 98.27%. This approach balances out the weaknesses of each classifier while taking advantage of its strengths. As a result, the approach as a whole is more reliable and has a reduced error rate.
- Classification of Android Malware Using Ensemble Classifiers (Chapter 5): This chapter describes ensemble multi-class classification for attribution of Android malware families. We gathered the feature vectors made up of the APK's static and dynamic features. The dataset for a specific APK includes the malware family label that is labeled with the feature vector. With an accuracy of 93.90%, the methodology outlined in this chapter classifies Android malware into known families, which makes it superior to individual classifiers.
- Text Processing–Based Malware-to-Vulnerability Mapping for Android (Chapter 6): This chapter uses the M2VMapper

framework to illustrate malware vulnerability mapping. This can assist in determining the attack's primary cause by assisting in the investigation of malware's malicious activity. M2VMapper models malware description reports using BoW and NLP techniques. The target variable is then transformed using a multi-label binarizer and further tweaked with regard to a number of hyper-parameters before being supplied to supervised machine learning classifiers. Using MLP for unigram, M2VMapper produced encouraging results with an accuracy of 98.04%.

- Android Vulnerabilities Impact Analysis on the Confidentiality, Integrity, and Availability Triad at the Architectural Level (Chapter 7): Based on CIA, this chapter provides an empirical impact study of several vulnerabilities impacting Android layers and components. The effect of 4,707 vulnerabilities over the period from 2009 to 2021 was examined. It is obvious that bottom layers are more vulnerable than top layers; hence, improving the Android OS's foundation should receive more attention. Researchers and Android developers can use the information offered in this chapter to identify the most vulnerable parts of their systems. This could help rethink the Android stack and provide safer features.

It's critical to research the fundamental vulnerabilities in order to comprehend the Android threat landscape. This chapter seeks to present a research study that examines Android OS vulnerabilities. The main emphasis is placed on the many layers and subsystems of the Android OS that are vulnerable, as well as how these vulnerabilities affect the CIA trinity. Such analysis can assist Android developers in concentrating on validating and verifying security flaws and redesigning the development processes of the underlying platform and Android apps to make them safer.

8.2 Future Directions

The strategies and methods put forth make clear a number of research voids and issues with Android security analysis approaches that require additional attention. The following prospective research directions are discussed:

- A major research emphasis on Android security: Because Android is open source, cybercriminals are enticed to use sophisticated malware to attack its surface. This has attracted the attention of many researchers.
- Combining different analytical approaches for more accurate and precise results: Due to inherent constraints, a single analytical methodology cannot be used to produce accurate results. The best outcomes can be achieved by combining the benefits of static, dynamic, and hybrid approaches using more sophisticated ML and DL algorithms.
- A greater focus on anti-analysis tactics: The most common anti-analysis strategies employed by malware to circumvent static and dynamic analysis are code obfuscation and packing. For precise analysis, it is necessary to eliminate obfuscated apps; hence, more precise and effective tools must be developed.
- The need for a more reliable permission system: Apps can be installed with an unlimited number of permissions, which makes it possible for privilege escalation attacks. Only those permissions that are required by the applications to carry out necessary tasks should be granted by users. Consequently, a stronger, more exploitation-resistant permission mechanism is required.
- Evaluating the malware description report's quality: M2VMapper's efficacy is reliant on the malware description report's level of quality. M2VMapper's present architecture allows investigators to select different malware reports but is unable to assess the quality of the description report. As part of ongoing study, this problem can be resolved.
- The need for robust verification and validation tasks: It is clear that hardware drivers are the parts of the Linux kernel that are most susceptible to attack. Therefore, it is necessary to strengthen the verification and validation tasks. Before committing to the AOSP repository, automated vulnerability detection technologies could be used as an integration pipeline.
- Examining more impact-related metrics, such as economic loss brought on by financial malware, is necessary when examining impact-related metrics caused by Android malware.

A framework for Android malware detection must be created and developed in order to fully analyze and profile Android applications.

- Use secure coding techniques: Android layers are subject to a wide range of vulnerabilities. In the hardware, memory corruption and buffer overflows are frequent, privilege escalation and access control problems are frequent in system apps, and code execution and initialization errors commonly affect the middle levels of the Android stack. Therefore, developers of various Android OS layers could employ secure coding standards.

Appendix A
Android Malware Behavior

LEGENDS

Installation—Drop (DR), Drive-By Download (DD) **Composition**—Standalone (ST), Repackaging (RPKG), Library (LIB)

Activation—Event (EV), By Host App (BHA), Scheduling (SC) **C&C**—Internet (IN), Command Encoding (CE): JSON (J), Java Script (JS), XML (X), Custom Protocol (P)

Anti-Analysis—Renaming (RN), String Encryption (SE), Dynamic Code Loading (DCL), Native Payload (NP), Evade Dynamic Analysis (EDA)

		INSTALLATION		COMPOSITION			ACTIVATION			C&C			ANTI-ANALYSIS				
MALWARE	MALWARE TYPE	DR	DD	ST	RPKG	LIB	EV	BHA	SC	IN	SMS	CE	RN	SE	DCL	NP	EDA
AdDown	Adware	✓			✓	✓	✓			✓				✓			
Agent-Smith	Adware	✓			✓		✓			✓							✓
Chamois	Adware		✓		✓			✓									
Copycat	Adware	✓			✓		✓			✓			✓				
Falseguide	Adware		✓		✓												
Ghostteam	Adware	✓			✓		✓	✓								✓	
Gunpowder	Adware				✓	✓				✓	✓	JS				✓	✓
Hiddnad	Adware	✓	✓		✓	✓	✓			✓					✓		
Judy	Adware		✓		✓		✓			✓		JS	✓				
Lightsout	Adware	✓			✓	✓											
Skinner	Adware		✓		✓	✓	✓			✓		JS					
Airpush	Adware					✓		✓	✓	✓		JSON	✓				
Dowgin	Adware	✓				✓		✓		✓		JSON	✓	✓	✓		✓
Kuguo	Adware	✓				✓	✓	✓		✓		CP	✓				
Minimob	Adware					✓	✓	✓	✓	✓		JSON	✓				

Utchi	Adware	✓				✓	✓	✓					✓				
Youmi	Adware	✓				✓		✓		✓		CP	✓				
Andup	Adware	✓				✓	✓	✓				JS	✓	✓			
Kyview	Adware		✓		✓												
Ewind	Adware, Trojan		✓		✓		✓			✓	✓	JS					
Androrat	Backdoor	✓		✓			✓		✓	✓		CP					
Dendroid	Backdoor		✓	✓					✓	✓							✓
Dresscode	Backdoor	✓			✓					✓			✓				
Ghostctrl	Backdoor	✓			✓			✓		✓	✓	JS					
Godless	Backdoor	✓	✓	✓	✓		✓	✓		✓		JSON				✓	
Guerilla	Backdoor		✓		✓		✓				✓	JSON					✓
Hummingbad	Backdoor	✓			✓			✓		✓		CP				✓	
Kevdroid	Backdoor			✓				✓	✓	✓		CP					
Milkydoor	Backdoor		✓		✓							CP		✓			✓
SMS-Thief	Backdoor	✓			✓		✓			✓							
Tizi	Backdoor	✓			✓					✓		CP					
Toastamigo	Backdoor		✓		✓		✓	✓		✓		JS					
Triada	Backdoor	✓		✓			✓		✓	✓		CP	✓	✓	✓		✓
DroidKungFu	Backdoor	✓		✓	✓		✓	✓	✓	✓		CP	✓	✓		✓	
FakeAngry	Backdoor	✓			✓		✓			✓		CP	✓	✓			

(*Continued*)

		INSTALLATION			COMPOSITION			ACTIVATION			C&C		ANTI-ANALYSIS				
MALWARE	MALWARE TYPE	DR	DD	ST	RPKG	LIB	EV	BHA	SC	IN	SMS	CE	RN	SE	DCL	NP	EDA
Fjcon	Backdoor	✓			✓		✓			✓		XML					
Fobus	Backdoor	✓		✓			✓			✓	✓	XML		✓	✓		✓
GingerMaster	Backdoor	✓			✓		✓	✓	✓	✓		CP	✓	✓			
GoldDream	Backdoor	✓		✓	✓		✓			✓		CP					
Obad	Backdoor	✓	✓	✓			✓		✓	✓	✓	JSON	✓	✓			✓
Spambot	Backdoor			✓			✓										
Univert	Backdoor			✓			✓		✓	✓		JSON					
xLoader	Backdoor, Trojan	✓	✓		✓			✓		✓	✓	JS		✓			
Lotoor	Hackertool	✓		✓			✓						✓		✓	✓	
Penetho	Hackertool			✓			✓										
FakeDefender	Ransomware	✓		✓				✓		✓		JS					
SimpLocker	Ransomware		✓		✓		✓			✓		CP					
Aples	Ransomware			✓			✓		✓	✓		CP					
Fusob	Ransomware			✓			✓		✓	✓		JSON	✓	✓	✓		
Jisut	Ransomware			✓			✓										
Koler	Ransomware			✓			✓			✓		CP	✓				✓
Roop	Ransomware			✓			✓			✓		JS	✓				
Agent-jl	Trojan		✓		✓			✓									

Calljam	Trojan	✓			✓						✓					
Cepsohord	Trojan		✓	✓				✓		✓		JS				
Chargeb	Trojan	✓			✓		✓			✓		JS	✓	✓		✓
Deathring	Trojan		✓	✓					✓		✓					
Dvmap	Trojan		✓		✓	✓										
Expensivewall	Trojan		✓		✓			✓			✓	JS	✓			
Fakeapp	Trojan	✓			✓		✓			✓		JS				
Fakebank	Trojan	✓		✓				✓			✓	JSON				
Ghost-push	Trojan	✓		✓		✓		✓	✓			CP				
Gooligan	Trojan	✓		✓		✓		✓	✓			CP				
Gustuff	Trojan		✓		✓		✓				✓	JSON				
Lokibot	Trojan	✓			✓		✓	✓		v	✓	JS				
Mordar-A	Trojan		✓		✓											
Pawost	Trojan		✓		✓						✓					
Rootnik	Trojan	✓		✓	✓		✓	✓				JS, XML		✓	✓	
Rootnikb	Trojan	✓		✓	✓		✓	✓				JS		✓	✓	
Skyfin	Trojan		✓		✓			✓		✓	✓	XML				
Slembunk	Trojan		✓		✓		✓			✓		JS, JSON		✓	✓	
Sockbot	Trojan		✓		✓			✓		✓		CP				
Spydealer	Trojan	✓	✓		✓		✓	✓		✓	✓	JS				

(Continued)

		INSTALLATION			COMPOSITION			ACTIVATION			C&C		ANTI-ANALYSIS				
MALWARE	MALWARE TYPE	DR	DD	ST	RPKG	LIB	EV	BHA	SC	IN	SMS	CE	RN	SE	DCL	NP	EDA
Twitoor	Trojan	✓			✓		✓			v	✓						
Xhelper	Trojan	✓		✓		✓			✓	✓		JS					
Xiny	Trojan		✓	✓				✓		✓							✓
Ztorg	Trojan	✓			✓			✓		✓		JSON	✓	✓	✓		✓
FakeAV	Trojan			✓			✓		✓								
FakeDoc	Trojan			✓			✓		✓				✓				
FakeTimer	Trojan			✓			✓		✓								
FakeUpdates	Trojan	✓			✓		✓	✓	✓	✓		XML	✓	✓			
Ksapp	Trojan	✓			✓		✓	✓	✓	✓		CP					✓
Lnk	Trojan				✓			✓									
Mmarketpay	Trojan	✓			✓		✓		✓	✓		CP					
MobileTX	Trojan	✓					✓										
Mseg	Trojan		✓		✓		✓			✓	✓	JSON					
Mtk	Trojan	✓			✓		✓	✓	✓	✓		CP	✓	✓	✓		
Nandrobox	Trojan	✓			✓	✓	✓	✓		✓		JSON					
UpdtKiller	Trojan				✓		✓	✓	✓	✓		XML	✓			✓	
Svpeng	TrojanBanker	✓	✓	✓			✓			✓	✓	CP					
Acecard	TrojanBanker		✓		✓		✓				✓	JS					

Asacub	TrojanBanker	✓			✓		✓		✓	✓	JSON	✓	✓		✓	✓
Bankbot	TrojanBanker	✓	✓	✓		✓		✓	✓	✓	CP	✓	✓	✓		✓
Bankosy	TrojanBanker		✓		✓		✓	✓		✓	JS					
Bianlian	TrojanBanker	✓			✓		✓		✓		JS		✓			
Cerberus	TrojanBanker	✓			✓		✓		✓		JSON					
Emotet	TrojanBanker	✓		✓				✓								
Exobot	TrojanBanker	✓	✓	✓	✓	✓	✓		✓	✓	JS					✓
GM-bot	TrojanBanker			✓		✓		✓	✓	✓	JS, XML					
Gugi	TrojanBanker			✓		✓				✓						
Marcher	TrojanBanker	✓		✓			✓	✓		✓	JS					
Pluginpahntom	TrojanBanker		✓	✓			✓		✓		JS				✓	✓
Roaming-Mantis	TrojanBanker		✓		✓		✓		✓		XML					
Swearing	TrojanBanker	✓			✓	✓										
Switcher	TrojanBanker	✓			✓	✓			✓		JS					
Tordow	TrojanBanker	✓			✓		✓		✓		JS					
Bankun	TrojanBanker	✓	✓	✓		✓		✓	✓		JSON, XML					✓
Zitmo	TrojanBanker			✓		✓		✓			CP	✓				

(*Continued*)

		INSTALLATION			COMPOSITION			ACTIVATION			C&C		ANTI-ANALYSIS				
MALWARE	MALWARE TYPE	DR	DD	ST	RPKG	LIB	EV	BHA	SC	IN	SMS	CE	RN	SE	DCL	NP	EDA
Mysterybot	TrojanBanker, Ransomware	✓			✓			✓		✓		JS	✓		✓		
Steek	TrojanClicker			✓			✓										
Winge	TrojanClicker	✓			✓		✓			✓		XML	✓				
Viking-horde	TrojanDropper	✓			✓		✓		✓	✓		JSON				✓	
Boqx	TrojanDropper	✓			✓												
Gorpo	TrojanDropper	✓			✓					✓		JSON	✓	✓			✓
Kemoge	TrojanDropper	✓			✓		✓			✓		CP					
Ramnit	TrojanDropper				✓			✓									
Gazon	Trojan-SMS		✓		✓		✓				✓	JS					
Podec	Trojan-SMS	✓			✓			✓		✓		CP	✓				
Boxer	Trojan-SMS		✓	✓			✓						✓	✓			
Cova	Trojan-SMS	✓		✓			✓			✓		CP	✓				
FakeInst	Trojan-SMS	✓		✓			✓			✓		JS	✓				
FakePlayer	Trojan-SMS			✓			✓						✓				
Gumen	Trojan-SMS				✓		✓		✓	✓		XML				✓	✓
Leech	Trojan-SMS	✓			✓		✓	✓	✓	✓		JSON	✓	✓	✓		✓

OpFake	Trojan-SMS		✓	✓		✓		✓	✓		CP		✓			
RuMMS	Trojan-SMS	✓	✓	✓		✓		✓	✓		JSON	✓	✓	✓		
SpyBubble	Trojan-SMS	✓		✓		✓		✓	✓		XML					
Stealer	Trojan-SMS	✓		✓		✓		✓	✓		JS	✓				
Tesbo	Trojan-SMS				✓	✓			✓		XML					
Vidro	Trojan-SMS			✓		✓		✓	✓		JSON					
Erop	Trojan-SMS			✓		✓										
Ogel	Trojan-SMS			✓		✓		✓	✓		CP	✓				✓
SmsKey	Trojan-SMS			✓		✓	✓					✓				
Chrysaor	Trojan-Spy		✓		✓											
Desert-scorpion	Trojan-Spy	✓	✓		✓	✓	✓			✓		✓	✓		✓	
Exaspy	Trojan-Spy		✓	✓			✓									
Faketoken	Trojan-Spy		✓	✓			✓		✓	✓	JS, XML					✓
RedDop	Trojan-Spy		✓		✓	✓			✓		CP	✓	✓			
SmsVova	Trojan-Spy		✓	✓	✓	✓		✓		✓	JS					
Sonicspy	Trojan-Spy	✓			✓		✓			✓	JS		✓			✓
Super-clean-plus	Trojan-Spy		✓	✓			✓		✓	✓	JSON				✓	✓
Triout	Trojan-Spy	✓			✓	✓			✓	✓	JS					

(Continued)

		INSTALLATION			COMPOSITION			ACTIVATION			C&C		ANTI-ANALYSIS				
MALWARE	MALWARE TYPE	DR	DD	ST	RPKG	LIB	EV	BHA	SC	IN	SMS	CE	RN	SE	DCL	NP	EDA
ViperRat	Trojan-Spy	✓			✓			✓		✓	✓						
Zoopark	Trojan-Spy		✓		✓	✓	✓										
Finspy	Trojan-Spy			✓			✓				✓	CP	✓				✓
Smszombie	Trojan-Spy	✓		✓			✓		✓		✓	XML					
Vmvol	Trojan-Spy	✓		✓			✓			✓		JSON					
Mecor	Trojan-Spy			✓			✓			✓		JS					
WannaHydra	Trojan-Spy, TrojanBanker	✓		✓			✓										

References

[1] Fling, B., *Mobile design and development: Practical concepts and techniques for creating mobile sites and Web apps*. O'Reilly Media, Inc., 2009.

[2] Hodara, H., & Skaljo, E., "From 1G to 5G", *Fiber and Integrated Optics*, v. 40, n. 2–3, pp. 85–183, 2021.

[3] Chataut, R., & Akl, R., "Massive MIMO systems for 5G and beyond networks—overview, recent trends, challenges, and future research direction", *Sensors*, v. 20, n. 10, p. 2753, 2020.

[4] Mobile Threat Catalogue, "Mobile ecosystem", Available Online: https://pages.nist.gov/mobile-threat-catalogue/background/mobile-attack-surface/mobile-ecosystem.html, Accessed: 21 September, 2022.

[5] Federal Mobility Metrics Working Group, "An overview of the mobile security ecosystem", Available Online: https://atarc.org/project/wp-mobile-security-ecosystem/, Accessed: 5 October, 2022.

[6] Luke Irwin, "6 reasons why software is becoming more vulnerable to cyber attacks", Available Online: www.itgovernance.eu/blog/en/6-reasons-why-software-is-becoming-more-vulnerable-to-cyber-attacks#:~:text=The%20demand%20for%20interconnectivity%2C%20integration,demands%2C%20which%20exacerbates%20the%20problem/, Accessed: 10 July, 2022.

[7] Skybox Security, "Vulnerability and threat trends report 2022", Available Online: www.skyboxsecurity.com/trends-report/, Accessed: 13 July, 2022.

[8] O'Neill, P. H., "2021 has broken the record for zero-day hacking attacks", Available Online: www.technologyreview.com/2021/09/23/1036140/2021-record-zero-day-hacks-reasons/, Accessed: 15 July, 2022.

[9] IBM, "2021 cost of a data breach report", Available Online: www.ibm.com/in-en/security/data-breach#:~:text=Data%20breach%20average%20cost%20increased,million%20in%20the%202020%20report, Accessed: 28 July, 2022.

[10] Ericson, "Ericson mobility report, 2022", Available Online: www.ericsson.com/en/reports-and-papers/mobility-report, Accessed: 10 August, 2022.

[11] Statcounter GlobalStats, "Mobile operating system market share worldwide", Available Online: https://gs.statcounter.com/os-market-share/mobile/worldwide/, Accessed: 20 July, 2022.

[12] Skybox Security, "Vulnerability and threat trends report 2020", Available Online: www.skyboxsecurity.com/trends-report/, Accessed: 9 August, 2022.

[13] Swati Khandelwal, "New IoT Botnet malware discovered; infecting more devices worldwide", Available Online: http://thehackernews.com/2016/10/linux-irc-iot-botnet.html, Accessed: 20 July, 2022.

[14] Statcounter GlobalStats, "Mobile operating system market share worldwide", Available Online: https://gs.statcounter.com/os-market-share/mobile/worldwide/, Accessed: 15 July, 2022.

[15] Posey, B., Wigmore, I., & Westervelt, R., "Mobile security (wireless security)", Available Online: www.techtarget.com/whatis/definition/mobile-security, Accessed: 28 October, 2022.

[16] 42 Gears Team, "What is the difference between MDM, EMM, and UEM?", Available Online: www.42gears.com/blog/difference-between-mdm-emm-uem/, Accessed: 27 October, 2022.

[17] Ranaweera, P., Jurcut, A., & Liyanage, M., "MEC-enabled 5G use cases: A survey on security vulnerabilities and countermeasures", *ACM Computing Surveys (CSUR)*, v. 54, n. 9, pp. 1–37, 2021.

[18] Kshirsagar, D., & Kumar, S., "A feature reduction based reflected and exploited DDoS attacks detection system", *Journal of Ambient Intelligence and Humanized Computing*, pp. 1–13, 2021.

[19] Garg, S., Singh, R. K., & Mohapatra, A. K., "Analysis of software vulnerability classification based on different technical parameters", *Information Security Journal: A Global Perspective*, v. 28, n. 1–2, pp. 1–19, 2019.

[20] Farahmand, F., Navathe, S. B., Enslow, P. H., & Sharp, G. P., "Managing vulnerabilities of information systems to security incidents", In *5th International Conference on Electronic Commerce*, Association for Computing Machinery, New York, NY, pp. 348–354, 2003.

[21] National Vulnerability Database, Available Online: https://nvd.nist.gov/vuln-metrics/cvss/, Accessed: 15 May 2020.

[22] Alhazmi, O. H., Woo, S. W., & Malaiya, Y. K., "Security vulnerability categories in major software systems", In *3rd International Conference on Communication, Network, and Information Security*, pp. 138–143, 2006.

[23] Vulnerability Details: CVE-2016–7182, Available Online: www.cvedetails.com/cve/CVE-2016-7182/, Accessed: 15 December 2020.

[24] Li, X., Chang, X., Board, J. A., & Trivedi, K. S., "A novel approach for software vulnerability classification", In *Annual Reliability and Maintainability Symposium (RAMS)*, IEEE, pp. 1–7, 2017.

[25] Bozorgi, M., Saul, L. K., Savage, S., & Voelker, G. M., "Beyond heuristics: Learning to classify vulnerabilities and predict exploits", In *16th ACM SIGKDD International Conference on Knowledge Discovery and Data Mining*, Association for Computing Machinery, New York, NY, pp. 105–114, 2010.

[26] Heiderich, M., "Towards elimination of XSS attacks with a trusted and capability-controlled DOM", DEng Thesis, University in Bochum, 2012.

[27] Atashzar, H., Torkaman, A., Bahrololum, M., & Tadayon, M. H., "A survey on web application vulnerabilities and countermeasures", In *6th International Conference on Computer Sciences and Convergence Information Technology*, IEEE, pp. 647–652, 2011.

[28] Woo, S. W., Alhazmi, O. H., & Malaiya, Y. K., "An analysis of the vulnerability discovery process in web browsers", In *10th IASTED International Conference on Software Engineering*, v. 6, pp. 13–15, 2006.

[29] Dinh, H. T., Lee, C., Niyato, D., & Wang, P., "A survey of mobile cloud computing: Architecture, applications, and approaches", *Wireless Communications and Mobile Computing*, v. 13, n. 18, pp. 1587–1611, 2013.
[30] Surendran, R., Thomas, T., & Emmanuel, S., "GSDroid: Graph signal based compact feature representation for android malware detection", *Expert Systems with Applications*, v. 159, p. 113581, 2020.
[31] Fraunhofer Institute For Secure Information Technology, *How Smartphones and Co. May be cheating on you.* Fraunhofer Institute For Secure Information Technology, 2022.
[32] Kshirsagar, D., & Kumar, S., "A feature reduction based reflected and exploited DDoS attacks detection system", *Journal of Ambient Intelligence and Humanized Computing*, pp. 1–13, 2021.
[33] Mahaffey, K., & Murray, M., "Understanding the spectrum of mobile risk", Available Online: www.lookout.com/spectrum-of-mobile-risk/, Accessed: 21 December 2021.
[34] Tam, K., Feizollah, A., Anuar, N. B., Salleh, R., & Cavallaro, L., "The evolution of android malware and android analysis techniques", *ACM Computing Surveys*, v. 49, n. 4, pp. 1–41, 2017.
[35] Joh, H., & Malaiya, Y. K., "Periodicity in software vulnerability discovery, patching and exploitation", *International Journal of Information Security*, v. 16, pp. 673–690, 2017.
[36] Hatamian, M., "Engineering privacy in smartphone apps: A technical guideline catalog for app developers", *IEEE Access*, v. 8, pp. 35429–35445, 2020.
[37] Vega, R. V., Quintián, H., Calvo-Rolle, J. L., Herrero, Á., & Corchado, E., "Gaining deep knowledge of android malware families through dimensionality reduction techniques", *Logic Journal of the IGPL*, v. 27, n. 2, pp. 160–176, 2019.
[38] Android vs iOS, "Mobile operating system market share statistics you must know", Available Online: www.appmysite.com/blog/android-vs-ios-mobile-operating-system-market-share-statistics-you-must-know/, Accessed: 15 November 2022.
[39] Hidhaya, S. F., & Geetha, A., "Detection of vulnerabilities caused by webview exploitation in smartphone", In *9th International Conference on Advanced Computing*, IEEE, pp. 357–364, 2017.
[40] Zhang, L., "Smartphone app security: Vulnerabilities and implementations", Ph.D. Thesis, University of Michigan-Dearborn, 2018.
[41] Ahvanooey, M. T., Li, Q., Rabbani, M., & Rajput, A. R., "A survey on smartphones security: Software vulnerabilities, malware, and attacks", arXiv preprint arXiv:2001.09406, 2020.
[42] Talal, M., Zaidan, A. A., Zaidan, B. B., Albahri, O. S., Alsalem, M. A., Albahri, A. S., Alamoodi, A. H., Kiah, M. L. M., Jumaah, F. M., & Alaa, M., "Comprehensive review and analysis of anti-malware apps for smartphones", *Telecommunication Systems*, v. 72, n. 2, pp. 285–337, 2019.
[43] Shrestha, B., Ma, D., Zhu, Y., Li, H., & Saxena, N., "Tap-wave-rub: Lightweight human interaction approach to curb emerging smartphone malware", *IEEE Transactions on Information Forensics and Security*, v. 10, n. 11, pp. 2270–2283, 2015.
[44] Lee, S., "Assessment of malicious applications using permissions and enhanced user interfaces on Android", In *IEEE International Conference on Intelligence and Security Informatics*, IEEE, pp. 270–270, 2013.
[45] Rashidi, B., & Fung, C. J., "A survey of android security threats and defenses", *Journal of Wireless Mobile Networks, Ubiquitous Computing, and Dependable Applications*, v. 6, n. 3, pp. 3–35, 2015.

[46] Cho, T., & Seo, S. H., "A strengthened android signature management method", *KSII Transactions on Internet & Information Systems*, v. 9, n. 3, 2015.

[47] Loftus, R., Baumann, M., van Galen, R., & de Vries, R., "Android 7 file based encryption and the attacks against it", Informal Report, University of Amsterdam, p. 33, 2017.

[48] Garg, S., & Baliyan, N., "Comparative analysis of Android and iOS from security viewpoint", *Computer Science Review*, v. 40, p. 100372, 2021.

[49] Davi, L., Dmitrienko, A., Sadeghi, A. R., & Winandy, M., "Privilege escalation attacks on Android", In *International Conference on Information Security*, Springer, pp. 346–360, 2010.

[50] Bhatt, A. J., & Gupta, C., "Comparison of static and dynamic analyzer tools for iOS applications", *Wireless Personal Communications*, v. 96, n. 3, pp. 4013–4046, 2017.

[51] Werthmann, T., Hund, R., Davi, L., Sadeghi, A. R., & Holz, T., "Psios: Bring your own privacy & security to iOS devices", In *8th ACM SIGSAC Symposium on Information, Computer and Communications Security*, pp. 13–24, 2013.

[52] Groß, T., Ahmadova, M., & Müller, T., "Analyzing Android's file-based encryption: Information leakage through unencrypted metadata", In *14th International Conference on Availability, Reliability and Security*, Association for Computing Machinery, New York, NY, pp. 1–7, 2019.

[53] Shen, Y., & Wang, H., "Enhancing data security of iOS client by encryption algorithm", In *IEEE 2nd Advanced Information Technology, Electronic and Automation Control Conference*, IEEE, pp. 366–370, 2017.

[54] MacDuffie, J. K., & Morreale, P. A., "Comparing Android app permissions", In *International Conference of Design, User Experience, and Usability*, pp. 57–64, 2016.

[55] Lutaaya, M., "Rethinking app permissions on iOS", In *Extended Abstracts of the 2018 CHI Conference on Human Factors in Computing Systems*, Association for Computing Machinery, New York, NY, pp. 1–6, 2018.

[56] Pieterse, H., Olivier, M., & Van Heerden, R., "Detecting manipulated smartphone data on Android and iOS devices", In *International Information Security Conference*, Springer, pp. 89–103, 2018.

[57] Opoku, M., Davis, J., & Nimbe, P., "Security evaluation of the smartphone platforms: A case study with Android, iOS and Windows Phones", *Asian Journal of Mathematics and Computer Research*, v. 8, n. 3, pp. 234–259, 2015.

[58] CVE Details, Available Online: www.cvedetails.com/, Accessed: 9 October 2020.

[59] Web Scraper, "Making web data extraction easy and accessible for everyone", Available Online: https://webscraper.io/, Accessed: 22 October 2020.

[60] Garg, S., & Baliyan, N., "Machine learning based android vulnerability detection: A roadmap", In *International Conference on Information Systems Security*, Springer, pp. 87–93, 2020.

[61] Garg, S., & Baliyan, N., "Android security assessment: A review, taxonomy and research gap study", *Computers & Security*, p. 102087, 2020.

[62] Securelist by Kaspersky, "IT threat evolution in Q2 2022. Mobile statistics", Available Online: https://securelist.com/it-threat-evolution-in-q2-2022-mobile-statistics/107123/, Accessed: 27 August, 2022.

[63] Suarez-Tangil, G., Tapiador, J. E., Peris-Lopez, P., & Ribagorda, A., "Evolution, detection and analysis of malware for smart devices", *IEEE Communications Surveys & Tutorials*, v. 16, n. 2, pp. 961–987, 2013.

[64] Haris, M., Haddadi, H., & Hui, P., "Privacy leakage in mobile computing: Tools, methods, and characteristics", arXiv preprint arXiv:1410.4978, 2014.

[65] Shrivastava, G., Kumar, P., Gupta, D., & Rodrigues, J. J., "Privacy issues of Android application permissions: A literature review", *Transactions on Emerging Telecommunications Technologies*, v. 31, n. 12, p. e3773, 2020.
[66] Tan, D. J., Chua, T. W., & Thing, V. L., "Securing Android: A survey, taxonomy, and challenges", *ACM Computing Surveys*, v. 47, n. 4, pp. 1–45, 2015.
[67] Martin, W., Sarro, F., Jia, Y., Zhang, Y., & Harman, M., "A survey of app store analysis for software engineering", *IEEE Transactions on Software Engineering*, v. 43, n. 9, pp. 817–847, 2016.
[68] Faruki, P., Bharmal, A., Laxmi, V., Ganmoor, V., Gaur, M. S., Conti, M., & Rajarajan, M., "Android security: A survey of issues, malware penetration, and defenses", *IEEE Communications Surveys & Tutorials*, v. 17, n. 2, pp. 998–1022, 2014.
[69] Sadeghi, A., Bagheri, H., Garcia, J., & Malek, S., "A taxonomy and qualitative comparison of program analysis techniques for security assessment of Android software", *IEEE Transactions on Software Engineering*, v. 43, n. 6, pp. 492–530, 2016.
[70] Kitchenham, B., & Brereton, P., "A systematic review of systematic review process research in software engineering", *Information and Software Technology*, v. 55, n. 12, pp. 2049–2075, 2013.
[71] Bartel, A., Klein, J., Monperrus, M., & Le Traon, Y., "Static analysis for extracting permission checks of a large-scale framework: The challenges and solutions for analyzing Android", *IEEE Transactions on Software Engineering*, v. 40, n. 6, pp. 617–632, 2014.
[72] Lortz, S., Mantel, H., Starostin, A., Bähr, T., Schneider, D., & Weber, A., "Cassandra: Towards a certifying app store for Android", In *4th ACM Workshop on Security and Privacy in Smartphones & Mobile Devices*, pp. 93–104, 2014.
[73] Shuai, S., Guowei, D., Tao, G., Tianchang, Y., & Chenjie, S., "Modelling analysis and auto-detection of cryptographic misuse in Android applications", In *IEEE 12th International Conference on Dependable, Autonomic and Secure Computing*, pp. 75–80, 2014.
[74] Octeau, D., McDaniel, P., Jha, S., Bartel, A., Bodden, E., Klein, J., & Le Traon, Y., "Effective inter-component communication mapping in Android: An essential step towards holistic security analysis", In *22nd Security Symposium USENIX*, USENIX, pp. 543–558, 2013.
[75] Li, D., Tran, A. H., & Halfond, W. G., "Making web applications more energy efficient for OLED smartphones", In *36th International Conference on Software Engineering*, Association for Computing Machinery, New York, NY, pp. 527–538, 2014.
[76] Mirzaei, N., Bagheri, H., Mahmood, R., & Malek, S., "Sig-droid: Automated system input generation for Android applications", In *IEEE 26th International Symposium on Software Reliability Engineering*, IEEE, pp. 461–471, 2015.
[77] Mojica, I. J., Adams, B., Nagappan, M., Dienst, S., Berger, T., & Hassan, A. E., "A large-scale empirical study on software reuse in mobile apps", *IEEE Software*, v. 31, n. 2, pp. 78–86, 2013.
[78] Crussell, J., Gibler, C., & Chen, H., "Andarwin: Scalable detection of semantically similar Android applications", In *European Symposium on Research in Computer Security*, pp. 182–199, 2013.
[79] Ernst, M. D., "Static and dynamic analysis: Synergy and duality", In *WODA 2003: ICSE Workshop on Dynamic Analysis*, pp. 24–27, 2003.
[80] Rasthofer, S., Asrar, I., Huber, S., & Bodden, E., "How current Android malware seeks to evade automated code analysis", In *IFIP International Conference on Information Security Theory and Practice*, pp. 187–202, 2015.

[81] Yang, Z., Yang, M., Zhang, Y., Gu, G., Ning, P., & Wang, X. S., "Appintent: Analyzing sensitive data transmission in Android for privacy leakage detection", In *ACM SIGSAC Conference on Computer & Communications Security*, Association for Computing Machinery, New York, NY, pp. 1043–1054, 2013.

[82] Arzt, S., Rasthofer, S., Fritz, C., Bodden, E., Bartel, A., Klein, J., & McDaniel, P., "Flowdroid: Precise context, flow, field, object-sensitive and lifecycle-aware taint analysis for Android apps", *ACM Sigplan Notices*, v. 49, n. 6, pp. 259–269, 2014.

[83] Zhang, M., & Yin, H., "Automatic generation of vulnerability-specific patches for preventing component hijacking attacks", In *Android Application Security*, Springer, pp. 45–61, 2016.

[84] Hoffmann, J., Ussath, M., Holz, T., & Spreitzenbarth, M., "Slicing droids: Program slicing for smali code", In *28th Annual ACM Symposium on Applied Computing*, pp. 1844–1851, 2013.

[85] Egele, M., Brumley, D., Fratantonio, Y., & Kruegel, C., "An empirical study of cryptographic misuse in Android applications", In *ACM SIGSAC Conference on Computer & Communications Security*, Association for Computing Machinery, New York, NY, pp. 73–84, 2013.

[86] Bagheri, H., Sadeghi, A., Garcia, J., & Malek, S., "Covert: Compositional analysis of Android inter-app permission leakage", *IEEE Transactions on Software Engineering*, v. 41, n. 9, pp. 866–886, 2015.

[87] Li, L., Bartel, A., Bissyandé, T. F., Klein, J., Le Traon, Y., Arzt, S., Rasthofer, S., Bodden, E., Octeau, D., & McDaniel, P., "Iccta: Detecting inter-component privacy leaks in Android apps", In *IEEE/ACM 37th International Conference on Software Engineering*, v. 1, IEEE, pp. 280–291, 2015.

[88] Lam, P., Bodden, E., Lhoták, O., & Hendren, L., "The Soot framework for Java program analysis: A retrospective", In *Cetus Users and Compiler Infrastructure Workshop*, v. 15, n. 35, 2011.

[89] Fink, S., & Dolby, J., "WALA–The TJ Watson libraries for analysis", 2012.

[90] Jiang, Y. Z. X., & Xuxian, Z., "Detecting passive content leaks and pollution in Android applications", In *20th Network and Distributed System Security Symposium*, 2013.

[91] Sbîrlea, D., Burke, M. G., Guarnieri, S., Pistoia, M., & Sarkar, V., "Automatic detection of inter-application permission leaks in Android applications", *IBM Journal of Research and Development*, v. 57, n. 6, pp. 10–1, 2013.

[92] Huang, J., Zhang, X., Tan, L., Wang, P., & Liang, B., "Asdroid: Detecting stealthy behaviors in Android applications by user interface and program behavior contradiction", In *36th International Conference on Software Engineering*, pp. 1036–1046, 2014.

[93] Bartel, A., Klein, J., Le Traon, Y., & Monperrus, M., "Dexpler: Converting Android Dalvik bytecode to JIMPLE for static analysis with SOOT", In *ACM SIGPLAN International Workshop on State of the Art in Java Program Analysis*, Association for Computing Machinery, New York, NY, pp. 27–38, 2012.

[94] Octeau, D., Enck, W., & McDaniel, P., "The DED decompiler", In *Network and Security Research Center, Department of Computer Science and Engineering*, Pennsylvania State University, 2010.

[95] Octeau, D., Jha, S., & McDaniel, P., "Retargeting Android applications to Java bytecode", In *ACM SIGSOFT 20th International Symposium on the Foundations of Software Engineering*, Association for Computing Machinery, New York, NY, pp. 1–11, 2012.

[96] dex2jar, Available Online: https://code.google.com/p/dex2jar/, Accessed: 7 November 2020.

[97] Hao, S., Li, D., Halfond, W. G., & Govindan, R., "Sif: A selective instrumentation framework for mobile applications", In *Proceeding of the 11th Annual International Conference on Mobile Systems, Applications, and Services*, Association for Computing Machinery, New York, NY, pp. 167–180, 2013.

[98] Enck, W., Gilbert, P., Han, S., Tendulkar, V., Chun, B. G., Cox, L. P., Jung, J., McDaniel, P., & Sheth, A. N., "Taintdroid: An information-flow tracking system for realtime privacy monitoring on smartphones", *ACM Transactions on Computer Systems*, v. 32, n. 2, pp. 1–29, 2014.

[99] Lindorfer, M., Neugschwandtner, M., Weichselbaum, L., Fratantonio, Y., Van Der Veen, V., & Platzer, C., "Andrubis--1,000,000 apps later: A view on current Android malware behaviors", In *3rd International Workshop on Building Analysis Datasets and Gathering Experience Returns for Security*, pp. 3–17, 2014.

[100] Bagheri, H., Kang, E., Malek, S., & Jackson, D., "Detection of design flaws in the Android permission protocol through bounded verification", In *International Symposium on Formal Methods*, Springer, pp. 73–89, 2015.

[101] Chen, S., Xue, M., Tang, Z., Xu, L., & Zhu, H., "Stormdroid: A streaminglized machine learning-based system for detecting Android malware", In *11th ACM on Asia Conference on Computer and Communications Security*, Association for Computing Machinery, New York, NY, pp. 377–388, 2016.

[102] Zarni Aung, W. Z., "Permission-based Android malware detection", *International Journal of Scientific & Technology Research*, v. 2, n. 3, pp. 228–234, 2013.

[103] Mahindru, A., & Sangal, A. L., "Feature-based semi-supervised learning to detect malware from Android", In *Automated Software Engineering: A Deep Learning-based Approach*, pp. 93–118, 2020.

[104] Vuong, T. A. T., & Takada, S., "Semantic analysis for deep Q-network in Android GUI testing", In *31st International Conference on Software Engineering and Knowledge Engineering*, pp. 123–170, 2019.

[105] Pang, Y., Xue, X., & Wang, H., "Predicting vulnerable software components through deep neural network", In *International Conference on Deep Learning Technologies*, pp. 6–10, 2017.

[106] Mehtab, A., Shahid, W. B., Yaqoob, T., Amjad, M. F., Abbas, H., Afzal, H., & Saqib, M. N., "AdDroid: Rule-based machine learning framework for Android malware analysis", *Mobile Networks and Applications*, v. 25, n. 1, pp. 180–192, 2020.

[107] Appice, A., Andresini, G., & Malerba, D., "Clustering-aided multi-view classification: A case study on Android malware detection", *Journal of Intelligent Information Systems*, v. 55, n. 1, pp. 1–26, 2020.

[108] Liu, X., Zhang, J., Lin, Y., & Li, H., "Atmpa: Attacking machine learning-based malware visualization detection methods via adversarial examples", In *IEEE/ACM 27th International Symposium on Quality of Service*, IEEE/ACM, pp. 1–10, 2019.

[109] Yuan, Z., Lu, Y., & Xue, Y., "Droiddetector: Android malware characterization and detection using deep learning", *Tsinghua Science and Technology*, v. 21, n. 1, pp. 114–123, 2016.

[110] Wang, R., Enck, W., Reeves, D., Zhang, X., Ning, P., Xu, D., Zhou, W., & Azab, A. M., "EaseAndroid: Automatic policy analysis and refinement for security enhanced Android via large-scale semi-supervised learning", In *24th Security Symposium USENIX*, USENIX, pp. 351–366, 2015.

[111] Fadadu, F., Handa, A., Kumar, N., & Shukla, S. K., "Evading API call sequence based malware classifiers", In *International Conference on Information and Communications Security*, Springer, pp. 18–33, 2019.

[112] Garg, S., & Baliyan, N., "A novel parallel classifier scheme for vulnerability detection in Android", *Computers & Electrical Engineering*, v. 77, pp. 12–26, 2019.

[113] Han, H., Lim, S., Suh, K., Park, S., Cho, S. J., & Park, M., "Enhanced android malware detection: An SVM-based machine learning approach", In *IEEE International Conference on Big Data and Smart Computing*, IEEE, pp. 75–81, 2020.

[114] Han, X., & Olivier, B., "Interpretable and adversarially-resistant behavioral malware signatures", In *35th Annual ACM Symposium on Applied Computing*, Association for Computing Machinery, New York, NY, pp. 1668–1677, 2020.

[115] Hsien-De Huang, T., & Kao, H. Y., "R2-d2: Color-inspired convolutional neural network (CNN)-based Android malware detections", In *IEEE International Conference on Big Data*, IEEE, pp. 2633–2642, 2018.

[116] Mantoo, B. A., & Khurana, S. S., "Static, dynamic and intrinsic features based Android malware detection using machine learning", In *2nd International Conference on Recent Innovations in Computing*, Springer, pp. 31–45, 2020.

[117] Martín, I., Hernández, J. A., & de los Santos, S., "Machine-Learning based analysis and classification of Android malware signatures", *Future Generation Computer Systems*, v. 97, pp. 295–305, 2019.

[118] Nguyen-Vu, L., Ahn, J., & Jung, S., "Android fragmentation in malware detection", *Computers & Security*, v. 87, p. 101573, 2019.

[119] Chen, L., Hou, S., & Ye, Y., "Securedroid: Enhancing security of machine learning-based detection against adversarial Android malware attacks", In *33rd Annual Computer Security Applications Conference*, Association for Computing Machinery, New York, NY, pp. 362–372, 2017.

[120] Sharif, A., & Nauman, M., "Function identification in Android Binaries with deep learning", In *7th International Symposium on Computing and Networking*, IEEE, pp. 92–101, 2019.

[121] Sharmeen, S., Huda, S., Abawajy, J., & Hassan, M. M., "An adaptive framework against Android privilege escalation threats using deep learning and semi-supervised approaches", *Applied Software Computing*, v. 89, p. 106089, 2020.

[122] Sourav, S., Khulbe, D., & Kapoor, N., "Deep learning based android malware detection framework", arXiv preprint arXiv:1912.12122, 2019.

[123] Spreitzenbarth, M., Schreck, T., Echtler, F., Arp, D., & Hoffmann, J., "Mobile-Sandbox: combining static and dynamic analysis with machine-learning techniques", *International Journal of Information Security*, v. 14, n. 2, pp. 141–153, 2015.

[124] Tian, K., "Learning-based cyber security analysis and binary customization for security", Ph.D. Thesis, Virginia Polytechnic Institute and State University, 2018.

[125] Bugiel, S., Heuser, S., & Sadeghi, A. R., "Flexible and fine-grained mandatory access control on Android for diverse security and privacy policies", In *22nd Security Symposium USENIX*, USENIX, pp. 131–146, 2013.

[126] Ham, Y. J., Lee, H. W., Lim, J. D., & Kim, J. N., "DroidVulMon--Android Based mobile device vulnerability analysis and monitoring system", In *7th International Conference on Next Generation Mobile Apps, Services and Technologies*, pp. 26–31, 2013.

[127] Zhang, Y., Yang, M., Xu, B., Yang, Z., Gu, G., Ning, P., Wang, X. S., & Zang, B., "Vetting undesirable behaviors in Android apps with permission use analysis", In *ACM SIGSAC Conference on Computer & Communications Security*, Association for Computing Machinery, New York, NY, pp. 611–622, 2013.

[128] Chen, K. Z., Johnson, N. M., D'Silva, V., Dai, S., MacNamara, K., Magrino, T. R., Wu, E. X., Rinard, M., & Song, D. X., "Contextual policy enforcement in Android applications with permission event graphs", In *Network and Distributed System Security Symposium*, v. 234, 2013.

[129] Andronio, N., Zanero, S., & Maggi, F., "Heldroid: Dissecting and detecting mobile ransomware", In *International Symposium on Recent Advances in Intrusion Detection*, pp. 382–404, 2015.

[130] Denis Crăciunescu, "The layers of the Android security model", Available Online: https://proAndroiddev.com/the-layers-of-the-Android-security-model-90f471015ae6/, Accessed: 15 October 2020.

[131] Faruki, P., Ganmoor, V., Laxmi, V., Gaur, M. S., & Bharmal, A., "AndroSimilar: Robust statistical feature signature for Android malware detection", In *6th International Conference on Security of Information and Networks*, pp. 152–159, 2013.

[132] Zheng, M., Sun, M., & Lui, J. C., "Droid analytics: A signature based analytic system to collect, extract, analyze and associate Android malware", In *12th IEEE International Conference on Trust, Security and Privacy in Computing and Communications*, IEEE, pp. 163–171, 2013.

[133] Felt, A. P., Chin, E., Hanna, S., Song, D., & Wagner, D., "Android permissions demystified", In *18th ACM conference on Computer and Communications Security*, pp. 627–638, 2011.

[134] Sato, R., Chiba, D., & Goto, S., "Detecting Android malware by analyzing manifest files", *Proceedings of the Asia-Pacific Advanced Network*, v. 36, n. 17, pp. 23–31, 2013.

[135] Sanz, B., Santos, I., Laorden, C., Ugarte-Pedrero, X., Bringas, P. G., & Álvarez, G., "Puma: Permission usage to detect malware in Android", In *International Joint Conference Special Sessions*, pp. 289–298, 2013.

[136] Burguera, I., Zurutuza, U., & Nadjm-Tehrani, S., "Crowdroid: Behavior-based malware detection system for Android", In *1st ACM workshop on Security and Privacy in Smartphones and Mobile Devices*, Association for Computing Machinery, New York, NY, pp. 15–26, 2011.

[137] Shabtai, A., Kanonov, U., Elovici, Y., Glezer, C., & Weiss, Y., "Andromaly: A behavioral malware detection framework for Android devices", *Journal of Intelligent Information Systems*, v. 38, n. 1, pp. 161–190, 2012.

[138] Zhao, M., Ge, F., Zhang, T., & Yuan, Z., "AntiMalDroid: An efficient SVM-based malware detection framework for Android", In *International Conference on Information Computing and Applications*, Springer, pp. 158–166, 2011.

[139] Yan, L. K., & Yin, H., "Droidscope: Seamlessly reconstructing the {OS} and Dalvik semantic views for dynamic Android malware analysis", In *21st Security Symposium USENIX*, USENIX, pp. 569–584, 2012.

[140] Bläsing, T., Batyuk, L., Schmidt, A. D., Camtepe, S. A., & Albayrak, S., "An Android application sandbox system for suspicious software detection", In *5th International Conference on Malicious and Unwanted Software*, IEEE, pp. 55–62, 2010.

[141] Spreitzenbarth, M., Freiling, F., Echtler, F., Schreck, T., & Hoffmann, J., "Mobile-sandbox: having a deeper look into Android applications", In *28th Annual ACM Symposium on Applied Computing*, Association for Computing Machinery, New York, NY, pp. 1808–1815, 2013.

[142] Arshad, S., Shah, M. A., Wahid, A., Mehmood, A., Song, H., & Yu, H., "Samadroid: A novel 3-level hybrid malware detection model for Android operating system", *IEEE Access*, v. 6, pp. 4321–4339, 2018.

[143] Zhou, Y., Wang, Z., Zhou, W., & Jiang, X., "Hey, you, get off of my market: Detecting malicious apps in official and alternative Android markets", In *Network and Distributed System Security Symposium*, v. 25, n. 4, pp. 50–52, 2012.

[144] Wu, W. C., & Hung, S. H., "DroidDolphin: A dynamic Android malware detection framework using big data and machine learning", In *International*

Conference on Research in Adaptive and Convergent Systems, Association for Computing Machinery, New York, NY, pp. 247–252, 2014.

[145] Baskaran, B., & Ralescu, A., "A study of Android malware detection techniques and machine learning", In *27th Modern Artificial Intelligence and Cognitive Science Conference*, pp. 15–23, 2016.

[146] Yerima, S. Y., Sezer, S., & Muttik, I., "Android malware detection using parallel machine learning classifiers", In *8th International Conference on Next Generation Mobile Apps, Services and Technologies*, IEEE, pp. 37–42, 2014.

[147] Google Playstore Apps. Available Online: https://play.google.com/store/apps/, Accessed: 15 July 2017.

[148] Wandoujiaapps. Available Online: www.wandoujia.com/apps/, Accessed: 15 July 2017.

[149] Wei, F., Li, Y., Roy, S., Ou, X., & Zhou, W., "Deep ground truth analysis of current Android malware", In *International Conference on Detection of Intrusions and Malware, and Vulnerability Assessment*, Springer, pp. 252–276, 2017.

[150] Allix, K., Bissyandé, T. F., Klein, J., & Le Traon, Y., "Androzoo: Collecting millions of Android apps for the research community", In *IEEE/ACM 13th Working Conference on Mining Software Repositories*, IEEE/ACM, pp. 468–471, 2016.

[151] APK Pure. Available Online: https://apkpure.com/, Accessed: 15 July 2017.

[152] Li, L., Gao, J., Hurier, M., Kong, P., Bissyandé, T. F., Bartel, A., Klein, J., & Traon, Y. L., "Androzoo++: Collecting millions of Android apps and their metadata for the research community", arXiv preprint arXiv:1709.05281, 2017.

[153] AMD Data Access Policy. Available Online: http://amd.arguslab.org/sharing/, Accessed: 15 July 2017.

[154] Garg, S., & Baliyan, N., "Data on vulnerability detection in Android", *Data in brief*, v. 22, pp. 1081–1087, 2019.

[155] APKTool. Available Online: https://ibotpeaches.github.io/Apktool/, Accessed: 10 August 2017.

[156] Ham, Y. J., Moon, D., Lee, H. W., Lim, J. D., & Kim, J. N., "Android mobile application system call event pattern analysis for determination of malicious attack", *International Journal of Security and Its Applications*, v. 8, n. 1, pp. 231–246, 2014.

[157] Shen, F., Del Vecchio, J., Mohaisen, A., Ko, S. Y., & Ziarek, L., "Android malware detection using complex-flows", *IEEE Transactions on Mobile Computing*, v. 18, n. 6, pp. 1231–1245, 2018.

[158] Garcia, J., Hammad, M., & Malek, S., "Lightweight, obfuscation-resilient detection and family identification of Android malware", *ACM Transactions on Software Engineering and Methodology*, v. 26, n. 3, pp. 1–29, 2018.

[159] Cai, H., Meng, N., Ryder, B., & Yao, D. D., "Droidcat: Unified dynamic detection of Android malware", Informal Report, Virginia Polytechnic Institute & State University, 2016.

[160] Milosevic, N., Dehghantanha, A., & Choo, K. K. R., "Machine learning aided Android malware classification", *Computers & Electrical Engineering*, v. 61, pp. 266–274, 2017.

[161] Fan, M., Liu, J., Luo, X., Chen, K., Chen, T., Tian, Z., Zhang, X., Zheng, Q., & Liu, T., "Frequent subgraph based familial classification of Android malware", In *IEEE 27th International Symposium on Software Reliability Engineering*, IEEE, pp. 24–35, 2016.

[162] VirusTotal Documentation. Available Online: www.virustotal.com/en/documentation/public-api/, Accessed: 16 October 2018.

[163] Sebastián, M., Rivera, R., Kotzias, P., & Caballero, J., "Avclass: A tool for massive malware labeling", In *International Symposium on Research in Attacks, Intrusions, and Defenses*, Springer, pp. 230–253, 2016.

[164] Yan, S., Khan, F. N., Mavromatis, A., Gkounis, D., Fan, Q., Ntavou, F., Nikolovgenis, K., Meng, F., Salas, E. H., Guo, C., & Lu, C., "Field trial of machine-learning-assisted and SDN-based optical network planning with network-scale monitoring database", In *European Conference on Optical Communication*, IEEE, pp. 1–3, 2017.

[165] Taheri, L., Kadir, A. F. A., & Lashkari, A. H., "Extensible Android malware detection and family classification using network-flows and API-calls", In *International Carnahan Conference on Security Technology*, IEEE, pp. 1–8, 2019.

[166] Bajwa, G., Fazeen, M., Dantu, R., & Tanpure, S., "Unintentional bugs to vulnerability mapping in Android applications", In *IEEE International Conference on Intelligence and Security Informatics*, pp. 176–178, 2015.

[167] Google, "Android tools project site—android lint", Available Online: http://tools.android.com/tips/lint, Accessed: 18 October, 2021.

[168] FindBugs™, "FindBugs™—Find bugs in Java programs", Available Online: https://findbugs.sourceforge.net/, Accessed: 18 October, 2021.

[169] Poudyal, S., Dasgupta, D., Akhtar, Z., & Gupta, K., "A multi-level ransomware detection framework using natural language processing and machine learning", In *14th International Conference on Malicious and Unwanted Software*, 2019.

[170] Karbab, E. B., & Debbabi, M., "MalDy: Portable, data-driven malware detection using natural language processing and machine learning techniques on behavioral analysis reports", *Digital Investigation*, v. 28, pp. S77–S87, 2019.

[171] Karbab, E. B., Debbabi, M., Alrabaee, S., & Mouheb, D., "DySign: Dynamic fingerprinting for the automatic detection of Android malware", In *11th International Conference on Malicious and Unwanted Software*, IEEE, pp. 1–8, 2016.

[172] Wang, S., Yan, Q., Chen, Z., Yang, B., Zhao, C., & Conti, M., "Detecting Android malware leveraging text semantics of network flows", *IEEE Transactions on Information Forensics and Security*, v. 13, n. 5, pp. 1096–1109, 2017.

[173] Booz, J., McGiff, J., Hatcher, W. G., Yu, W., Nguyen, J. H., & Lu, C., "Tuning deep learning performance for Android malware detection", In *19th IEEE/ACIS International Conference on Software Engineering, Artificial Intelligence, Networking*, IEEE/ACIS, pp. 140–145, 2018.

[174] Pendlebury, F., Pierazzi, F., Jordaney, R., Kinder, J., & Cavallaro, L., "TESSERACT: Eliminating experimental bias in malware classification across space and time", In *28th USENIX Security Symposium (USENIX Security'19)*, USENIX Association, pp. 729–746, 2019.

[175] Karbab, E. B., Debbabi, M., Derhab, A., & Mouheb, D., "MalDozer: Automatic framework for Android malware detection using deep learning", *Digital Investigation*, v. 24, pp. S48–S59, 2018.

[176] Mikolov, T., Sutskever, I., Chen, K., Corrado, G. S., & Dean, J., "Distributed representations of words and phrases and their compositionality", In *27th Conference on Neural Information Processing Systems*, Curran Associates, Inc., pp. 3111–3119, 2013.

[177] Pennington, J., Socher, R., & Manning, C. D., "Glove: Global vectors for word representation", In *19th Conference on Empirical Methods in Natural Language Processing*, pp. 1532–1543, 2014.

[178] Trendmicro. Available Online: www.trendmicro.com/vinfo/dk/security/news/cybercrime-and-digital-threats/, Accessed: 9 November, 2021.

[179] kaspersky. Available Online: www.kaspersky.co.in/resource-center/threats/mobile/, Accessed: 9 November, 2021.

[180] F-Secure. Available Online: www.f-secure.com/en/home/products/mobile-security/, Accessed: 9 November, 2021.

[181] Malwarebytes. Available Online: www.malwarebytes.com/mobile/, Accessed: 9 November, 2021.

[182] CNET. Available Online: www.cnet.com/news/Android-malware-that-comes-preinstalled-are-a-massive-threat/, Accessed: 9 November, 2021.
[183] ZDNet. Available Online: www.zdnet.com/topic/security/, Accessed: 9 November, 2021.
[184] Checkpoint. Available Online: https://research.checkpoint.com/category/Android-malware/, Accessed: 9 November, 2021.
[185] NJCCIC. Available Online: www.cyber.nj.gov/threat-center/threat-profiles/Android-malware-variants/, Accessed: 9 November, 2021.
[186] Jurafsky, D., *Speech & language processing*. Pearson Education India, 2000.
[187] Papagiannopoulou, E., & Tsoumakas, G., "Local word vectors guiding keyphrase extraction", *Information Processing & Management*, v. 54, n. 6, pp. 888–902, 2018.
[188] Robertas, D., Venˇckauskas, A., Toldinas, J., & Grigali¯unas, ˇS., "Ensemble-based classification using neural networks and machine learning models for windows PE malware detection", *Electronics*, v. 10, n. 4, p. 485, 2021.
[189] The AV-Test Security Report 2018/19. Available Online: www.av-test.org/en/news/heightened-threat-scenario-all-the-facts-in-the-av-test-security-report-2018–2019/, Accessed: 4 October 2020.
[190] Review, Refocus, and Recalibrate the 2019 Mobile Threat Landscape. Available Online: www.trendmicro.com/vinfo/hk-en/security/research-and-analysis/threat-reports/roundup/review-refocus-and-recalibrate-the-2019-mobile-threat-landscape/, Accessed: 12 October 2020.
[191] Garg, S., & Baliyan, N., "Android malware classification using ensemble classifiers", In *Cloud Security*, pp. 133–145, CRC Press, 2021.
[192] Wang, K., Zhang, Y., & Liu, P., "Call me back! Attacks on system server and system apps in android through synchronous callback", In *ACM SIGSAC Conference on Computer and Communications Security*, Association for Computing Machinery, New York, NY, pp. 92–103, 2016.
[193] Huang, H., Zhu, S., Chen, K., & Liu, P., "From system services freezing to system server shutdown in Android: All you need is a loop in an app", In *22nd ACM SIGSAC Conference on Computer and Communications Security*, Association for Computing Machinery, New York, NY, pp. 1236–1247, 2015.
[194] Cao, C., Gao, N., Liu, P., & Xiang, J., "Towards analyzing the input validation vulnerabilities associated with Android system services", In *31st Annual Computer Security Applications Conference*, Association for Computing Machinery, New York, NY, pp. 361–370, 2015.
[195] Ahmad, W., Kästner, C., Sunshine, J., & Aldrich, J., "Inter-app communication in Android: Developer challenges", In *IEEE/ACM 13th Working Conference on Mining Software Repositories*, IEEE/ACM, pp. 177–188, 2016.
[196] Backes, M., Bugiel, S., & Derr, E., "Reliable third-party library detection in Android and its security applications", In *ACM SIGSAC Conference on Computer and Communications Security*, Association for Computing Machinery, New York, NY, pp. 356–367, 2016.
[197] Ghafari, M., Gadient, P., & Nierstrasz, O., "Security smells in Android", In *IEEE 17th International Working Conference on Source Code Analysis and Manipulation*, IEEE, pp. 121–130, 2017.
[198] Jimenez, M., Papadakis, M., Bissyandé, T. F., & Klein, J., "Profiling Android vulnerabilities", In *IEEE International Conference on Software Quality, Reliability and Security*, IEEE, pp. 222–229, 2016.
[199] Linares-Vásquez, M., Bavota, G., & Escobar-Velásquez, C., "An empirical study on Android-related vulnerabilities", In *IEEE/ACM 14th International Conference on Mining Software Repositories*, IEEE/ACM, pp. 2–13, 2017.

[200] Garg, S., & Baliyan, N., "Android stack vulnerabilities: Security analysis of a decade", *Accepted in International Conference on Paradigms of Communication, Computing and Data Sciences*, Springer, 2021.

[201] Android Issue Tracker. Available Online: https://issuetracker.google.com/issues?q=status:open/, Accessed: 22 October 2020.

[202] A Complete Guide to the Common Vulnerability Scoring System. Available Online: www.first.org/cvss/v2/guide/, Accessed: 24 October 2020.